es the typical communication that dominates most organizations, ...en there's communicating like a compassionate, influential leader. Keith's book teaches you to become not only a strategic, coach and thinker, but a strategic, intentional communicator who truly inspires positive change. Even after decades of my own experience as a senior executive, *Sales Leadership* has provided new insights in how to best support my team and organization to more effectively achieve our business objectives."

Scott Bell, Regional Vice President, Volkswagen Group of America

"Keith's framework around the 'Art of Enrollment' particularly jumped out as a critical conversation to creating the alignment and buy-in needed around sales coaching, as well as the company vision, business objectives and agile change. By weaving in some proven leadership strategies through artful storytelling and practical examples, Sales Leadership is a book for the sales manager who truly wants to create a thriving sales culture and make a difference.'"

Robert A. David, Berkley, Director of Corporate Education, University of California, Berkeley

"*Sales Leadership* is not just for sales leaders. This is a visionary book for every leader and salesperson. Keith is spot on regarding how the next generation of top salespeople are going to coach their customers, and this book shows you how. It's packed with concrete steps on what it takes to transform from a spreadsheet manager and into an authentic sales leader, how to effectively coach to each person's individuality and motivations that align personal goals with our business objectives, and so much more. Truly a game changer."

Al Guido, President at San Francisco 49ers and CEO of Elevate Sports Ventures

"This book is even more insightful, more specific with the "how to's", and even more enlightened. Keith's global tours and vast amount of direct experience in this coaching arena have made him an expert and a bit of an oracle on the concepts. One should not doubt him, one should pay attention and execute to what he offers."

Mitch Little, V.P. WW Sales & Applications, Microchip Technology Inc., Author of Shiftability

"Keith's personal experiences made the book relevant, and accurately reflected a global leadership point of view that is refreshingly effective."

Thomas de Buhr, Managing Director, Twitter Germany

"As a sales leader, I have sought to help my teams in a simple direct and pragmatic way to guide them to their success. But coaching sales organizations that is simple conceptually is not always easy to implement, or at least until I met Keith Rosen. With this new book and the evolution of Keith's approach to sales coaching, this complex but necessary skill is even simpler and easier to implement and use all day, every day, supporting your sales teams to be motivated and successful."

Giuseppe Rossi, Vice President, Solution Sales EMEA,
CA Technologies

"Anyone who wants to help their team do the best work of their careers not only needs to read this book but should have it on the corner of their desk for daily reference. If you want to know how to exponentially transform your team, culture and results, follow Keith's prescriptive coaching advice and templates without hesitation. I have, and it's evident in the success of our company's results and engagement scores. With this follow on to *Coaching Salespeople into Sales Champions*, the new playbook is complete, thorough, exact and off-the-chart insightful."

David Turner, CEO, Contegix

"Every leadership book does not apply to sales leadership. Salespeople are uniquely special, and the lifeline of every business. They need to be trained, coached, respected and supported in a way that aligns with their sales DNA and individuality. Keith has created a coaching code designed by and for salespeople that's sure to optimize performance, loyalty, and retention. Clearly the best book on sales leadership I've seen in a decade."

Gerhard Gschwandtner, Founder and CEO, Selling Power

"This is the most practical coaching framework I've seen, especially for busy sales leaders. No filler, or abstract theory that you have to decipher to apply. You'll find the questions and tools can be easily applied in every conversation, every day. An insightful and knowledgeable guide, full of everything you need to know on how to coach your team to excellence – and become the leader you want to be."

**Frédéric Chauvire, Vice President EMEA North General Business
and Channel at SAP**

"Keith has beautifully captured what caring, busy managers can do to avoid impatience, frustration and instead, to make coaching actually easy and impactful, and their own jobs more fulfilling. Exceptional companies and leaders realize that to ignite engagement, innovation and growth, the ability to execute and over-perform requires the right coaching conversations and a supportive culture. Keith lays out in practical detail, not only how to implement a successful coaching initiative but also provides practical guidance to ensure you and your company are adequately prepared to do so."

**Simon Frewer, Global Director of Sales & Marketing Solutions
("Challenger" practice) and Talent Development Practices
at CEB/Gartner**

"Implementing Keith's Sales Leadership playbook will drive the success and scalability of your team to achieve superior results, while making every manager's job easier. The templates and coaching talk tracks to handle the essential management conversations, especially the difficult ones, will help you develop happy, productive people who enjoy coming to work."

Colleen Honan, Chief Sales Officer, Brainshark

"Keith Rosen has written a must-read guide for every sales leader regardless of industry or organization. In our fast-paced business, being able to productively coach anyone in 15 minutes, 5 minutes or using just one defining question, Sales Leadership accelerates greater results."

**Vincent Lombardo, Chief Sales Officer
at Heartland Payment Systems**

"When everyone is effectively coaching and unconditionally supporting each other That's when you know a healthy coaching culture has emerged. Sales Leadership is the best book ever written on how to do it well. This book is the ultimate reference guide to drive maximum performance and engagement."

Conor Gleeson, VP Alliances and Channel, Oracle Direct, EMEA

"The days of, "I promoted my top rep to manager and they're struggling" are over, when you make your salespeople great coaches. The way companies make purchasing decisions is continually evolving, which is why your salespeople and managers need to transform into influential, outstanding coaches. Keith shares a simple, yet effective strategies every leader needs to become a great coach, and his magic is in showing the *how* around what great coaching sounds like – with proven tactics and techniques to make you a better leader, whether you're a salesperson, new manager or a seasoned veteran."

Tony Rodoni, Executive Vice President, Salesforce

"As a Vice President of Sales for both Oracle and Microsoft for over 20 years, I've had the fortune of leading the greatest sales teams in the technology industry. I've read all the sales leadership books you can think of and have sponsored all the sales and leadership trainings you can imagine. Many of these books and workshops were written or delivered by people who never lived in the trenches. Zero scars. Keith is different. He gets it. As VP of Sales at Microsoft, I hosted Keith multiple times to work with my sales leaders. He connected with them with his unique approach that inspired and motivated them into taking action. Results? He turned my sales leaders into great coaches that developed sales champions. Our C- level relationships and revenue results during this time speak for themselves. ***Number one team in the country multiple times.*** His new book, *Sales Leadership*, takes this critical role and coaching conversation to another level. I'm proud to say that Keith has been an Executive Sales Coach for me. I strongly recommend this book. His coaching and workshops changed the game for our teams at Microsoft. Lastly, his approach is not limited to sales Leaders. Keith's approach is for anyone who has the honor, privilege and responsibility to help others grow and succeed."

John Fikany, CEO The Fikany Group, previous VP of Sales for Microsoft and Oracle

"Being a great leader takes much more than leveraging a coaching framework and developing your coaching acumen. It's the inner game of leadership, the mindset and way of being that expands your thinking to create that coaching magic and exceptional results you never thought possible. Before you change your behavior and the outcome, you need to change your mindset, and this book coaches you to do so flawlessly. Keith's authentic, honest, candid and caring approach to coaching is exactly how to coach individuals rather than manage a team uncover powerful coaching moments that often go unnoticed."

Vala Afshar, Chief Digital Evangelist at Salesforce

SALES LEADERSHIP

SALES LEADERSHIP

The Essential Leadership Framework to

Coach Sales Champions, Inspire Excellence, and

Exceed Your Business Goals

KEITH ROSEN, MCC

WILEY

Published by John Wiley & Sons, Inc., Hoboken, New Jersey.
Published simultaneously in Canada.

If you want to buy a bunch of these books to share this gift with others, we can help. We can also co-brand and customize this book specifically for you or your organization and you may even qualify for a complimentary workshop with Keith.

For general information on our other products and services or for technical support, please contact our Customer Care Department within the United States at (800) 762–2974, outside the United States at (317) 572–3993 or fax (317) 572–4002.

Wiley publishes in a variety of print and electronic formats and by print-on-demand. Some material included with standard print versions of this book may not be included in e-books or in print-on-demand. If this book refers to media such as a CD or DVD that is not included in the version you purchased, you may download this material at http://booksupport.wiley.com. For more information about Wiley products, visit www.wiley.com. For more information on Keith Rosen, visit www.KeithRosen.com.

Library of Congress Cataloging-in-Publication Data:

Names: Rosen, Keith, author.
Title: Sales leadership: The essential leadership framework to coach sales champions,
    inspire excellence, and exceed your business goals / Keith Rosen.
Description: Hoboken, New Jersey : John Wiley & Sons, Inc., [2018] | Includes index. |
    Identifiers: LCCN 2018022526 (print) | LCCN 2018025346 (ebook) | ISBN
    9781119483243 (Adobe PDF) | ISBN 9781119483274 (ePub) | ISBN 9781119483250
    (hardcover)
Subjects: LCSH: Sales force management. | Employees—Coaching of. Classification:
    LCC HF5439.5 (ebook) | LCC HF5439.5 .R669 2018 (print) |
    DDC 658.3/1245—dc23
LC record available at https://lccn.loc.gov/2018022526

Cover Design: Wiley
Cover Image: © kyoshino / iStockphoto

Printed in the United States of America

V10003513_081518

To my extraordinary wife, best friend, and soul mate, and my three miraculous children, you are the center of my universe and fill my life with meaning, laughter, joy, fulfillment, peace, and purpose. My life is truly perfect because of you. Thank you for your patience, support, and for tolerating me through this writing process so that I can honor my commitment and passion to making the world a better place, one person at a time.

You will forever be my guiding light, my inspiration, my reason for living, and what keeps me focused on the priorities that truly matter most in life. I love you deeply and forever.

Contents

CHAPTER FIVE

CHAPTER SIX

CHAPTER SEVEN

The Power of Why

Years ago, there lived a wise and noble king. The king lived a happy life with his beautiful wife. A few years after their marriage, his wife got sick and died soon after. Unfortunately, this tragedy occurred before having children, leaving the king to rule the kingdom alone.

While devastated by the loss of his wife, the king stayed true to his commitment to rule with honor and take care of the people in his kingdom.

The love for his wife was so strong, the king couldn't bear the thought of ever getting married again. As the years passed, having no children of his own, the king knew the time would come when he would have to find the right man who, upon his death, would take his place as king. Since there was no bloodline and no son who could rightfully take the king's place, he called upon the people of the kingdom to help him find a suitable heir to the throne. The king knew there would have to be a test of some sort that would help identify the most promising candidate.

One day, while the king was taking a stroll through the countryside, he came upon a massive sinkhole that must have been about 750 meters long and 100 meters wide. "I've got it!" exclaimed the king. "I know the test that would help me identify the next king." And with that, he quickly returned to the castle to share his idea with his advisors. The very next day, the king issued a decree throughout the kingdom. "Come one, come all. In three weeks' time, those who feel worthy enough to take my place will meet in the town square to demonstrate why they should be heir to the kingdom."

The day finally arrived. Thousands of people had traveled for miles from every corner of the kingdom to reach the town square, each carrying the dream of being chosen as the heir to the throne.

The king took these promising candidates out to the countryside to show them what he had found. "Here is the question that, if answered correctly, will earn you the rightful place as our next king."

Pointing to the massive hole, he simply asked, "What should I do?"

After several days and hundreds of responses later, no one had yet to come up with the right answer. Repeatedly, the king would hear the same responses. "Fill it with rocks and dirt." "Fill it with water." "Build a bridge across the sinkhole." "Build a wall around it." "Put warning signs around the sinkhole." "Make it a graveyard." "Fortify it." "Camouflage the sinkhole to protect us from our enemies." While some of these may be interesting ideas, none of them were the answer the king was hoping for.

Two days went by. The king was getting discouraged, wondering if anyone was capable of thinking and acting like a successful king. As the number of candidates dwindled to a remaining few, it was time for one young man to answer the king's question; a poor farm boy from the countryside who was ridiculed by those older and wiser than he for even considering the possibility of becoming king. "So," the king began with a disheartened and skeptical tone. "What should I do?"

The young man hesitated for a moment and then responded with, "Why do anything?"

Suddenly, the king's disposition changed. He looked at the young man and asked with hope, "Why? When everyone else advised me what I could do with the sinkhole, why are you the only one not to advise me at all, nor tell me what I should do? Why do you come to me with only a simple question?"

The young man respectfully answered. "Because I cannot answer your question, my king. I don't know your *why*. Until I understand not only what you want to do, but also why you want to do anything and what your intentions are, only then can we start to formulate the vision of your desired outcome and how we can go about creating it, even if you decide to do nothing."

How insightful! Instead of telling the king what *he* would do, this young man simply presented the king with one question, a question so simple yet so powerful and often overlooked.

Why? After all, how could this young man align and collaborate effectively with the king if he didn't understand the king's motivations, intentions, and the *why* behind his beliefs, actions, opinions, decisions, behavior, goals, or values?

"Congratulations," exclaimed the king. "You are the next heir to the throne of our kingdom."

The town was shocked. The elders of the town questioned the king. "Why this boy?"

To which the king replied, "I never wanted to fix anything. That was not my intention. Everyone came to me with a solution to fix what they assumed was a problem that needed fixing. They never took the time to uncover and understand my *why* or my desired intentions and point of view.

"This young man was the only one who was insightful enough to seek out my intention—my point of view—and uncover my *why*," the king concluded.

CREATE THE UNIFIED *WHY*

The key to being a great leader is understanding what your people want and expect from you, but more important, *why* they want it. When leading your team to a shared goal and vision, they need to understand not only what they need to do but also *why* they are doing it and what's in it for them, so they can see how they personally benefit.

To set and manage people's expectations and create alignment in thinking and action requires understanding people's *why*, who they are, their values, goals, and their intentions, while ensuring they are aligned with the company's *why*. This is what it takes to transform the culture and performance of any organization. What would it mean to you, your team, and to your organization if you could achieve companywide, unified alignment in thinking and action?

These leadership principles apply in every area of our lives. And when leading an organization or a team, when you can discover and articulate your *collective why*, only then can you harness the power of coaching as a cornerstone to develop your champion team and create a shared vision and a healthy, top-performing culture.

What you do, *what* you sell, and *what* value you provide is the by-product. The journey to cultural greatness begins with *why, your one clear thing or vision. Your beacon*. Why you do what you do is the essence of who you and your company are—your values, goals, and priorities as an individual and as a unified organization.

Which eloquently transitions our conversation to the first of many self-reflective questions I'll be asking you.

WHY ARE YOU A LEADER?

It's one of the first questions I ask when working with a management team. On one end of the spectrum, managers tell me, "Keith, one day my boss came to me and asked if I wanted to be a manager. And *poof!* Just like that, I became a manager. No training or onboarding, of course. Just a scorecard, a quota, and a whole bunch of responsibilities."

On the other end of the spectrum, regardless of what country or company I'm in, managers in every position report that they became a leader because the following priorities and core values are important to them.

1. Making an impact by being a trusted advisor and guiding people down the best path for their career.
2. Developing people to help them succeed and observing them advance in a career they love.
3. Achieving team goals that are bigger than the one.
4. Family, contribution, life balance, integrity, patience, living in the moment.
5. Helping people achieve things they didn't think were possible.

When asked what values they compromise most due to the pressure to perform and do their job well, they listed:

6. Making an impact by being a trusted advisor and guiding people down the best path for their career.
7. Developing people to help them succeed and observing them advance in a career they love.
8. Achieving team goals that are bigger than the one.
9. Family, contribution, life balance, integrity, patience, living in the moment.
10. Helping people achieve things they didn't think were possible.

There's a *big* problem. Managers are super conflicted in their role between what's asked of them and what's expected, while honoring who they are and their values.

New systems, processes, or technology do not transform your organization; they help manage it. That's why you must start by transforming your people. To create collective alignment and a shared vision and direction, you need to understand, respect, and support everyone's *why*. It is the impetus to a successful cultural transformation and to opening the door to your ideal kingdom. Here's to becoming the king of your domain. Well, maybe not king, but definitely a world-class leader.

SUPPORTING YOUR QUEST FOR COACHING GREATNESS

Since writing *Coaching Salespeople into Sales Champions* in 2008, I've had the privilege of working with managers on five continents and in over 75 countries. This inspired me to further develop and refine what is now considered to be the top, universally applied coaching model used by the world's leading sales organizations.

Sales Leadership is the result of my 10-year global quest to discover how to ignite unprecedented human achievement by developing leadership titans. *Coaching Salespeople into Sales Champions* was the first book of its kind that poured the foundation for coaching mastery. *Sales Leadership* further supports your journey to become an elite leader and trailblazing coach, reinforced by stories from across the world. In fact, you'll be thrilled to know that this book and the revised L.E.A.D.S. coaching framework will enable every busy, caring manager to have effective coaching conversations in 10 minutes or less!

FROM THE SIDELINES

I use the words, *coach*, *manager*, *boss*, and *leader* synonymously throughout this book. Why? Because at the end of the day, you're still responsible for your business objectives. However, the best managers *are* the best leaders. They encapsulate all of the great qualities and competencies of a manager, leader, and coach, including the language of leadership—*coaching*. Title means nothing, nor does it denote or exemplify your character and true value. It's who you are, your actions, and how you show up that counts.

Regardless of your position, experience, or industry, implementing the strategies throughout this book will make you part of the next generation of leaders who do remarkable things.

This leads us into the first chapter of our journey, where we begin to answer the question: *Why is coaching the lynchpin that will either lead you and your company to greatness or toward mediocrity and inevitable failure?*

CHAPTER 1

Preparing for the Cultural Evolution

P *eople create the mindset, mindset shapes behavior, behavior defines culture, and ultimately, culture determines success. That's why the primary business objective is to make your people more valuable.*

WHAT'S YOUR BUSINESS DNA?

We were ending the second day working with a team of managers in Beijing, China. During every program I deliver, I want to ensure that expectations are met, know what their biggest learning moment is, and capture their commitment after our time together was over. This is necessary to make sure that what we worked on becomes embedded in the way the managers lead and coach.

As we went around the room, Pierre, one of the managers, paused to share a horrific experience he had just a week earlier.

"I received some disturbing news from our corporate office last week. During last month's quarterly senior leadership meeting, Chan, one of the VPs had a heart attack in the middle of the meeting. Of course, we called an ambulance immediately. Within minutes, he was rushed to the hospital.

"As you can imagine, everyone else in the meeting was extremely concerned about Chan. And yet, the meeting continued. Reports were reviewed. Business plans evaluated. Priorities reaffirmed. Team performance and scorecards assessed.

"An hour passed. The hospital called the main office to share the devastating news. Chan had died moments after arriving at the hospital."

While there's nothing worse than the sudden and untimely passing of a good person, here's what I found most troublesome about this horrific story. The administrator from the hospital asked one of the other VPs in that meeting, "Who would be the proper family member to contact and let them know about Chan's death?"

Ten people were in that meeting. Some of them had worked together for over 12 years. And yet, when the hospital administrator asked how to contact Chan's family, not one person in the room had an answer.

No one really knew who Chan was. They knew him as an employee and a peer, but certainly not as a human being. It's a disturbing story, but it's one we can all learn from.

Think about your company. Think about your team, your peers, your customers. How much do you really know about them, personally? How much time and attention do you invest in fostering a deeper connection with people?

Keeping HR compliance in mind, do you really *know* the people you work with?

I can't think of anyone who would *want* to work at a company like Chan's. The sad truth is, there's a good chance most people already do.

BURN THE BRIDGE OF MEDIOCRITY

Countless studies detail the business impact that effective coaching has on performance, productivity, attitude, employee engagement, and of course, company culture. Which is why I won't be focusing on any of that.

Data isn't going to help you create a coaching culture, but it clearly shows that you need one.

THE SCATHING TRUTH

What about those companies that do not have fantastic DNA? How can struggling and great companies alike achieve enduring success?

If you want to change the face of your business, you need to alter the most fundamental composition of your organization. To do so, every employee must focus their thoughts, listening, and attention on the heart-beat of the business, which comes not from products and services, but from people.

CHOOSE NO INITIATIVE OVER A FAILED INITIATIVE

Every time you put profit over people, the promise of improving the work environment will fail. Employees will perceive any course you roll out or coaching offered as an event-based flavor of the month. Your good intentions to develop people into champions become overshadowed by the company's underlying, self-serving agenda to achieve business objectives.

The frustration rises on both sides.

Company leaders: "We just invested in our people! They should be following what they learned."

Your Employees: "Nothing new here. The company was hot on coaching this month, but it's always going to be about the results. Things always go back to the way they were."

No traction is created, no positive change can be sustained, and cultures inevitably backslide to a fear-based, results-driven workplace. The additional cost of a failed initiative is that companies learn the wrong lesson: that coaching doesn't work.

So what's the secret to developing a thriving, top-performing coaching culture that people want to be part of? How do you prepare any company for this transformational journey? How do you prevent it from being just another fleeting idea due to the cultural volatility that exists within your company?

Before we answer this question, let's create some alignment around the definition of *culture*.

EXAMINING CULTURE

Merriam-Webster's dictionary defines culture as, "the customary beliefs, social forms, and material traits of a racial, religious, or social group. The characteristic features of everyday existence shared by people in a place or time."

This definition applies to any organized group, such as universities, networking events, trade associations, conferences, social networks, non-profits, a neighborhood fitness center, and even governments. It seems we're all part of and operate in a variety of cultures as we move through the world around us.

BOARDROOM OR *BORED ROOM*: DEFINING CORPORATE CULTURE

The infamously stodgy word *corporate* refers to the collective body that makes up any organization. Merriam-Webster's definition of *culture* also includes:

> b: the set of shared attitudes, values, goals, and practices that characterizes an institution or organization; a corporate culture focused on the bottom line; c: the set of values, or social practices associated with a field, activity, or societal characteristic ... d) the integrated pattern of human knowledge, belief, and behavior that depends upon the capacity for learning and transmitting knowledge to succeeding generations.

THE COMPANY ECOSYSTEM

Many pieces must be addressed to solve this cultural puzzle. It's an environment that encapsulates a shared feeling, belief system, attitude, and set of values. Culture dictates how people should behave, perform, and treat one another.

Every company's culture exists within a network of unique individuals engaging and interacting with each other. A healthy culture is a consistent culture—especially in the face of adversity. It's one where people feel their workplace, like their home, is a safe place to live by their values and authentically express themselves.

People live within the culture of their company. Ultimately, it determines their fulfillment, growth, purpose, contributions, success, quality of life, and peace of mind.

WHEN COMPANY AND PERSONAL VALUES CLASH

Does your company culture reflect your people and their personal values? Are your people a reflection of your culture? Does the attitude and behavior within your organization reflect your desired culture? Does your culture reflect not just your corporate vision but your team vision, as well as your team's and your personal vision and values?

COACHING CONUNDRUM

There is no more line between work and life. There's just life! So, if you're not honoring and living your values at work, then you're compromising your integrity by not fully living your values in life.

Companies and *leaders* with good intentions struggle to break free from the monotony of their current business because they face the daily pressures of metrics, performance expectations, quotas, employee challenges, customer needs, deadlines, hiring, forecasting, emails, impromptu meetings, employee development, reporting—the list runs on.

Inevitably, the reversion to a dysfunctional culture is a by-product of the primary directive: to achieve results.

MINDFUL MOMENT

Having a shared company consciousness is the same as having a shared vision.

You're Not Coaching Effectively

Like most leaders, you've probably had some exposure to coaching, either through a book, a keynote, a half-day coaching workshop, or a full-blown course. Unfortunately, the majority of managers now think they know how to coach. *If only it were that easy!* The following story illustrates this common misconception.

As a newly promoted manager, Carlos was excited about his position and was already a huge advocate of coaching. As you could imagine, Carlos was thrilled when his boss told him they were going to start scheduling one-to-one coaching sessions, the first one being next Monday.

Immediately, Carlos began preparing. When Monday finally arrived, Carlos sat down with his boss for their first coaching session. As Carlos began sharing some of his goals and challenges, his boss sat, apparently engaged, listening, even asking some leading, closed-ended questions along the way.

After Carlos explained one challenge he was experiencing with one of his sales reps, the first bit of coaching Carlos received started with: *Here's what you should do ...*

This isn't coaching! Did you catch the punchline? Many people don't. Some managers think coaching entails listening and asking a few questions, then giving the answer. As we journey throughout this book, you'll be reading many similar conversations that portray managers as ineffective, directive, and manipulative.

There are four main reasons why managers don't coach:

1. **They think they're coaching but they're not.** This inevitably leads managers to learn the wrong lessons. A telltale sign is a manager who says things like, "Coaching doesn't work," "Sometimes you have to just tell them what to do, which is much easier," or, my favorite, "Coaching just takes too long."

2. **They had awful training.** Sometimes managers go through terrible coaching training. They do everything they were told to, but it doesn't work, so they assume coaching doesn't fit the culture.

3. **There is no companywide alignment on what coaching is and how to do it.**

4. **There is no plan or process to ensure consistent, effective coaching.**

5. **They're not being effectively coached themselves.**

In fact, coaching doesn't have to be hard at all. In this book, you'll learn how most coaching conversations can be completed in less than 10 minutes!

Your Culture Sucks

I always try to come from a positive place. For example, I believe that failure is an opportunity to learn; fear can become your greatest ally; and confidence is a choice you make by not allowing external situations dictate your internal state of well-being.

But we don't have time for *sugar coaching* or feel-good statements. Let me be direct, in case no one has shared this memo with you: *Your culture sucks, your people are disengaged because they're not coached effectively, you're only maximizing about 40 percent of their potential, and you're spending most of your time focused on the wrong activities. In short, you've lost sight of your top priority,* your people.

You may think I'm being presumptuous. You're shaking your head saying, "You're wrong, Keith. You never experienced our culture. We have a great culture."

My questions are: How do you know? What measurable criteria are you using? What results are you experiencing? The upcoming pages will provide you with a quick assessment to determine if your coaching is generating worthwhile results or not.

A 10-YEAR COACHING STUDY

While data is an essential need of any business, it doesn't transform anyone into an exceptional leader.

That's why I focus on the soft skills and transformation of people rather than on the data.

For those who appreciate validated data points to justify decisions (such as the need for coaching excellence), here's one that supports my prior statement: Over the last 10 years, my free ebooks have been downloaded approximately 350,000 times.

In the download request form, there's one required question: "Do your sales and management teams consistently use an effective coaching framework that creates a healthy, top-performing culture and wins more sales?"

A whopping 88 percent of respondents say no. These people represent a global population from a variety of different industries, including HR, sales, management, operations, marketing, engineering, IT, finance, and C-suite leadership. Moreover, these are people from some of the most prestigious, successful, and well-known companies in the world.

Even though my free resources were never meant to be used as surveys, that one question captured honest and objective data. After all, the downloaders' intention was to get the ebook, not to consciously complete a survey.

COACHING CONUNDRUM

Companies collapse a great culture with great results. Not true. These two ideas are mutually exclusive. While results are critical for business success, you know if you have a great culture when you're enjoying the ride, feel that your work complements your life, are living your values, and are self-motivated to attain your business objectives.

Assessing Your Culture and the Measurable ROI of Coaching

Whether you *think* your culture is healthy or toxic, here are 14 questions to quickly assess your culture and coaching.

1. Do you have more turnover than your industry average?
2. Do you struggle with departmental silos or creating a cohesive team functioning as one?
3. Are your managers spending 70 percent of their time putting out fires or developing, observing, and coaching their people in a way that generates consistent, measurable results?
4. Is *everyone* on your team achieving their quota and business objectives, and not just the few top producers who managers rely on to hit your monthly goals?
5. Are your people seeking out coaching from you, their coworkers, and other departments?
6. Do you view your team as *direct reports* or peers, coworkers, and resources? Do you seek out coaching from others, regardless of their position?
7. Are your salespeople authentically *coaching* rather than *selling* to your customers?
8. Are you effectively developing a talented bench of future leaders?
9. Do you work in a safe, transparent, and trusting environment fueled by innovation and positivity, or a fear-based culture?
10. Are you retaining your top talent?
11. Are you gaining market share and growing steadily each year?
12. Do you and your people come to work happy and fulfilled because you all want to be there?
13. Do you work from a place of intention or reaction? Do your company priorities seem to be changing daily?
14. Is everyone committed to holding themselves and others personally accountable to sustain and reinforce the culture you want?

These are just a few questions to assess your culture. If you can't answer *yes* to these questions, then you're lying to yourself about the type of culture you work in.

CHOOSE A CULTURE OF INTENTION OR REACTION

It's up to you whether you put this book down now and never pick it up again, or continue to honor your commitment to yourself, your team, and your company to be the best leader and coach you can be. Regardless of your conscious and intentional effort, your team and company culture will naturally emerge.

Unfortunately, taking this passive approach comes at a cost, especially when most companies default to a results-driven, fear-based culture. In fact, 99 percent of companies I've worked with would admit their culture is driven by results and not by people. It's an occupational hazard when every person, manager, team, department, and organization has a target on their back because every company's primary business objective is to evaluate the result.

You likely hear otherwise from every executive, find it on every company website, and read a framed company vision proudly displayed in every office. There, the message is always: *We put people first.* Maybe that's their *intention*, or, maybe it's true when times are good and easy, but when there's a deal on the line and a massive revenue-generating opportunity that can make or break quota, the coaching stops. Instead of using a high-stakes situation as a powerful coaching moment, results take priority over developing people every time.

Sadly, when results are the priority, regardless of the collateral damage that follows, most company cultures develop in a reactionary way. Creating a great culture requires conscious intention, focus, and a clear vision that becomes the blueprint for your organization. When coaching becomes unconsciously consistent—and when it aligns with the way people naturally engage and communicate with one another—that's the sign of a healthy coaching culture.

MINDFUL MOMENT

Instead of having your culture define your people, have your people define your culture.

A CULTURE OF STRATEGIC COMMUNICATORS

Whether you're focused on becoming an extraordinary leader, or you're looking to implement a coaching program within your organization, it's easy to become overwhelmed. Fear creeps in and people wonder, "What if there's no consistent or companywide adoption? What if it's just another failed project and short-term event? What if I'm not a good coach? What if I don't want to coach? What if my team doesn't embrace the coaching? What if I'm the only manager doing this? What if performance actually slips?" No one wants to find themselves in a position like this, or have egg on their face after a poorly implemented initiative.

Instead of letting fear rule, reframe your perspective. Consider the failure of any initiative to be a consequence of the overlooked components to be mindful of to ensure coaching success. This applies whether the initiative is for you, a team, or other managers. Developing a culture and becoming an inspirational, respected sales leader is not limited to a series of strategies, processes, reports, or surveys to develop a baseline. Like coaching, it's not a checkbox you put on a scorecard. The tipping point for developing a coaching culture begins with a series of strategic, well-timed changes in thinking and behavior, then putting it into practice. This includes the questions you'll be using in your coaching conversations, all of which are precisely scripted using what I refer to as *coach tracks*. These templates are for you to use to achieve a baseline of coaching best practices, and you will need them to facilitate highly valuable coaching conversations. This is necessary to create a culture of strategic communicators.

Why a culture of strategic communicators? Because the foundation of all positive change, whether it's external or within ourselves is communication. The transformation of human magnitude can only happen when thinking and behavior change.

Ask yourself, where do you begin when you want to change something for the better? What is the first thing you do? You conduct an inner dialog in your mind. We tell ourselves what we want, why we want it, and how it's possible to achieve it if we believe we are capable of doing so. Or, we have a conversation that does just the opposite: we get in our own way as we become our worst nemesis.

Before you continue, it's essential that you keep this top of mind: It will be your internal communication that will create your external experiences, results, happiness, fulfillment, confidence, personal success, and ability to become a transformational, influential leader. If you possess any self-doubt, here's a life-changing exercise to take on: Grab your laptop, tablet, or phone and schedule enough time to write out the story of your life and why you are the way you are. Then write down all the reasons why you can't become or achieve more of what and who you want to be.

Once you write out your limiting story, throw it out. It's time for you to write you new story. The story you have is old and stale. You're comfortable with it only because you've been carrying it around your whole life, using it to justify every decision and action you have made. If that's no longer working for you, consider today to be your first birthday! It's in your power to create your reality through language and that includes your inner dialog as well.

You are not defined by your experiences and the beliefs you hold. This book will guide you through not only a transformation of action and behavior, but also a transformation of thought. You will adopt the habit of thinking like a talented, valued sales leader, and your past experiences will lose their power over you. You will respond to and learn from them. And that begins by asking yourself the right questions to challenge the reality you don't want and create the one you do.

MINDFUL MOMENT

If your primary focus is on changing your company and your people, you will fail. Change starts with you. When you change yourself, you exemplify what is possible for others and inspire organic, positive change.

34 CHARACTERISTICS OF A COACHING CULTURE

It's one thing to measure the impact of a coaching culture on your business. However, what would a coaching culture *look and feel* like? A coaching culture is a unified culture that everyone wants to be part of. Here are some characteristics that exemplify a coaching culture:

1. Acceptance
2. Accountability
3. Authenticity
4. Care
5. Collaboration
6. Communication
7. Confidence
8. Creativity
9. Efficiency
10. Empowerment
11. Ethics
12. Excellence
13. Family first
14. Fearlessness
15. Fun

16. Growth
17. Honesty
18. Healthy relationships
19. Innovation
20. Integrity
21. Lifelong learning and development
22. Living your personal values
23. Love and connection
24. Positivity
25. Professionalism
26. Self-awareness
27. Self-care
28. Selflessness
29. Service
30. Support
31. Top performance
32. Teamwork
33. Transparency
34. Trust

How would your culture measure up? Can you cite specific examples of how each of these characteristics were present?

FROM THE SIDELINES

Ultimately, a coaching culture is a people culture.

PREPARING FOR YOUR CULTURAL EVOLUTION

Now that you have a more well-defined picture of what a coaching culture looks and feels like, there are seven pillars in every company that determine the overall health and success of your organization.

The Seven Pillars to Achieve Cultural Excellence
1. **Purpose—The Why.** Why do you do what you do?
2. **People—The Who.** Do you have the right people in the right roles who share similar values?

3. **Proficiency—The Mastery.** Skill, knowledge, acumen.

4. **Process—The How.** Onboarding, sales, coaching, interviewing, procurement, handling performance issues, compliance, and all the other processes developed in each department that sustain consistency, efficiency, growth, and success.

5. **Product—The What.** What do you sell? A product, service, or both? Where would you score your product or service on the spectrum of excellence, if you did a competitive analysis?

6. **Perception—The Attitude.** Your attitude, your customer's attitude, as well as the organizational attitude determines your company's level of engagement, collaboration, accountability, loyalty, integrity, motivation, excellence, and all characteristics of a positive coaching culture. Strategy, service, and skill encompass part of the outer game: the rules of engagement and execution. Your attitude and mindset determine the inner game or the core of success. This is the heartbeat of your organization and where your journey begins. Without the right attitude, everything you build will crumble from the pressure of toxic thinking.

7. **Performance—The Score.** How is individual and organizational productivity and success being measured?

If there is a gap or breakdown in any of these seven areas, it will be difficult to achieve and sustain cultural excellence.

Before we start building a culture, we need to start with an impenetrable foundation. Remember, the tallest buildings have the deepest foundation.

IS YOUR COACHING WORKING? ASSESS YOUR CURRENT CULTURE

Some leaders want to take the pulse of the company's current culture, so they have a baseline from which they can measure progress. An anonymous, brief survey with a few questions could suffice. Some companies use more detailed, third-party assessments. Other companies ask one or two questions to assess the level of employee engagement, using any of the survey platforms you can find online.

If the intention of the survey is clear, you increase the chance of aggregating more objective data, rather than people using this to air their grievances or lambast the managers and company, knowing it's anonymous.

Keep in mind, most people have their own definition of what coaching is. To ensure consistency, include a universal definition of coaching on the top of the survey to ensure they are evaluating the company based on a shared understanding of coaching. Finally, make sure you clarify the intention of the survey and what the benefit is for each employee, so they see what's in it for them, since people will resist what they don't understand.

What follows are 10 sample questions you can use in your survey. While there's value in asking all of them, you'll get a better response rate with fewer questions. Modify them as you see fit, as well as the style of question you want to use. (Open text box, multiple choice, scale 1–5, checklists, and so on.)

1. Would you refer people to work for our company?
2. How would you rate the environment or health of our culture? (Scale of 1–5 where 1 is the lowest score you can give.)
3. What five words would you choose that best describe our culture? (Text box or multiple choice.)
4. How would you rate your manager's support and commitment to your success?
5. How would you rate your manager's effectiveness around developing and coaching you to achieve your goals?
6. How consistent is the coaching you receive from your manager?
7. Does coaching measurably improve your (performance, productivity, attitude, job satisfaction)? (Note that each question should only measure <u>one</u> outcome at a time. In this example, "performance, productivity, attitude, and job satisfaction" would be broken up into four distinct questions.)
8. On a scale of 1–5, how fulfilled and satisfied are you at your job?
9. What do you love most about the company?
10. If you could change three things about the company, what would they be?

PREPARING FOR YOUR CULTURAL JOURNEY

Many companies think they already have a healthy coaching culture, when in fact, they do not. This happens because you can be blinded by success. You might be thinking, "We're hitting our growth goals and quotas, so we must be doing everything right." These are the same companies who also tell me they have little visibility, if any at all, around how their managers develop, support, and coach their teams.

Other companies and leaders realize they need help, regardless of performance. These leaders are more self-aware, have let go of their corporate ego, and like you, seek out resources to continually learn, grow, and perform like champions.

While you may feel you need the answers to move forward, the answers are only as good as the questions that are asked. Rather than provide a checklist, I developed 38 questions to spark creativity, innovation, and strategic thinking, and ensure you are well-positioned for your cultural evolution. Please note these questions are not listed in any particular order, so feel free to arrange them in the order you prefer.

TIP FROM THE COACH

The question is always more important than the answer because the answer you get is only as good as the question you ask.

COACHING CULTURE QUESTIONNAIRE

1. What is the universal definition of *coaching* and a *coaching culture* that will create companywide alignment and adoption?

2. What are the challenges you're experiencing that would be minimized or resolved if you transformed and upskilled your managers to become elite performance coaches?

3. Why do you want to create a coaching culture?

4. What are your measurable objectives and the results/ROI you expect that would determine the success of this initiative?

5. What is your ideal profile and the top characteristics of (a leader/coach, salesperson, employee, etc.)?

6. What practical, easy-to-incorporate coaching framework and methodology will you use to ensure consistency throughout your organization?

(continued)

(*continued*)

7. Who is the subject matter expert outside of your company who will support you around this initiative and ensure all best practices are being incorporated and adopted?

8. Will you be building this in-house or partnering with a credible company or leader in the field to create and deliver this for you?

9. Who will be the facilitator/trainer and coach who would deliver the coaching program? (The program will fail with the wrong trainer and coach, regardless of how good the content is.)

10. Will you be leveraging outside coaches to support your internal coaches and those who may require individualized coaching?

11. Who will own this initiative and be responsible for its launch, implementation, and success? Who will be the evangelists, advocates, and stakeholders? Will they have coaches of their own to support them throughout this initiative?

12. When is the launch date? When would be the best possible time to launch this coaching initiative and schedule the onsite or virtual leadership coach training, as well as the coach training for your salespeople and every department?

13. Who would be participating in the initial training program? The senior leadership, executives, or midlevel or frontline managers? What team, function or department would be the first to participate in this course?

14. Will you start with individual coaching, a pilot, or a full rollout?

15. What are the milestones that will be achieved and results measured throughout the implementation of this initiative that will ensure success?

16. How many people would be participating in the *initial* coach training course?

17. How many simultaneous days of training are you allocating to deliver the leadership coaching program?

18. How many employees in each department would be taking this course?

19. How are you introducing this initiative, and to whom? (A companywide email, team meeting, individual meetings, or will you incorporate all these communication platforms?)

20. Once announced, what is your timeline and path to progress? What are the defined phases of this initiative, the order in which they are introduced, and over what period of time? (Refer to the appendix for an outline of the steps to take and the order of the critical conversations that need to happen. After the initial rollout, ongoing coaching, observation, and enrollment becomes part of your daily, habitual rhythm of business.)

21. How will you ensure you have the support, commitment, and backing of your senior leadership team to ensure that this is a non-negotiable priority and will not compete against other initiatives? Is senior leadership just as committed to going through the same training and coaching that every other employee will participate in?

22. Do you have the right people in the right positions?

23. What will be the initial training format? An initial onsite delivery? Virtual delivery? Teleconference? Videos? Developing online courses?

24. Are you taking people out of the office (which would include travel expenses and more time for logistical planning) or are you doing the training onsite?

25. How will you reinforce, sustain, and embed the coaching after the initial coach training? Onsite training/coaching reinforcement, an advanced course, virtual delivery/ videoconference, online training and resources, webinars, videos, team coaching, scheduled one-on-one and group peer-to-peer coaching to reinforce best practices and learn from each other?

26. Do you have well-defined job descriptions for your managers? Is it clear that the top priority for every manager and where they need to invest the majority of their time is in the development and coaching of their team?

(continued)

(*continued*)

27. How are you going to manage the coaching process? What technology, if any, might you consider (an online coaching platform) to further support and manage the coaching process and progress for each coachee?

28. How are you going to measure the *quality* of each manager's coaching? How will you ensure you have the visibility you need around the quantity and quality of each manager's coaching to avoid it becoming a "check-the-box" activity?

29. How will you leverage your CRM to uncover coaching and developmental opportunities?

30. How are you going to ensure consistency around peer-to-peer coaching?

31. What would be the structure and cadence of coaching? Team coaching and individual coaching for each person within the company? Scheduled coaching? Dynamic, situational coaching? Observation? How often?

32. How will you ensure the fundamental principles of coaching are being honored? Will you choose "always be coaching" (ABC), "always be peer coaching" (ABPC), or "always be enrolling" (ABE)

33. What modules and topics would you like to see covered in the coaching course that your managers would participate in? How will you ensure there are no missing modules or critical topics in your program?

34. How will you budget for an investment like this? If you can't make the proper investment of time and money, then save both and don't do it at all.

35. What are the possible barriers that can lead to coaching failure when attempting make this the daily responsibility of every manager, salesperson, and peer?

36. How will you ensure global adoption throughout the company? How are you going to hold people accountable when it comes to delivering consistent coaching and being coached?

37. What kind of coaching evangelists, advocates, group, or coaching consortium can you put together who would

support the stakeholders and participants throughout this initiative and beyond? Who will take the role of being the accountability partner to ensure the coaching culture is sustained? Who will become your chief coaching officer?

38. Rather than push people to coach and be coached, using forced scorecard/HR compliance, how will you enroll people to the point they want to engage in and are fully committed to coaching?

CAN'T CHANGE YOUR COMPANY'S CULTURE? CREATE A SUBCULTURE INSTEAD

While many companies may not be ready to take on this initiative, there will be managers who want to learn how to become inspiring, transformational leaders and masterful coaches. That's what the rest of this book is about. At this point in the reading, we will look at the best way to support an organization by ensuring these managers have the foundation to build a coaching culture. Unfortunately, many managers who try to initiate positive change in their company wind up feeling frustrated, disappointed, and disheartened from the pushback they receive from their boss or senior leadership. You've probably heard something along the lines of: "While this is important, it's not our priority. Enough with the coaching for now. We need results to make sure we hit our revenue goals for the year." That's ironic, because in order to hit your goals without the stress of last-minute decisions, late nights, impromptu meetings, and using your last bit of physical and intellectual energy to crawl over the finish line, *you need to be coaching your people!*

FROM THE SIDELINES

It is the responsibility of every manager to insulate their people from the pressure felt from the top.

Rather than trying to change your company's culture in the short term, create a subculture instead.

CAN YOU TRULY CHANGE A METRICS-DRIVEN CULTURE?

As an author and a wordsmith, I truly believe that reality is created in the language we use. Therefore, when you change the language, you have the power to change your thinking, which in turn creates new and better results. In the following story, I describe how one group of senior leaders experienced this very powerful universal principle.

I presented a workshop in Madrid, Spain, to about 80 senior sales leaders of a Fortune 50 company. They were there to learn how they could further impact their team and influence their organization by effectively coaching their sales teams, peers, and cross-functional teams. The group questioned whether a manager truly has the power to impact or influence a culture without authority, to the point where they can effectively coach their team in a sustainable way, especially in an environment where the leaders doing so are in the minority.

Their concern was how effectively their coaching could be over the long term if their boss and the organization's overall culture is not a coaching culture but instead a results-driven culture that valued performance over everything else, including their people.

Demoralized, dejected, and discouraged, these managers truly wanted to initiate positive change, but they felt helpless. They believed they had no influence over their company culture and could do nothing to make the positive changes that were desperately needed. So, instead of trying to become the change they wanted to see, they tried to work around the system and tolerated the toxic culture.

Think of our global society for a moment. Pick any country and consider the cultures that exist and even coexist among each other within an overarching larger culture. Now consider your company culture. Regardless of the size of your company, managers struggle to figure out what they can do to measurably impact their work environment.

This frustration typically manifests itself in a comment from a manager that sounds like this.

> Keith, I get that coaching works. You just put us through a powerful simulation that demonstrated what could be possible when we lead conversations with questions and more effectively <u>engage</u> with each other. I'm a huge believer in the power of coaching. But the message we hear from my boss, and my boss's boss, and the senior leadership team in this company is, "Get the results or die trying."
>
> So, coaching is great during good times, but it gets tossed out the window during a heated performance review or when your team is 30 percent down from your sales targets and you're a month away from closing out the quarter.

At that point, all I'm thinking is, my scorecard isn't looking very green and that's going to affect my team, my bonus, reputation, and career. We work for one of the largest companies in the world. We are a KPI-, scorecard-, results-driven organization. While I'd love to see this change, to date, we're not measured around how effective we are as coaches, but around our quota and goal attainment, and performance.

I've heard this a couple of times. I'm sensitive to this and deeply empathize with these managers. As much as I may understand their situation and how they believe there's no hope of change, as a coach, I'm not serving anyone by jumping on the bandwagon of despair and limiting thinking, nor telling people what they already know.

However, I truly understand and deeply respect the feeling that, regardless of the company you work for, trying to change a culture can often feel like trying to quickly turn a battleship, especially if you're a large global sales organization. Instituting any type of transformational change can feel overwhelming, risky, discouraging, and time consuming, especially when there are business objectives that need to be achieved *now*.

CREATE A SUBCULTURE

While continuing the facilitation of this workshop in Madrid, an idea came to me. I didn't plan on saying this nor was it in my presentation. I turned to the senior leaders and asked, *"What if you create your own subculture instead?"*

Being in a room with some very intelligent and experienced people, I needed to back up my statement. So, before I went deeper, I wanted to make sure I got my facts right. So, we all pulled out our phones and found how Merriam-Webster's dictionary defined the word *subculture* to ensure alignment around the definition and its relevance to this conversation.

Here's what we found.

b. an ethnic, regional, economic, or social group exhibiting characteristic patterns of behavior sufficient *to distinguish it from others within an embracing culture or society* [italics added for emphasis].

It sounded as if I was on to something. We then jumped over to Dictionary.com.

They defined subculture as:

a. the cultural values and behavioral patterns distinctive of a particular group in a society.

b. group within a society that has its own shared set of customs, attitudes, and values, often accompanied by jargon or a different way of communicating. A subculture can be organized around a common activity, occupation, age, status, ethnic background, race, religion, or any other *unifying social condition.*

This definition helped further reinforce the next question that I posed to every manager who wants to create positive change. I responded to their concern by asking a question very few could answer: If creating the type of subculture you want is a possibility, then how do you change a culture? How do you develop and transform talent?

The answer? *One person at a time. One conversation at a time.*

Regardless of the company you work for, look at your team for a moment and ask yourself, "Who created the culture and environment that exists within my team?" You did. You created that environment. In every conversation and during every interaction. Whether it's during a face-to-face meeting, a telephone conversation, a text, IM, or email.

Because in every interaction, you are doing one of two things. You are building trust, or you are eroding trust. You are building and developing people or you are eroding them.

And don't lose sight of the fact that it is your responsibility to create the desired coaching culture, or subculture—the positive environment that can coexist and thrive within a larger culture. It is entirely in your power to create a subculture of collaborative, coachable, and self-driven champions.

In an ideal scenario, the entire company would shift to creating a culture where they authentically put their people before the results. But until that happens, your team, department, or division can be the voice and example for what is possible, regardless of what is going on around you or throughout the company. From there, the subculture you create spreads organically throughout your organization. That's how to change a culture—from the inside out.

FROM THE SIDELINES

When you wake up, the first question to ask yourself before starting your work day is not, "What can I do to achieve my business objectives?" The question you want to ask yourself is, "What can I do today to make my people more valuable than they were yesterday?" The by-product is, you achieve your business objectives while developing a strong bench of future leaders.

Let's be clear, your job description hasn't changed. What has changed is the way you engage with and support your direct reports, peers, boss, and customers. Regardless of the culture you work within, how you communicate with and support people is always entirely in your power. And where you tap into that power to inspire positive change is in the language of leadership, the language of coaching.

THE CULTURE IS YOU

Honoring this philosophy and opening your thinking to create a subculture creates the changes and the type of environment that you and your team desperately want and need to thrive.

Regardless of your culture, your people interact with you every day. And how does that translate into the impact you can make? You're the culture or, at least, you're the subculture.

Therefore, creating the subculture you want on your team is all in your power because you control how you communicate, respond, and engage with each person on your team, including your peers, cross-functional teams, and customers.

Think of it this way: It doesn't matter what train you get on and whether the conductor of the train is a leader whose style is different than your own. As they lead you down the path to achieve your shared business objectives and desired destination, keep this in mind. When you get on that train, you get to choose your cart, seat, and your view. That's why, ultimately, the culture is you.

FROM THE SIDELINES

If the entire organization is part of this cultural journey, then everyone's a coach.

STOP SELLING, START COACHING

The question every company wants answered when it comes to accelerating growth, revenue, employee development, and productivity, is: How can we maintain our competitive edge, build our brand, outsell our competition, and consistently achieve our sales goals?

Your customers have evolved. So must your salespeople. That's why top salespeople are great coaches. Instead of training salespeople with outdated techniques your competitors use, you must transform your salespeople into *consultative sales coaches* who coach customers to succeed.

THE CONSULTATIVE SALES COACH

Being the innovator of executive sales coaching and the first to create a course that specifically focuses on developing sales leaders and all people managers into world-class coaches, I continually noticed the parallel between sales leadership coaching and professional selling.

My clients started recognizing it too. In practically every sales leadership coaching program I delivered, I would hear from at least one of the participants, "Keith, when reading your book, *Coaching Salespeople into Sales Champions*, this model can also apply to sales. If the art of coaching is to create new possibilities and it's always about the coachee, then the same model can apply to selling."

Actually, this *is* how I sell. Well, I don't *sell*. Instead, I coach prospects, which is why the definition of coaching and the definition of selling are the same.

Selling is the art of creating new possibilities.

THE SECRET TO MAKING TOP SALESPEOPLE GREAT MANAGERS

Ever promote a great salesperson into a management position, only to watch them struggle with managing, developing, and coaching their team? To solve this eternally universal contagion, here's how to prepare your future managers for their next position.

Sales training isn't the answer. To build a bench of next-gen successful leaders, start developing your salespeople into consultative sales coaches. Now, when they get promoted into a management position, they already possess the core competency and proficiency of a leader—coaching! Moreover, since these directs embraced the coaching methodology as a salesperson, you mitigate the risk of promoting the wrong people into management.

Imagine if every person within your company learns and embraces the language and methodology of coaching. Only then can you create corporate alignment, a united front, shared vision, the future leaders of your organization, and a top-performing coaching culture.

THE BEST LEADERS—AND SALESPEOPLE—COACH

Do you need a coaching model for your salespeople and a different one for your managers? Not at all. And that's great news. While my coaching model remains the same, the only thing that really changes is the conversation.

Instead of limiting the coaching conversation between a manager and a direct report, salespeople are now leveraging coaching conversations with every prospect, customer, peer, boss, coworker, friend, and family member, including your children, spouse, or significant other.

Now salespeople can coach their customers in a way that empowers them to find their own solution; one they would have greater ownership of, rather than being told what to buy.

MINDFUL MOMENT

The new language of leadership is coaching. The language of selling is coaching. The language across every department is coaching. Subsequently, the language of your culture is coaching, which creates full organizational alignment:

The Manager Coach + The Selling/Nonselling Coach = A Top-Performing Coaching Culture.

The first step to creating a coaching culture that inspires greater innovation and talent is by transforming everyone into a world-class coach. When everyone in your organization is speaking one language, and everyone, regardless of tenure, title, department, or position gets coached effectively and consistently, the results are extraordinary.

This is how you create and sustain your position as a market leader and get your peers, team, and company focused on one unified vision, strategy, and shared goal.

FROM THE SIDELINES

Another quick note about word choice: I use the words *framework* and *model* interchangeably, as I also do with the words, *manager*, *boss*, *leader*, and *coach*. This note is especially for any perfectionists who find these inconsistencies annoying.

We've finished discussing what's needed to prepare your company for a cultural journey into coaching. The rest of the book gets even more exciting because it focuses on the one thing that's going to make or break your company's success—*you!*

L.E.A.D.S.:
Your Guiding
Framework for
Transformational
Coaching

B efore introducing the newly revised L.E.A.D.S. coaching model that will be your communication strategy for every conversation, here's an email I received from a manager who had attended my coaching course the day before.

As you read this story, notice how coaching isn't something that happens in the office, but every day, in every situation, and every conversation.

Hi Keith,

I wanted to share an interaction I experienced this morning that gave me a bit of an *ah-hah* moment after attending your program this past week.

I will start off by saying, I was not in the best mood this morning. I was waiting to order a bagel at the only place that I know of in my town that makes a proper bagel. There's usually a pretty long line, and this morning was no exception. I tend to be somewhat impatient while standing in lines. My mind tends to race when I feel like I'm idling …

While standing there, hungry, impatient, and irritable, I had the feeling that someone was looking at me. I looked down to see a little girl, maybe 5 or 6 years old, peering up at my face with a warm smile. I smiled back at her briefly and returned to my racing thoughts, while checking my texts and emails. A few minutes later, she turned to her mother and started talking, which pulled my attention back to the moment.

The interaction between the daughter and her mother was as follows: The daughter said, "Mommy, that lady is really pretty."

Her mother replied, "Do you think you can tell me who you are talking about without pointing your finger?"

"She's right behind us," the daughter said.

After looking at me and smiling, asked her daughter, "What do you think would happen if you told her that you think she's pretty?"

Pausing for a second, the daughter responded with, "Ummm ... I don't know."

"Well. How do you feel when someone says something nice to you?"

The daughter giggled and said, "Pretty gooood."

"So, how do you think she would feel if you told her that?"

The daughter didn't respond to her mother's question, but instead smiled at her, and then turned to me. Very politely and confidently the little girl said, "Um. Excuse me. Hi. My name is Libby. I think you're very pretty."

Libby had just made my wait in line a little more enjoyable, and my day a lot better. I sincerely thanked her and told her that she just made me feel really good. Continuing to talk to Libby for a few minutes, she explained to me that Sundays are her favorite day of the week.

She also told me, very factually, "I think bagels are like cupcakes. They're really yummy, but things like that are only healthy when they're special. We can't eat them all of the time, because they wouldn't be special anymore if we did." This little person had some insightful wisdom! Libby's self-assured confidence and liveliness were engaging and remarkable to me.

First, as I observed, this mother seems to be quite the master of the whole mom thing. I don't have children, so I am not a subject matter expert. However, after my interaction with Libby and her mom, I thought about several ways a similar situation could have played out between other parents and children, and of course, between myself and my team.

A well-intentioned parent who might have seen an opportunity to make someone else's day a little better could have responded to their child's initial statement with something along the lines of, "You should tell the lady that you think she's pretty. It will make her feel good." The child might have awkwardly stepped outside of his or her comfort zone and offered the compliment to the stranger. This directive approach could also backfire. If Libby's mom never took the time to uncover how she felt and expand her daughter's perspective, Libby may not have said anything out of fear or discomfort.

This mother, on the other hand, seemed to recognize an opportunity to increase Libby's confidence, instead of just pushing her out of her comfort zone. The use of open-ended questions seemed to encourage little Libby to arrive at her own conclusion of what the next action should be. When Libby acted, she was visibly confident in her decision. It was neat to watch.

Personally, I am grateful that I had the opportunity to experience this interaction from a perspective that I might have otherwise missed. I wanted to reach out and share this story with you and thank you for directly impacting my awareness in this way. It's amazing how different things can look when you start looking through different lenses.

With gratitude,

Amanda

This story is a great illustration of the power of coaching, patience, and being present in the moment. It doesn't matter what the situation is, or who the person is, whether at work or at home, coaching is simply the most effective form of communication, and the preferred language of elite leaders.

QUESTIONS ARE THE UNIVERSAL LANGUAGE

Every coaching framework consists of well-crafted, precision-based questions to facilitate the conversation, which empowers people to self-reflect and arrive at a solution or new insight on their own.

At the core of coaching, the theory is simple: To tap into each person's individuality by starting every conversation with the intention to understand each person's point of view, goals, motivation, skill set, priorities, strengths, behavior, and way of thinking through the strategic use of well-timed, open-ended questions. Powerful questions encourage people to develop their own problem-solving skills and amplify their self-awareness. If they can't see their own gap, limiting thinking, what they need to change, or create an effective solution, only then is the timing right for the coach to share an observation that the person would benefit from which they could not see on their own.

Well-crafted coaching questions empower people to:

- Become better strategic thinkers who solve their own problems and create their own solutions.
- Take ownership and accountability over every area of their life.
- Tap into their individuality.
- Pause, process, talk through, and reflect on each situation to expand their peripheral view and self-awareness.

- Challenge what they do and how they think to recognize any assumptions, limitations, and gaps in their belief system, activity, behavior, or attitude that they could not see otherwise.
- Get to the root cause of a challenge so it can be resolved fully, rather than treat symptoms, solve the wrong problems, and continually have redundant conversations that consume your time.
- Build confidence, self-esteem, and the coaching skills needed to become an all-star salesperson and a leader in your organization.
- Recognize that, most of the time, they have the right answer within them!
- Trust their manager and develop healthy relationships. Questions, combined with proactive listening, show people that you care and they are being heard and respected—all because you're giving them your time and undivided attention they deserve!

If you ask people questions that challenge them to rethink their assumption or belief or help them arrive at a new idea, solution, or answer on their own, then they in turn have created the very thing that they were looking for from you. That is, *the answer.*

FROM THE SIDELINES

It doesn't matter if you have the perfect answer. People often resist what they hear, but they believe what they say. That's why the question is always more powerful than the answer.

What people create, they own. And if they own their ideas, they're more apt to act on their solution or adopt healthier thinking, rather than being told what to do. Leveraging people's abilities builds their confidence and skill set, creates the accountability every manager wants and needs on their team, and frees up the time to focus on their primary objective—coaching champions.

Moreover, consistent coaching not only develops but reinforces and sustains the skills, attitude, and behavioral changes needed to achieve more than you and your team thought was possible.

A UNIVERSAL DEFINITION OF COACHING

If you went around to each person in your company or on your team and asked them to define coaching, it's a safe bet you will not hear a consistent definition. So, before you start coaching, there needs to be a universal understanding and definition of what coaching is.

After all, based on experience or assumptions, everyone is going to have their own definition of what coaching is, and how effective it can be. That's why I've provided you with a universal definition of coaching that every manager, team, and company can embrace.

As you reach through the definition, notice how it encapsulates the responsibilities of the coach, the expectations of the coachee, and what it means to communicate and act like a world-class leader.

COACHING CONUNDRUM

Many managers operate under the faulty belief that you only coach when solving a problem, dealing with underperformance, or jumping in to help close a sale. Coaching transcends beyond this myopic view. *Every* conversation is a coaching conversation.

Coaching is a way of communicating, connecting, and engaging with someone in an empowering way that:

1. *Co-creates* new possibilities to bring out a person's best through deeper, open-ended questions and by sharing your observations at the right time.
2. *Challenges* current thinking and assumptions to stimulate self-awareness, accountability, and problem-solving skills.
3. *Guides* the person to set and/or reinforce best practices or a new direction in behavior, skill, attitude, or strategy around their goals.

This is achieved through a process of consistent interaction, observation, and *unconditional* support in a safe and trusting environment that focuses on the unique and specific needs and talents of each individual in a way that facilitates long-term, positive change.

FROM THE SIDELINES

Here's the abbreviated definition of coaching: *the art of creating new possibilities.*

THE REVISED L.E.A.D.S. MODEL FOR MASTERFUL COACHING

Now that we've established a universal definition of coaching, how do you achieve these objectives during every conversation?

I first introduced my L.E.A.D.S. Coaching Model in *Coaching Salespeople into Sales Champions*. You'll notice that I've kept the foundation and steps of my coaching framework intact.

However, since its initial introduction, the L.E.A.D.S. Coaching Model has exponentially evolved. (After working with more than three million people on five continents in over 75 countries, you're bound to learn a few things.) It's now more effective, intuitive, tactical, and easily implemented for the sales manager, salesperson, all managers, and anyone who wants to coach!

What excites me most is how it transcends all industries, company cultures, and geographic boarders. I was intentionally mindful of the unique global cultures to avoid creating a framework that's solely from an American point of view. I wanted to validate and ensure worldwide adoption would be possible.

While the acronym and intention behind each step has remained the same, it's now the L.E.A.D.S. model on steroids. This section is meant to be very tactical, so you can keep this as a template in front of you every time you have a conversation. Instead of sharing a few hundred coaching questions like I did in my last coaching book, I've narrowed it down to *15 questions* you can use in virtually every situation and conversation, along with 7 non-negotiable coaching questions, which will get you in the habit of consistent coaching.

Let's begin with taking a behind-the-scenes look at the science and methodology of the L.E.A.D.S. Coaching Model.

TIP FROM THE COACH

Coaching disclaimer: While I guarantee coaching will work famously with everyone you coach, I make no guarantees when it comes to your significant other! Why? Simply because you're way too vested in the situation and outcome! Besides, when I first attempted to coach my wife, she made her dissatisfaction clear when she said, "Don't try that Jedi mind stuff on me!" Now, she does all the coaching in our relationship (although I'm not always convinced it's authentic *coaching*).

A SIMPLE COACHING FRAMEWORK

Regardless of the conversation you're having, or the person you're speaking with, there are always three questions that need to be answered in every interaction.

1. **What?** What's going on? What's the topic of this conversation? What's the objective? What help is the coachee looking for? Gather the facts by asking questions to accurately assess the situation.

2. **Why?** Why is this happening? Why is the coachee in this situation? Uncover the gap or the **root cause**. Is this a training (mindset and skill set), coaching, advising, or observation-sharing moment?

3. **How?** Tactical action-oriented. How are you going to move forward and create a new outcome, possibility, or healthier way of thinking?

Unfortunately, the coaching and communication framework that most of the world's leaders use sounds like this.

1. What's going on?
2. Here's what you need to do.

Ouch. In case you haven't noticed, this is not coaching! Now you're reverting to the destructive role of the *chief problem solver*. The greater cost here is, many managers believe this is what good coaching sounds like and why companies often assume their managers are already coaching consistently and effectively!

What's missing here? Questions. The *why*. In addition to the *why*, this ineffective model doesn't take into consideration the *who*, the *how*, or the *when*. If you're only hearing *what's* going on, assume rather than assess and validate the facts, and subsequently provide a solution, then the root cause, the gap, the assumptions, the detrimental thinking, or the developmental moments have not been identified.

A few intentional, open-ended questions need to be asked in a particular order during every coaching conversation. We're now going to deep dive into every step of the newly revised, super-charged, L.E.A.D.S. Coaching Model.

FROM THE SIDELINES

Hang up your cape, chief problem solver. If you really want to be a hero, bring out the hero in those around you.

THE ANATOMY OF THE L.E.A.D.S. COACHING MODEL

I've been told that my framework is practical, non-theoretical, and easy to implement. Most coaching "frameworks" are nothing more than theoretical, 100-foot coaching overviews that list the objectives you need to achieve. They leave it up to you to figure out what questions to ask, and when to ask them. However, the L.E.A.D.S. framework is as easy as plug and play (see Figure 2.1).

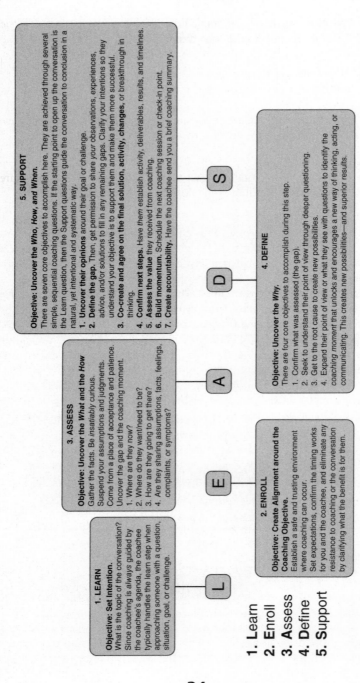

1. LEARN

Objective: Set Intention.
What is the topic of the conversation? Since coaching is *always* guided by the coachee's agenda, the coachee typically handles the learn step when approaching someone with a question, situation, goal, or challenge.

2. ENROLL

Objective: Create Alignment around the Coaching Objective.
Establish a safe and trusting environment where coaching can occur.
Set expectations, confirm the timing works for you and the coachee, and eliminate any resistance to coaching or the conversation by clarifying what the benefit is for them.

3. ASSESS

Objective: Uncover the *What* and the *How*
Gather the facts. Be *insatiably* curious.
Suspend your assumptions and judgments.
Come from a place of acceptance and patience.
Uncover the gap and the coaching moment.
1. Where are they now?
2. Where do they want/need to be?
3. How are they going to get there?
4. Are they sharing assumptions, facts, feelings, complaints, or symptoms?

4. DEFINE

Objective: Uncover the *Why*.
There are four core objectives to accomplish during this step.
1. Confirm what was assessed (the gap).
2. Seek to understand their point of view through deeper questioning.
3. Get to the root cause to create new possibilities.
4. Expand their point of view or what they see with questions to identify the *coaching moment* that unlocks and encourages a new way of thinking, acting, or communicating. This creates new possibilities—and superior results.

5. SUPPORT

Objective: Uncover the *Who, How, and When.*
There are seven core objectives to accomplish here. They are achieved through several simple, sequential coaching questions. If the starting point to open up the conversation is the Learn question, then the Support questions guide the conversation to conclusion in a natural, yet intentional and systematic way.
1. **Uncover their opinions** around their goal or challenge.
2. **Define the gap.** Then, get permission to share *your* observations, experiences, advice, and/or solutions to fill in any remaining gaps. Clarify your intentions so they understand your objective is to support them and make them more successful.
3. **Co-create and agree on the final solution, activity, changes,** or breakthrough in thinking.
4. **Confirm next steps.** Have *them* establish activity, deliverables, results, and timelines.
5. **Assess the value** they received from coaching.
6. **Build momentum.** Schedule the next coaching session or check-in point.
7. **Create accountability.** Have the coachee send you a brief coaching summary.

L   E   A   D   S

1. Learn
2. Enroll
3. Assess
4. Define
5. Support

FIGURE 2.1 The L.E.A.D.S. Coaching Framework.

34

If you have not read *Coaching Salespeople into Sales Champions*, the L.E.A.D.S. Coaching Model is an acronym for:

Learn

Enroll

Assess

Define

Support

That's it! Let's take an exploratory walk through this framework to ensure you have a solid understanding of the objective behind every step.

FROM THE SIDELINES

One company, one coaching model. That's why, in the spirit of consistency, flexibility, and simplicity, the L.E.A.D.S. Coaching framework and the Enrollment framework never change, regardless of who you're speaking with. The only thing that changes is the conversation, the topic, and the coachee.

Learn

Objective: Establish the Objective of the Conversation

- What are the topic and expectations of the conversation?
- Since coaching *always* follows the coachee's agenda, coachees determine the *learn* step when approaching you with a question, situation, goal, or challenge. So, identify the topic they want to discuss, whether it's an impromptu, situational coaching conversation or a scheduled coaching session. (If you're wondering what to do when you have an agenda or something that you need to discuss or address, that's where "The Art of Enrollment," Chapter 7, comes into play.)

FROM THE SIDELINES

Lead every conversation with questions, rather than answers. That's why in every conversation, you're either assessing the facts or assuming them.

Enroll

Objective: Create Alignment around the Objective

- Establish a safe and trusting environment where coaching can occur.
- Set expectations around the conversation, confirm the timing works for you and the coachee, and eliminate any resistance to having the conversation by clarifying what the benefit is for them.

Assess

Objective: Uncover the *What* and the *How*

- Gather the facts. Be *insatiably* curious.
- Suspend your assumptions and judgments.
- Come from a place of acceptance and patience.
- Uncover the gap and coaching moment.
  1. Where are they now?
  2. Where do they want/need to be?
  3. Who do they want to be? (Someone who is confident, fearless, caring, respected, patient, supportive, and so on. This answer should get at a person's internal characteristics.)
  4. What's missing for them to achieve their objectives?
  5. How are they going to get there?
  6. Are they sharing assumptions, facts, feelings, complaints, or symptoms?

MINDFUL MOMENT

Being curious is no longer enough. Great coaches are *insatiably* curious. You have an unwavering desire to learn, explore, and deeply understand every situation, person, and point of view.

Define

Objective: Uncover the *Why*

There are four core objectives to accomplish during this step.

1. Confirm what was assessed to ensure alignment and under-standing (the gap).

2. Seek to understand their point of view through deeper questioning.

3. Identify and define the root cause (if it hasn't surfaced during the Assess step) to resolve a challenge or create new possibilities.

4. If needed, expand their point of view or what they see with additional deep dive, *expansion questions* to identify the *core coaching moment* that unlocks and encourages a new way of thinking, doing, or communicating.

Support

Objective: Uncover the *Who*, *How*, and *When*

There are seven core objectives to accomplish here. If it feels overwhelming, have no fear. These objectives are achieved through several simple, sequential coaching questions. If the starting point to open up the conversation is the Learn question, then the Support questions guide the conversation to conclusion in a natural, yet intentional and systematic way.

1. **Uncover their opinions** on how to resolve a situation, eliminate a problem, achieve a certain outcome, create a shift in attitude, or make a positive change in their behavior, skill, strategy, activity, resources, and communication. What do they need to change to improve results and become who they want to be?

2. **Close the gap.** Once you've walked through what they've learned and what they've committed to, whether in action, thinking, or strategy, this is when you get permission to share *your* observations, experiences, advice, and/or solutions to fill in any remaining gaps they missed. Clarify your intention prior to sharing your observations so they understand that your prime objective is to support them and make them more successful. For example: "Are you open to hearing some ideas that would make you more successful/eliminate this problem and enable you to generate the results you want?"

3. **Co-create and agree on the final solution** or change in thinking, strategy, skill, or behavior.

4. **Confirm next steps** and any associated deadlines. Have *them* establish activity, deliverables, results, and timelines. When they own it, they're accountable for it.

5. **Assess the value** they received from coaching and what, if anything, needs to change, whether it's related to the topic or your coaching style.

6. **Build momentum.** Schedule the next coaching session or check-in point. If applicable, determine if you need to follow up on something they committed to or they need to follow up with you regarding any progress or results achieved prior to your next conversation or meeting.

7. **Create accountability.** Have the coachee send you a brief coaching summary, also known as the Coaching Action Plan (Chapter 5), to demonstrate alignment, accountability, what they've learned, the commitments they've made, along with any associated deadlines.

TACTICAL APPLICATION OF THE L.E.A.D.S. COACHING MODEL

Now that we've broken down the anatomy and objective of each step in the coaching framework, it's time to get tactical! What follows are the questions to use in every step of the coaching framework.

You'll find that these questions are applicable for practically every conversation you'll have, forever.

Keep in mind, this isn't only a framework for coaching, it's also your new language and daily communication model for how you begin and end every conversation.

This includes how to:

1. Prepare for and begin the conversation.

2. Gather all the facts and opinions and eliminate costly assumptions.

3. Uncover and work through the coaching, learning, and alignment moment.

4. Establish next steps.

5. Build personal accountability.

6. Confirm the value of the conversation and interaction with you to reinforce learning, development, and the power of coaching, a connection they're likely to miss.

7. Gather feedback to ensure your coaching is aligned with how the coachee wants to be coached. This cements your value, while building your brand and strengthening your reputation as a great leader.

8. Conclude the conversation.

24 TYPES OF QUESTIONS IN THE L.E.A.D.S. COACHING FRAMEWORK

In *Coaching Salespeople into Sales Champions*, I created an appendix with more than 300 coaching questions you can use in more than 40 of the most common scenarios managers find themselves in.

In this book, I've named the 24 types of common questions you'll use that are embedded throughout each step of the L.E.A.D.S. framework. Rather than waste time on the theoretical mumbo jumbo that cannot be put into action, I've given you a few examples to use when coaching.

Every step in the L.E.A.D.S. framework has questions labeled under that step. This part goes one step further to assign more specific categories to give context to the more precise questions for coaching in certain scenarios.

1. The Accountability Question
2. The Alignment Question
3. The Assumptive Question
4. The Celebration Question
5. The Challenge Question
6. The Core Question
7. The Coding Question
8. The Contrarian Question
9. The Empowerment Question
10. The Enrollment Question
11. The Expansion Question
12. The Expectation Question
13. The Implication Question
14. The Learning Question
15. The Messaging Question
16. The Momentum Question
17. The Phraseology Question
18. The Relationship Question (e.g., inner game, fear, confidence, transparence, self worth, etc.)
19. The Reset Question
20. The Role-Switch Question
21. The Self-Reflective Question
22. The Springboard Question
23. The Strategic Question
24. The Who-Based Question

TIP FROM THE COACH

Why try to memorize something that's brand new to you? It's legal to keep the framework and questions nearby when coaching! Keep your notes, the L.E.A.D.S., and the enrollment model in front of you until it becomes innate. Whether in-person or remote coaching, I suggest sharing this with your coachees. Show them what you're learning. This will develop transparency, connection, and greater trust, demonstrating you're both going through this learning curve together. So, keep the book handy, make a copy, put it on your computer, send it to your mobile phone, or tattoo it on your arm. (Tattoo is optional.)

As you review these questions, be mindful about the number and type of questions you ask.

Learn

- Learning Question: "What's going on?"
- Learning Question: "What's on your mind?"

These are two simple questions to ask during the learn step. Especially during an impromptu, situational coaching conversation, you'll find that the coachee is typically prepared and has their agenda for the conversation. So, you may not have to ask.

Now, if it's a scheduled coaching session, you would have received the Coaching Prep Form at least 24 hours in advance of a scheduled coaching session and have the Coaching Action Plan handy. (Refer to Chapter 5 for several templates, including two newly designed coaching prep forms and a Coaching Action Plan.)

Remember, when it comes to coaching, it is *always* the coachee's agenda, since they're the one coming to you, whether it's during a scheduled one-to-one coaching session or an impromptu, situational conversation.

One more thing: I would never want you to ask all of these questions. You don't need to! While many of the questions are non-negotiable since it's information you need to coach effectively, use the ones you feel are most appropriate.

Later in this chapter, I'll provide you with an abbreviated L.E.A.D.S coaching framework that will make it possible for you to coach in 10 minutes or less!

Enroll

- Is now a good time to discuss how you can achieve the results you want?
- What would be possible if we can redefine your role in a way that would work better for you?

- Imagine if … [fill in the blank]. It's often most effective to follow this with a goal they've shared with you. For example, "Imagine if you were able to get that promotion and increase in salary by the end of the year. What would that mean to you?" Or, "What if you were able to meet your sales goals? How would that impact you (your family, quality of life, peace of mind, and so on)?"
- If we could achieve the success you want and minimize the stress and overwhelm you said you're experiencing, are you open to discussing this?

As you may have noticed, all of these questions are closed-ended. I never have to coach managers on how to ask closed-ended questions, since they've already mastered those; especially if they have a sales background! But sometimes you need a yes or a no so that you can determine the path you need to travel down in the conversation. And in the unlikely event you ask these questions and hear a *no*, this becomes another coaching moment! Seek to understand the *why* behind the *no*!

Assess

- Expectation Question: What are your objectives here? Where do you want to be when you get to the other side of this (situation, goal, challenge)? What's the ideal result you want to achieve?
- Empowerment Question: What would it mean to you if you achieved this?
- Strategic Question: Walk me through the details (of this situation, conversation with the customer, steps you've taken, and so on).
- Strategic Question: What have you tried so far? How did you do it? Messaging Question: What did the conversation sound like? How did you respond?
- Strategic Question: How have you handled a similar situation before? (First, seek to understand their point of view and their approach *before* sharing your opinion.)
- Phraseology Question: When you say (*difficult, frustrated, pushing back, qualified, overwhelmed, value, uncooperative, success*), how do you mean? ("Phraseology," Chapter 10.)

Define

First: Recap what you've heard: "To ensure I've captured what you've shared, what I'm hearing is …"

Then: Once you've confirmed alignment around the message sent and received, it's time to dive deeper with the following questions to uncover the root cause.

TIP FROM THE COACH

Keep in mind, the gap or root cause can easily reveal itself during the assess step, which saves you time, as you can skip the define step and move right into the support step.

- Core Question: Why do you think this is happening? Why do you think you're in this situation?
- Assumptive Question: What assumptions might you be making about (the customer, situation/conversation, the other person, yourself)?
- Assumptive Question: How do you know that to be true? To ensure we're not making any assumptions, what are the facts here?
- Expansion Question: What else is possible? What else could be true? (Expand their line of vision around the situation by peeling the proverbial conversational onion to get to the facts or root cause. Remember, "And?" and "What else?" are complete and very effective questions.)
- Expansion Question: What's another way to look at this?
- Self-Reflective Question: What are you recognizing or hearing that, if successfully addressed, would create a new and better outcome?
- Self-Reflective Question: What questions haven't you asked? Challenge Question: Ideally, what is it you really want that you may not think is possible?
- If you were to describe the ideal situation/outcome what would it be?
- What would the best-case scenario look like?
- Implication Question: What would the worst-case scenario look like? (This question is effective in uncovering any irrational fears and negative assumptions people harbor in their mind.)
- Challenge Question: What, if anything, needs to change?
- Who-Based Question: Who do you need to be in order to (achieve your goal, improve that relationship, build your brand, improve your self-worth)?
- Implication Question: If this doesn't get resolved/nothing changes/you aren't able to attain your quota, how will this

impact you? (This is an *implication-based question* so they can recognize the cost of not changing, taking action, resolving, or achieving something.)

- Alignment Question: What's the common ground that we share? What's the common objective that you see here? What do you feel we agree on? (You and your peer, coworker, direct report, customer, family member, friend, etc.)
- Coding Question: What new habits do you need to develop to replace the ones that don't serve you?
- Empowerment Question: What would be possible if ...? (For example, ... *you were able to book ten meetings a week?*) This question encourages people to focus on the benefits they will realize if they do make the needed changes.

Support

- Self-Reflective Question: What's your **opinion** on how to (resolve this/achieve the results you want)?
- I trust you on this, so if I wasn't here, and you had to come up with something, what would you do?
- Role-Switch Question: If we switched roles and you were in my position, how would you handle this? (You may know what life looks like through their eyes if you've been in their role before, but do *they* know what your world looks like? Let's see how comfortable and effective they are when wearing your shoes!)
- Contrarian Questions: What if that wasn't true? What if you had no limitation? What if the opposite were true? What if your boss, customer, or significant other was in alignment with you and your thinking? How would that change things?
- Challenge Question: If you couldn't use that as a reason/excuse anymore, how would you move forward and resolve/achieve this? (A fantastic question to eliminate the opportunity for the coachee to use excuses, and instead, focus on a solution they're accountable for.)
- Challenge Question: We can focus on what we can control, or we can focus on what we can't. Let's focus on what we can control in activity and strategy, so that you can achieve the results you want, okay? (This question shifts the conversation away from the complaints and what is out of the coachee's or manager's control, to what the coachee can do to achieve their goals.)
- Accountability Question: If you did know, what would it be? (While this sounds like an awkward question, it's a powerful

one to use when you hear the coachee say, "I don't know." Use this question and you'll notice how the majority of the time, the coachee will come up with a response, and because you have positioned it as a hypothetical question, it's less intimidating than a question with a "right" answer! You just have to ask it with a straight face.)

Now Coach the Gap!

You've uncovered your coachee's opinion, perspective, the gap, and a learning moment! Now you know what they know, how they think, what they've done, how they've done it and what was missed. (Refer to the last section in this chapter to learn about the only three scenarios and responses your coachee will share in every situation.)

Now, if they nailed it and came up with a great solution or insight, congratulations! That is a testament to great coaching. Now, let them take their solution and execute on what they created, so that you no longer have to do their job!

However, if their solution isn't fully developed, begin by saying, "Thanks for sharing your ideas. Let's walk through them together to ensure your strategy/solution will achieve the results you want."

Then, if they miss anything, and most of the time they will, get permission to share your additional observations that will fill in any remaining gaps to ensure they're open to hearing them.

Here's what that can sound like. "Can I share some observations that would help you achieve the results you want and make you more successful?"

Wrap-Up and Next Steps

Maintain Progress and Momentum: While still in the support step, confirm their action plan and commitments, build accountability, schedule a time to follow up or schedule the next coaching session, assess the value they received from coaching, and request an email recap of the conversation.

- Accountability Question: What are you willing to commit to in activity and/or result? By when?
- Coding Question: What can you do to ensure you honor the successful daily habits that will enable you to achieve your goals?
- Empowerment Question: How can I best support you around this and be a supportive accountability partner to ensure you achieve the results you want? (Caution: Don't say, "How can I help?"

This question translates in the coachee's mind as, "What part of your job do you want me to do for you?")

- Momentum Question: When should we reconnect to ensure you have achieved the result you want?
- Accountability Question: If for some reason you don't follow through with the commitments you make, how would you like me to handle it?
- Accountability Question: How would you like me to approach you and bring this up in a way you'd be open to?
- Coding Question: How can you handle this the next time you're in a similar situation?
- Learning Question: How are you feeling about our conversation?
- What new possibility did we create? What did you learn?
- How has this changed your opinion/perspective?
- What did you find most valuable/helpful/useful?
- Calibration Question: What, if anything, would you like me to change regarding the way I'm coaching you?
- Momentum Question: When do you want to schedule your next coaching session?
- When can I expect the Coaching Action Plan to recap our conversation, what you've learned, and your commitments?

TIP FROM THE COACH

Before ending the coaching session, make sure you have scheduled the next coaching session or time to follow up. If you don't have the opportunity to schedule this, follow up to ensure you both get this on your calendar or use an online calendar app to do so.

HOW TO COACH IN 10 MINUTES OR LESS

I hope the revised framework will help you adopt coaching faster than ever, especially since I further defined the types of different questions that reside in each step. But why stop here?

I know you're busy. And if you're reading this book, I know you care about your company, your people, and being the best you! While the model above is certainly more comprehensive, *what if you can coach anyone in 10 minutes or less?*

Sure, there will be times when a more in-depth conversation is needed. But for busy, caring managers, 10-minute conversations remove the fear that coaching takes too long. And what makes your coaching even more valuable is that you can more effectively honor the patience needed to coach, knowing you have a path to follow that will organically guide the conversation to its natural conclusion—in just about 10 minutes!

Managers often don't know what direction to take a coaching conversation, or how long the conversation will last. Instead, they flail around like someone thrown into a pool who doesn't know how to swim.

At my company, Profit Builders, we've trained more than 100,000 global managers in easily adaptable, practical, high-impact, and time-efficient coaching skills. Of course, some coaching conversations require more time and questions to do the deeper dive needed to uncover the root cause of what may be a more challenging situation.

However, in most cases, these 12 universally applied, non-negotiable coaching questions—and 10 minutes—are all you need to make a positive impact and coach people to achieve more on their own. Since knowing where to begin and where the end question is, you can more easily develop the habit of coaching.

LASER COACHING: 12 QUESTIONS AWAY FROM A BREAKTHROUGH

Each question below is a non-negotiable question to gather the information you need in order for the coaching to be effective. Can you achieve this in less than 12 questions? At times, this is most certainly true. In fact, in Chapter 4, you'll learn how you can actually use just one question to enable you to coach in sixty seconds!

1. Learning Question:
   - What's going on? What's on your mind?
2. Enrolling Question:
   - Is this a good time to discuss how we can work together and how I can support you so you can achieve the results you want?
3. Assessing Question:
   - What's the ideal outcome you're looking for? What's your objective?
   - Walk me through the details around what you've tried or done so far and how you did it. (Get specific around activity, written communications, verbal conversations, objection handling, qualifying prospects, project management, sales presentations, meetings, and results. Keep digging for facts by asking, "Then what happened?" and saying *and*. In addition, find out how they've handled similar situations in the past.)

4. Defining Question:
   - Now that you've shared with me (recap what you heard), if you were the coach, what do you think the root cause is behind this situation or outcome? (Why do you feel this is happening?)
   - What else can be true? (And what else?)
   - What assumptions might you be making about: the situation or conversation; their/your definition of words like *overwhelm, difficult, value, consistent,* and *best deal*; the outcome and what may happen; or the person, customer, manager, coworker, or yourself?
   - What questions have/haven't you asked (yourself, others) to validate what you believe is true?

5. Supporting Question:
   - What's your opinion on how to: achieve your goal; resolve this situation; improve your skill, will, attitude, and so on?
   - What needs to change?
   - Can I share some observations that would help you achieve the results you want and make you more successful? Use this if the coachee missed something you observed. Ask before sharing to get permission so they're open to discussing.
   - What are you willing to commit to in activity and/or results? What would that look or sound like? By when?
   - What did you find most helpful/useful?
   - When do you want to reconnect to ensure you have achieved the results you want?

Determine next steps, a time to reconnect, and the value received. Then, request the Coaching Action Plan recapping the conversation, learnings, and commitments.

COACHING SIMPLIFIED: THE ONLY THREE COACHING GAPS YOU'LL EVER UNCOVER

You learn a thing or two after clocking thousands of hours coaching people from all over the world. In the spirit of continually simplifying the coaching process, I'm happy to reveal that there are only three general responses you'll hear during the support step. Recognizing this will help you coach more efficiently, effectively, and make it a collaboration rather than an interrogation.

Let me be clear: I'm not referring to the countless topics to coach on. I'm talking about the three main categories of responses you'll encounter when uncovering and addressing the gap in the L.E.A.D.S. Coaching Model.

1. The coachee provides a fully developed solution and/or possesses a high level of self-awareness. They recognized the gap! The coachee provides an observation, insight, or a strategy that can work. Maybe it's aligned with what you had in your mind, or shockingly, a different insight or solution that you didn't think of but could work. As such, there's no need to fill in the gap or dissect the coachee's solution. Next, the coachee implements the plan and shares insights or observations through self-reflection.

2. The coachee provides a partial solution and/or an average degree of self-awareness. They recognized part of the gap, but there were still some holes in either their solution or thinking. The support step is your opportunity to share your observations and advice to fill in the gaps they may have missed.

3. You know for a fact that the solution or approach the coachee provided is inaccurate, would be ineffective, extremely risky, resource prohibitive, or achieve a low success rate, and/or the coachee has a very low degree of self-awareness. They did not recognize the gap in thinking, skill, knowledge, attitude, or strategy.

Once you've uncovered the other person's point of view and the scenario that's most applicable, walk through their solution *before* you share your observation or advice. You can position this in a positive way that would move the conversation forward to completion while still having them own the outcome: "Thanks for sharing your opinion, I really appreciate it. Let's walk through your strategy and ideas to see how this could play out and, if needed, refine it together to ensure it will achieve the results you want."

Then, get permission before sharing your observations, advice, experiences, or subject matter expertise. Here's what that can sound like. "Can I share an observation that would enable you to achieve the results you want and make you even more successful?"

Notice what this approach accomplishes. If you want people to be open, trusting, coachable, and collaborative, drilling people with closed-ended questions just makes them feel like they're being interrogated instead of engaging in a collaborative conversation.

As you walk through the conversation together, you'll notice the gaps to fill in that were missed; steps or skills to refine, develop, or reinforce;

assumptions and limited thinking that needs to be addressed; and best practices and healthy thinking that needs to be acknowledged. Now the coach and the coachee can leave that conversation feeling confident they have a solid course of action and strategy to win big.

TIP FROM THE COACH

Want to shorten the coaching model? Consider this. Once your team is enrolled and appreciates the value of coaching, you don't need to keep re-enrolling them in every conversation. Now the L.E.A.D.S. Coaching Model becomes the L.A.D.S. Coaching Model! And if you ever experience any resistance to your coaching or the observations you share, it's simply a re-enrollment opportunity to reset expectations and clarify your intentions.

We've now gone through the methodology and the tactical framework so you can start leveraging the revised L.E.A.D.S. model. Let's get practical and see how the L.E.A.D.S. Coaching Model works in a variety of common situations managers find themselves in. You'll notice how the coachee's response dramatically changes when the manager acts as the chief problem solver, compared to when the manager engages like a coach uses the L.E.A.D.S. model.

But before you move on, how about taking a few of these easy coaching questions out for a spin and see how they work for you? Remember, even using one great question per week will help build that coaching muscle, so you can develop a habit.

CHAPTER 3

The L.E.A.D.S. Coaching Model at Work

DIRECTIVE COACHING IS NOT A THING

Welcome, once again, to the life and times of the *chief problem solver*. Before we dive into best coaching practices, let's look at what coaching is not. What follows are examples of what *not* to do and in no way resembles what good coaching looks and sounds like. These are simply hollow statements, empty and devoid of substance. As you read through these examples of common conversations managers have, think about how much of the conversation is left on the table due to the assumptions being made.

FROM THE SIDELINES

Welcome, once again, to the life and times of the *chief problem solver.*

Failed Conversation 1: Coaching Performance and Behavior

Direct Report	Manager
I know my numbers are slipping. Do you have any advice for me?	Just make more calls. And take the time to learn more about our products/services. Also, make sure you really qualify every opportunity, so ask better questions during your next meeting.

Failed Conversation 2: Skill Coaching During a Deal Review

Direct Report	Manager
The customer is pushing back on moving ahead with us. Any suggestions for what I can do to turn this around?	Call the customer and find out what's getting in the way and we'll talk about this tomorrow.

Failed Conversation 3: Gap Analysis During a Pipeline Review

Direct Report	Manager
Here are all the current deals I'm working on in my pipeline. I think they should all close on schedule, but one may be in question.	Great news! So everything else is accurate? Regarding that one customer, just uncover their pain points and find out what their compelling reason is that's going to get them to buy now.

Failed Conversation 4: Urgency Around Closing a Sale to Make the Quarterly Sales Number

Direct Report	Manager
Just a heads up. You know that account I was working on that was going to give us more business? Well, there was a change in procurement and now they're asking for a bigger discount. What do you want me to do?	What? We really need this deal to close out the quarter strong. I'm sure you've tried everything. Call the customer and try to build more value. I'll call the CFO to see what we can work out.

Put your coaching hat on and assess these four scenarios by answering the following questions:

- Did the manager learn why this is happening?
- Did the manager deliver value with his or her response?
- Did the manager identify the gap, coaching moment, or root cause?
- Did the exchange build accountability or inspire any measurable behavioral change?

The answer to these four questions is a resounding *no!* The only thing this directive manager achieved is telling the person what to do, while simultaneously taking on some of their direct report's responsibility to close the sale. What did this salesperson learn that would make them a better performer? Nothing other than, "If I have a problem, I don't have to resolve it. My boss will do my job for me." That is the costly lesson that managers everywhere further reinforce with their team.

USING THE L.E.A.D.S. COACHING MODEL

Enough of those painful conversations. We're going to look at the same scenarios, but this time, notice how the manager changes the conversation using the L.E.A.D.S. coaching model.

Before we dig in, bear in mind there are many ways to facilitate these conversations. I'm providing just one coaching approach for each of the scenarios we just discussed. Aside from a scheduled coaching session, the following conversations can also occur dynamically or during an impromptu, situational conversation. If a deeper dive is needed, your coachee can always cover the topic, strategize around a goal, or work through a challenge during a scheduled, one-to-one coaching session.

This is when you'll have enough time to work through each topic to completion, instead of rushing through a critical conversation, only to leave it unresolved, along with a trail of bodies (or at least more unresolved problems) in your wake.

TEN-MINUTE COACHING MOMENTS

If done well, some of these conversations won't take more than 10 minutes— and your time investment will pay off exponentially.

Successful Coaching Conversation 1: Coaching Performance and Behavior

Direct Report	Manager
(Learn) I know my numbers are slipping. Any advice?	**L.** (Done by coachee.) **Enroll.** Are you open to exploring some ways to turn your performance around so that you can achieve the results you want? **Assess.** When do you feel this started? **A.** When were you performing at a level you were comfortable with? **A.** What can you think of that you may have done differently, better, or more of that made you successful before? **A.** Where do you feel you want to be at this point? **A.** Walk me though the process you're currently using when prospecting. **Define.** What do you feel has changed since then? **D.** What can you change or improve starting today? **Support.** What are you willing to commit to completing by our next meeting? **S.** What system can you put into place to ensure this becomes a daily habit that will improve performance? **Coach:** Now, you can continue with the final questions in the support step. Recap, set expectations and an action plan, schedule the next meeting, and bring this conversation to its conclusion.

Successful Coaching Conversation 2: Skill Coaching During a Deal Review

Direct Report	Manager
(Learn) The customer is pushing back on moving ahead with us. Any suggestions regarding what I can do to turn this around?	**L.** (Done by the coachee.) **Enroll.** Can you walk me through what that conversation sounded like, so together we can come up with a strategy that's going to help you win this customer's business? **Asses.** When you say the customer is "pushing back," how do you mean?

Direct Report	Manager
	A. How did you respond?
	A. How comfortable are you having another conversation with this customer?
	A. How have you handled something like this in the past that got you the results you wanted?
	Define. What do you think contributed to this pushback in the first place? Why do you feel you're in this position?
	Support. What would be the objective of this next call?
	S. What would your conversation *sound* like?
	S. Let's do a quick simulation/role play on how you can approach them so that you get the result you want, okay? Besides, it's always safer to practice on me than on your customers.
	Coach: Move to the last few questions in the support stage to recap and set expectations for the next coaching session.

Successful Coaching Conversation 3: Gap Analysis During a Pipeline Review

Direct Report	Manager
(Learn) Here are all the current deals I'm working on in my pipeline. I think they should all close on schedule, but one may be in question.	**L.** (Done by the coachee.)
	Enroll. Would you be open to outlining a strategy we can develop so that you're confident the deal in question actually closes? (I'm curious to know what you're doing to ensure these deals close. This way, you can feel confident that you'll hit your numbers and no sales fall through the cracks.)
	Assess. Can you walk me through the stage you're at with these opportunities?
	A. Regarding the opportunity you're not entirely certain about, how do you mean "it's in question"?
	Define. Where's this sense of doubt or uncertainty coming from around this particular deal?

Direct Report	Manager
	D. Why do you feel you may lose this sale?
	Support. To validate this, let's do a quick comparison against our benchmarked best practices and sales process. That will help us to determine what areas, if any, have been missed, and what skills you need to ensure there are no gaps, so you can avoid situations like this in the future.
	Coach: Move to the last few questions in the support stage to recap and set expectations for the next coaching session.

Successful Coaching Conversation 4: Uncovering Assumptions Through Coaching

Direct Report	Manager
(Learn) I know I keep cutting the customer off when I'm speaking with them. It's hard for me to just stay quiet and listen to them, especially when I know what they're going to say.	**L.** (Done by the coachee.)
	Enroll. Would you be open to exploring some ways to improve your conversations with customers so you can generate better results?
	Assess. Can you walk me though a time when this recently happened?
	A. When do you find this happening most? With who?
	Define. Why do you feel that you're *always* 100 percent sure you know what they're going to say?
	D. How would you feel if you were in the customer's shoes?
	D. How can this impact your performance and customer relationships when making this assumption?
	Support. What would be a better way to handle this the next time to avoid a similiar situation? What strategy could you put in place?

> ## COACHING CONUNDRUM
>
> There's no such thing as directive or prescriptive coaching! It's an oxymoron. If you're directive or prescriptive, by default, you're no longer coaching but telling people what to do! If you tell people you're coaching them, and instead act as the chief problem solver, you're diluting the integrity and impact of coaching. At this point, you're better off not coaching, because after a bad coaching experience, your people will not want to be coached!

THE COST OF NOT COACHING

Every manager has resolved a problem or closed a deal for someone, just to save the day. While they love you for doing this, it also comes at a great cost. Here's how to resign from the time-consuming role of super-salesperson and chief problem solver, so you can eliminate the messy problems that plague your team.

> After a week of enjoying the breathtaking sites and culture of India, I was in a conference room, halfway through the first day of delivering my leadership coaching program, when I heard this all too familiar response: But Keith, there are times that you just can't coach. I understand that in most cases, it makes sense to lead every conversation with questions. It's definitely the more effective way to develop people and have them create their own solutions. But if it's the 13th hour and there's a huge deal on the line or a blazing inferno with a customer that needs to be extinguished immediately—or if we're in jeopardy of losing a client—it's not like you can sit the rep down and take the time to start coaching them around what they need to do! At that point, you must jump in and take charge to resolve what could escalate into a bigger problem. That's why everything isn't always a coaching moment. Sometimes you have to jump in, which is part of our job.

If only I had a dollar for every time a manager said this!

You Can't Always Be Coaching—Or Can You?

As I looked across the room of managers who, for the most part, seem to agree with this manager's statement, I responded with four words they weren't expecting: "I agree. You're right."

I sensed the manager who shared this observation felt validated. Before I threw in the towel, there was a great coaching moment for every manager in the room:

> You're 100 percent right. If you find yourself in the position you described, you must react immediately. At that point, there is no time to coach.
>
> When your direct report comes to you with an ultra–time-sensitive issue, there isn't time to teach, coach, train, or wait for them to self-assess and come up with the right solution. The problem has already metastasized way beyond what your direct report can do to resolve it, and escalated to the point where only a manager could handle it. As such, the coaching moment is gone.

Silence blanketed the room. I took their silence as agreement and understanding. I continued sharing a few observations in a way that no one in the room was expecting.

JUSTIFYING YOUR ROLE AS THE SUPER SALESPERSON

Some managers enjoy playing the role of the hero or super-salesperson who can swoop down to save the day or the deal. That's because it fills the basic human need of wanting to be needed and valued. When the person you saved thinks you're the hero, it feeds your ego, and you feel the love, validation, and belief that this is your value as a manager and that your team can't survive without you.

Unfortunately, this behavior comes at a cost to the coachee, to you, and to the company.

Many managers believe getting this involved in the sales process or taking on each of your team's problems is their true value when, in fact, it's only a part of a leader's value.

Once the cost of playing the super-salesperson becomes too great, only then must the manager relinquish the chief problem solver role and coach effectively to avoid those time-consuming problems that shouldn't exist in the first place—the same problems that result in lost revenue.

Like exercising, ongoing coaching keeps you and your team healthy, operating at peak performance, and prepared for the championship game. This avoids the problems that are about to hit the fan, which cause stress and wastes your time when doing your direct report's job. Now it's a distraction from your core responsibilities, such as building a team of future leaders.

ENTER THE FAN

I then asked these managers for permission to get a bit crude with them. I wanted to ensure I wasn't offending anyone. Inevitably, in one universal voice, every manager chimes in and says, "Of course! Go for it!"

I walked up to one of the flip charts in the room, took out a marker, and proceeded on drawing an oscillating desk fan on the right side of the page. I then drew an oval shape on the middle of the page, closer to the fan, so that it looked like it was about to hit the fan. And again, in the spirit of wanting to avoid using crude words, I asked the managers if they knew what this oval-shaped object represented.

As people started to chuckle at my drawing, it was clear that they got it. After the laughter died down, I explained my illustration. "As you can see, it's about to hit the fan. So, what does this tell you?"

Another manager begins to interpret my illustration. "At this time, it's too late to coach. You're either telling the person what they need to do, doing it with them, or taking over their problem to resolve it yourself. You have no choice but to jump in, because time is of the essence. There's so much on the line that if the issue is not handled immediately and properly, there are going to be greater consequences."

I confirmed everyone's agreement.

Now comes their defining moment. I asked the managers, "Since we're all in agreement, the question to ask yourself is, 'Why?' That is, why are you in this reactionary situation at all? What's the root cause? *Why* is this happening in the first place?"

Before they responded, I asked these two questions around the level of accountability they own in these situations. "What if you are responsible for creating these situations that most of you want to avoid? What role are all of you playing in this?"

I returned to my flip chart and drew a horizontal dotted line from the fan on the right of the page, all the way to the left side of the page. At the end of the dotted line, I drew another small oval.

"If you're a great salesperson, do you wait until the end of your sales process, after you provide the solution, to overcome objections, or do you take the time in the beginning of the sales process to qualify and identify any potential barriers so you can defuse these objections when they're small?" I explained that when the *oval* is far from the fan, it's possible to do something to neutralize the issues or disqualify the opportunity.

I continued to create a new possibility for every manager in the room. "Similar to professional selling, if you are honoring the ABCs of leadership—*always be coaching*—then you would have been able to identify this potential catastrophe when it was much smaller and you could do something about it, before it metastasized into something so big that it was positioned to hit the fan."

I asked if anyone had a different point of view around this. The silence in the room was, once again, interpreted as agreement and understanding.

How to Prevent It from Hitting the Fan

It was evident that these managers agreed with the theory behind my example. It was time for them to self-assess. I asked, "Now that we've established how costly these situations are, how do you avoid these problems from happening in the first place?"

The solution was now glaringly obvious to the group. If the leaders had been coaching that person effectively and consistently from the start, they would have identified the potential pitfall in their process and seen a developmental opportunity. Doing so would avoid situations like these from surfacing and getting to the point where the manager must drop what they're doing and waste their limited time to reactively resolve it.

I had one final question for the group: "If you turn this into a developmental opportunity for your direct report to learn from this experience, what can you do next?"

One manager announced, "Discuss how this can be avoided in the future?"

"Exactly," I confirmed. "After the situation has been resolved, conduct what I call a, *post-mortem review*."

Once you resolve the situation, reconnect with that person and discuss what needs to be done (e.g., skill, mindset, resources, strategy) to avoid this type of situation in the future."

FROM THE SIDELINES

If you're doing a post-mortem review, you missed the initial coaching moment, but created a new one.

Consider this truth: The only reason to conduct a post-mortem review is because there wasn't consistent coaching that would have identified the smaller gaps at the onset. Think about selling: A salesperson who misses a key qualifying question in the beginning of their sales process can result in a lost sale when asking for the person's business, because they didn't initially uncover and address all potential roadblocks or their concerns.

LET THE FAN BLOW YOUR PROBLEMS AWAY

Why use the analogy of a fan to drive home such a critical lesson? If you hold up a piece of paper in front of a fan, it's easy for the fan to blow it away. Conversely, hold a large rock in front of a fan and see what happens. The rock doesn't move. This metaphor illustrates how smaller problems get resolved quickly, while larger problems cause stagnation and more effort to resolve.

The lesson here is that consistent, effective coaching is your air-conditioning on a blistering summer day. Without it, you'll wind up sweating over resolving daily problems that don't need to be there in the first place.

Of course, fans can also be used to put your face next to it and talk into the fan, so you make a cool-sounding voice, like Darth Vader. Don't pretend like you've never done that.

Since we're playing pretend, let's pretend that you think you have all the time in the world to coach. The reality is, you do.

COACHING VERSUS TRAINING: WHAT'S THE DIFFERENCE?

Two common questions about coaching and training are: 1) How do you differentiate between training and coaching? and 2) Do you collapse the two together or leverage each one to complement the other? Here's an analogy to help you understand how to distinguish between a coaching or a training opportunity and when to leverage both.

If you want to learn how to play golf, and you're going to take the game seriously, one of the first things you're going to do is find a great instructor or enroll in a golf training class. You find someone who can teach you the fundamentals of the game and help you develop your swing. Since you've never done this before, the instructor will demonstrate what a great golf swing looks like.

After that, the instructor will then ask you to swing the club and hit some balls. That's the *training* aspect: learning the game, best practices, and core competencies needed to become a great golfer.

After you've learned the basics, you're on the course, golfing on your own. You've taken what you learned from the golf pro and are doing your best to apply it. You noticed that you've hit a plateau and realize you need another lesson.

Since you want to take your game to the next level, you schedule another lesson with your instructor. The instructor doesn't take the same training approach as in your early lessons. Now it's time to take a *coaching* approach to build upon that foundation and refine your game. Unlike the trainer, the coach is going to assess what you want to work on and identify skills you don't even know you need to improve. Your coach is going to uncover what you really want and how great a golfer you want to be. What do you ultimately want to shoot? That's one measurable result or destination; your gauge for winning.

Rather than tell you *how* to play, now the coaching instructor is going to *observe* you play. So, you go out on the course to play a few holes. As you play, the coach is observing how you swing the club, how well you play, and your attitude and inner game. The coach needs to get a good sense of your style, strengths, and opportunities for improvement. As you play through a few holes, the instructor may ask some questions along the way, such as, "On that last shot, why did you choose your 9 iron?" or "I'm sensing you were a bit frustrated from that last hole. What was going through your mind?"

After observing you, the instructor will then share an observation or two. And that might sound like, "Okay, I've watched you play a few holes. On the next shot, just keep your head down." The instructor did not tell me several things to change. He gave me only one.

Think about your direct reports. Imagine if you were in the field making client visits with your salespeople. After the first meeting, you share several things they need to improve by the next meeting. In doing so, you've inadvertently sabotaged this salesperson and set them up for failure. Rather than focusing on the customer, they're focusing on what you told them *they* need to change! The point is, limit the observations you share in the field. You will always have the opportunity to discuss the other areas they need to improve during your next one-on-one.

TIP FROM THE COACH

Sales training is what you need to become a salesperson. Sales coaching is what you need to become a sales champion.

Table 3.1 shows a brief comparison of training versus coaching. A teacher, consultant, or trainer is going to show you *how* to do something you have limited or no experience with. They may share knowledge around a certain topic, product, or even company policies during your on-boarding process in a new role. The trainer is going to provide you with a foundation, a process, and a benchmark of best practices to give you a starting point in relation to where you would begin to build upon to create your path of development.

TABLE 3.1 Training versus Coaching

Training	Coaching
Providing new information, strategies, objectives, and required competencies through demonstration and the dissemination of fresh ideas.	Empower people to heighten their self-awareness and generate solutions using the right questions to assess what they've learned, know, and what they're doing to continually improve.
Directive: At this point, you're explaining what to do, how to do it, and why, rather than searching for gaps or blind spots.	Collaborative: Asking questions for them to self-assess and uncover areas they need to work on, some of which you share when they didn't see on their own.
Sharing and teaching of core competencies, processes, and best practices. This is the foundation.	Refinement and reinforcement of best practices through *consistent* observation, conversation, and feedback.
Training sessions are scheduled when needed, often event based.	Coaching never stops; it's ongoing and consistent.

A *coach*, however, is going to show you how to improve what you're doing through all modes of learning: reinforcement, practice, observation, conversation, training, simulations, role plays, and the sharing of best practices. Now, coaching becomes the process to reinforce and refine best practices, while tapping into the individuality and strengths of each player on your team.

Coaching is the discipline management uses to leverage all your salespeople's individual strengths and talents to keep them on top of their game and recognize their fullest potential today, rather than what could be tomorrow.

If you're learning how to do something for the first time, like golf, the instructor isn't going to let you invent your own swing. Initially, everyone is taught the same way, since you need a baseline around universally proven best practices and knowledge, and the rules of the game. Then, as you learn the fundamentals, coaching will refine your game so you can leverage your unique strengths and develop your own style, making the swing your very own.

Chronologically speaking, the first step as a manager is teaching best practices and training every business athlete the same way when they're learning something they've never done. Show them the correct way to carry out their tasks, develop their skills, and explain the rules of the position.

When it comes to refining your game, removing obstacles, and challenging limiting thinking, that's when coaching comes into play. By continually building upon their skills and developing their mindset, they can continue to excel in their position and perform like champions.

How to Coach in 10 Minutes or Less

I magine you're in a pressure situation: a deal needs to be closed, a customer issue needs to be resolved, or a decision needs to be made. At that point, do you have to be directive with your team and tell them what they must do?

Not exactly.

It took me three decades of innovation, testing, coaching, practice, research, and refinement to develop my L.E.A.D.S. framework, the undisputed, perfect, bulletproof coaching strategy, and the only coaching framework that works for every sales leader and coach on the planet. And after tens of thousands of managers have adopted this framework, they report back that it is the only one that always works. It sounds like a huge success, right?

Why isn't there another framework dedicated to sales leaders? Because, with all due respect, the authors who write other coaching books have often never managed anyone or been a salesperson! Those frameworks may be valuable in other industries, but when it comes to the world of sales, they will not work. They fall short of necessary, critical steps for coaching sales leaders, but my approach resolves this issue forever.

Of course, I just couldn't stop there. As the business community continues to evolve, coaching does, too, in order to keep up with the changes in our marketplace.

One major breakthrough presented in *Sales Leadership* comes from being able to deliver laser-precise coaching in 10 minutes. But what if there were a way to coach in just sixty seconds? Through some self-coaching, I challenged myself to realize this new possibility, and the following coaching strategy is what has emerged. It can make the difference between developing a mediocre team of dependent, transactional order takers or a team of accountable, top producers. It's all how you choose to communicate. So, if you still feel you don't *always* have time to coach, here's a powerful strategy you can use today and every day! (Then, send me a message and let me know how well it worked.)

"COACHING TAKES TOO LONG"

It saddens me to think how many senior leaders and frontline sales managers fall into this toxic, limiting thinking that breeds mediocrity and dependency instead of ingenuity and accountability. This very belief is also the reason why these leaders aren't developing, why their sales aren't increasing, why market share is dwindling, and why their people are just surviving or squeaking by rather than performing to their peak potential.

You might be wondering, "How can you expect me to consistently coach all my direct reports, especially when I have 25 people I'm managing, when I'm getting pulled in twenty different directions along with the additional tasks or projects that need to be completed? Fires need to be extinguished, customers need to be serviced, and deals need to be closed!"

For the most part, managers have successfully overengineered coaching, just like they have done with many other things.

It's a paradox. *Your strengths are also your weaknesses.*

Many of the leaders I work with are so smart that their intelligence and experience can hinder their ability to coach. They think it can't be so simple.

But what if it was? I'm not suggesting it will *always* be this simple or that the following 60-second coaching strategy will replace the need to use the L.E.A.D.S. coaching model. Every manager must complete a formal sales leadership coach training program delivered by a Master Certified Coach if they want to make the full transformation into a best-in-class leader and coach. However, this is a powerful, bulletproof coaching strategy to start exercising your coaching muscle. Here's something to consider: What if most of the conversations you have when you're in problem-solving, directive mode can be transformed into meaningful, engaging coaching conversations?

And here's a crazy thought: What if the coaching conversation takes less time than doling our your advice and telling someone what to do? Consider this: *If you have time to put out fires and provide someone an answer, then you have time to coach. Choose your path.*

The reality is, sometimes one coaching question can empower someone to come up with their own ideas and solutions.

And as we've learned, what you create, you own. And if you own it, you're more apt to act on it. That's why the greatest leaders don't struggle with building personal accountability within their team. They allow their team to do the work.

So, it's not that coaching takes too long; it's the *way* you're coaching that takes too long. Thanks to the approach presented in *Sales Leadership*, with a little refinement, some bodywork, and maybe a new engine, you can get where you want to go faster than ever and in a safe environment.

Let's set the stage. One of your salespeople approaches you with a timely, pressing issue.

> *Boss, I really need your help on closing this sale. As you know, I've been working this deal for the last year and have it in my forecast for this quarter. Unfortunately, now the customer is pushing back and they're looking for a better discount. Something's going on in procurement and I'm not sure what to do. I know you have a relationship with the CFO, so can you please call the CFO and help me out here, or just tell me what I need to do?*

Here's the defining moment that will create either a new possibility or something less desirable.

SALESHOG DAY

Option One: You call the CFO, tell the salesperson what to do to resolve this, or worse, you take on their problem, make it yours, and do all the work for them, believing that by doing so, it will save you time and allow you to move on to your next task.

The result? Failure. If you've seen the movie *Groundhog Day* with Bill Murray, then you know what I'm referring to. It's the story of a guy who wakes up every day, repeating the same day the same way. He finds himself trapped in a time loop, doomed to relive that day repeatedly until he gets it right.

If you've ever felt like you're having repetitive conversations or reliving the same day repeatedly, here's your chance to get it right.

COACHING CONUNDRUM

If you're having repetitive or redundant conversations, either they're not listening to you, not understanding you, or you didn't get to the root cause of the issue. And the reason why they may not be listening to you is because you may be telling them something that they already know. *Redundancy turns off listening.*

Once someone feels they're being manipulated, talked at, or not getting what they want or need, they stop listening. To compound this, if you're not asking questions, then you're assuming the facts and, consequently, you will wind up solving the wrong problems or providing ineffective solutions. That's when your employees decide, "My manager sucks."

Option Two: Rather than choose to be in reactive or directive mode, use this powerful coaching strategy instead. I call it the *Billion-Dollar Coaching Question*. It's a form of laser-precision coaching, *not* speed coaching. For context, a laser is defined as a device that generates an intense beam of coherent monochromatic light (or other electromagnetic radiation) by stimulated emission of photons from excited atoms or molecules. Lasers are used in drilling and cutting, alignment, and guidance, and in surgery; the optical properties are exploited in holography, reading bar codes, and in recording and playing compact discs.

This is exactly what you'll achieve with this strategy.

Here's what this coaching strategy sounds like in practice, using the example of the salesperson looking to close a sale with a customer who wants a discount:

> *I'm happy to share my opinion with you, Tim. However, you're much closer to this (customer, situation, etc.) than I am, and I trust you and your judgment. So, what's your opinion on how to (handle this, move forward, resolve this, land this account, communicate to the team in a way they would be open to hearing your ideas, etc.)?*

Then, depending upon how they answer, and being mindful of the only three scenarios when coaching (Chapter 2), follow up with:

> Thanks for sharing your opinion, I really appreciate it. Let's walk through your ideas to see how this situation could play out and then, if needed, refine it together to ensure your strategy will achieve the results you want.

Inevitably, there will come a time when you see a gap that needs to be filled. This could be something that either the salesperson missed or that needs further refinement. That's why, when sharing your observations, advice, experiences, or subject matter expertise, get permission before doing so to ensure they're ready and open to your ideas. Jumping right in with reactive, unsolicited feedback can make people defensive and shut down the conversation. You can get started with something like this:

> Can I share an observation that would enable you to achieve the results you want and make you even more successful?

That, my friend, is it! How long would it take to reposition the conversation by asking these questions? Conservatively speaking, let's go with 60 seconds or less! Said another way, you can not only coach in 10 minutes or less, but also be a 60-second coach! Let's see why this is so effective.

THE FIVE PARTS OF THE 60-SECOND COACHING QUESTION

The 60-Second Coaching Question, otherwise known as the Billion-Dollar Coaching Question (that's how valuable it is), is simple and direct. The following section will show you how to successfully leverage this coaching tool, so the conversation feels natural and the coachee does all the heavy lifting.

PART 1: "I'M HAPPY TO SHARE MY OPINION WITH YOU."

Acknowledge that you will be sharing exactly what they have asked for, keeping them engaged.

PART 2: "HOWEVER, YOU'RE MUCH CLOSER TO THIS SITUATION THAN I AM."

Many times, it's the salesperson who has the relationship with the customer and, therefore, is much closer to the customer than their manager. This statement acknowledges their position of importance and their role in the situation, which builds accountability in an empowering way.

PART 3: "AND I TRUST YOU AND YOUR JUDGMENT ON THIS."

This statement alone is powerful. How often does someone say this to you? Do you hear this often? And if you do, how does it make you feel? How does this positively impact your self-worth and confidence? Acknowledging you trust someone and believe in their abilities builds their confidence and creates a deeper, more trusting relationship with your team.

MINDFUL MOMENT

The sheer act of respecting, actively listening, and truly wanting to understand someone's point of view builds trust and stimulates the *law of reciprocity*. That is, if you respect their opinion, authentically care, are insatiably curious, transparent, vulnerable, are coachable and open to feedback, and give them the gift of your listening and attention, they will do the same for you. This fosters trust, loyalty, deeper collaboration, and is the formula to spark remarkable innovation. Besides, what people really want in their career and from their manager is to be acknowledged, heard, valued, and respected.

PART 4: "SO, WHAT'S YOUR OPINION ON HOW TO HANDLE THIS?"

Here's the coaching moment. Seek to understand their *opinion* and viewpoint *before* sharing yours. Otherwise, you may find yourself creating your own *Groundhog Day* scenario.

Asking this question certainly took less time than giving an answer. The added benefit is, you're empowering others to do the work and own it, rather than making them lazy. By pushing for action and strategic thinking, you're not doing all of their work for them!

PART 5: "THANKS FOR SHARING YOUR OPINION, I REALLY APPRECIATE IT. LET'S WALK THROUGH YOUR IDEAS TO SEE HOW IT COULD PLAY OUT AND THEN, IF NEEDED, REFINE IT TOGETHER TO ENSURE YOUR STRATEGY WILL ACHIEVE THE RESULTS YOU WANT."

Explore their opinion and ideas together. Ask questions from all angles to ensure they have thought through their idea completely. Then, if and when you need to share your observations, advice, experiences, or subject matter expertise to round out a final comprehensive solution, use this question.

Can I share an observation that would enable you to achieve the results you want and make you even more successful?

Once they share their opinion, depending upon what you hear, this question will continue to refine their solution in a collaborative way, without making them wrong.

Why does this work in every scenario? As discussed in Chapter 2, there are only three general responses you will hear after asking for their opinion, whether using the full-blown L.E.A.D.S framework or this laser-like version. If you use the shorter version, you're not changing the framework. You're simply assessing the situation and spending the appropriate amount of time, because the laser-precise coaching strategy still encapsulates every step in the L.E.A.D.S. framework. By leading with questions, you're collaborating, rather than telling coachees, "You suck and your solution will not work. I know better, so here's what you need to do." Taking the latter approach will shatter the trust between you and the person you're speaking with, in addition to invalidating them and making their opinion wrong. And opinions are not right or wrong; they're just opinions.

You know very well that once the boss tells you what to do, they've relapsed to becoming the chief problem solver. That's why you need to exercise *patience* to have them explore their opinion through to completion so the coachee can recognize the gaps themselves. Then, together you can refine and come up with the best possible solution or strategy.

TIP FROM THE COACH

In every conversation, you *always need to seek to understand* the other person's point of view and opinion *first* so that you can uncover what they know and what they don't, in order to identify the gap.

ASK FOR AN OPINION, NOT A SOLUTION

While delivering a one-day sales leadership coaching workshop for a team of senior leaders in Buenos Aires, Argentina, we were working through the Billion-Dollar Question and the need to uncover the coachee's opinion. After sharing this powerful coaching tool, one manager immediately questioned its validity: "Keith, I can see how this can work on some people, but other people will not want to give you an answer."

That's true. Whether it's because you're their manager, they don't want to look bad or be wrong, they don't trust you, they know you'll give them the answer anyway, or they truly don't know, chances are, you'll still hear, "*I don't know. You tell me, boss.*"

I repeated the exact question for this manager. However, this time, I enunciated the key word: "What's your *opinion* on how to handle this?"

"Oh," the manager said after listening to me. "I didn't hear you use the word *opinion* the first time. Or I guess I'm not seeing the difference between an opinion and a solution. Why is that so important?"

The answer? Because every person on the planet has an opinion. If you ask people for an *answer* or *solution*, you'll often hear, "I don't know." But even if someone may not have an answer, they most certainly have an opinion, because an opinion is not right or wrong. A strategy, answer, or solution can be.

If you ask someone about their favorite food, vacation, music, hobby, sports, or health regimen, you'll hear a variety of answers, none of which are wrong.

Like surgical precision, leaders must be mindful of the words they use, since they all carry a different meaning for each of us—especially in cases like *opinion* versus *solution*. The best part about this strategy is, you can use it immediately in your very next conversation!

Ideally, the manager would go through the proper questions in the L.E.A.D.S. framework to ensure there is trust; buy-in; clear expectations around coaching and alignment; and around the intention of the conversation, the outcome, and solution. However, when people are clear about your intentions, when there's a baseline of trust in the relationship combined with authenticity, transparency, care, and precise communication, this coaching strategy can achieve all these objectives at once.

Of course, tweak the positioning statement and question to best fit the situation. You will be pleasantly amazed how responsive and open people are to this approach and how much more of an impact you will make in even less time, regardless of how busy you are.

IMPROMPTU SITUATIONAL COACHING— THE ABCs OF LEADERSHIP

There are endless coaching opportunities to leverage beyond regularly scheduled coaching sessions. Therein lies the fundamental guideline to creating a coaching culture—embracing the ABCs of leadership: Always be coaching.

MASTERING SITUATIONAL COACHING

To make coaching a natural conversation, it's essential to understand, from a timing perspective, what kind of coaching needs to take place in certain situations. To keep it simple, Table 4.1 illustrates the differences, as well as similarities between situational and scheduled coaching, and why they are both an essential part of your comprehensive coaching strategy. (We'll do a deep dive in Chapter 7 around how to determine whether it's a coaching or enrollment conversation.)

TABLE 4.1   Situational versus Scheduled Coaching

Impromptu, Situational Coaching	Scheduled Coaching
Focuses on timely, reactive, more immediate needs, questions, objectives, or challenges.	Focuses on longer-term, personal, professional, or career goals, skill development, coaching through a win or challenge, working through a topic that requires more time, and reinforcing best practices.
Typically, these are shorter conversations. There's no such thing as speed coaching! Schedule additional time if needed.	Scheduled, one-on-one coaching sessions that typically last one hour.
ABC! Coaching happens in *every* conversation, meeting, or interaction, including deal, forecast, performance, pipeline, business plan reviews, field sales calls, customer visits, water cooler conversations, etc.	This includes ABC. In addition, the scheduled coaching calls happen between 1 and 4 times a month with each person on your team. (Frequency is dependent upon each person's goals, experience, performance, situation, and needs.)
Next steps, a follow-up, or a scheduled meeting time is identified to build momentum and accountability.	Next steps, a follow-up, or a scheduled meeting time is identified to build momentum and accountability.
Expectations are set around the agenda of the direct report. (If there's something you need to address, that's your agenda. Therefore, you need to enroll them in having the conversation. See Chapter 7.)	Coaching is *always* the coachee's agenda, not yours. However, you can make suggestions or share observations, experiences, and best practices that support their goals as long as you follow the L.E.A.D.S. framework. You just can't make demands or push a topic you want to cover. That's your agenda and where enrollment comes into play. (See Chapter 7.)

(continued)

TABLE 4.1   (Continued)

Impromptu, Situational Coaching	Scheduled Coaching
Impromptu, situational coaching happens all the time. In every conversation, you first need to understand the other person's intentions, expectations, needs, and point of view. This can only be achieved through well-crafted questions.	The coachee develops and sends their coach a preplanned agenda prior to the coaching session using the coaching pre-call planning form. (See Chapter 5.)
When a deeper dive is necessary, crossover to scheduled coaching can happen using the L.E.A.D.S. Coaching Framework. Alternatively, rather than crossing over to a scheduled coaching session, you can apply situational coaching when there's a need to follow up or hold people accountable to ensure the coachee honored their commitments.	When follow-up is necessary, crossing over to situational coaching can happen using the L.E.A.D.S. Coaching Framework to instill deeper personal accountability.

COACHING CONUNDRUM

While laser coaching is a thing, there's no such thing as speed coaching. Said a different way, speed coaching is when you cut corners, skip the non-negotiable questions, fill facts with assumptions, or rush through a coaching conversation because you either don't have the time or the patience to coach. If you need more time and patience, schedule it and prepare.

MINDFUL MOMENT

When do you coach? Honor the ABCs of leadership: Always be coaching. Rather than think of coaching as an event or something you do to someone, it's simply the language of leadership that you speak daily that enriches the lives of those around you, including yourself.

COACHING NEVER STOPS

Here's an all too common tale: There was a top performer who was typically left alone by his manager and, consequently, was not being coached consistently. One month, his numbers dipped. So, the manager observed, coached, advised, and gave recognition where it was deserved. Inevitably, his numbers went back up.

The following month, the manager left this top performer alone, and once again, his sales dipped. The lesson? Consistent coaching is non-negotiable! Like healthy eating or exercise, coaching is a way of life to preserve the health and performance of your team.

TEAM COACHING OR TEAM MEETINGS?

If I didn't hear this during every leadership program I deliver, I would have excluded this from the book: "Keith, what's the difference between one-to-one coaching and coaching a group of people?"

With all the humdrum, useless meetings people attend daily, here's how you can ignite that spark of innovation, collaboration, and engagement that will make your meetings worthwhile, and dare I say, even fun.

COACHING CONUNDRUM

Unless you have a team coaching strategy to follow, most managers who attempt to coach in a group setting find themselves back on their soapbox telling people what to do. The solution? Smash your soapbox.

YOUR MEETINGS SUCK: HOW MANAGERS FACILITATE INFLUENTIAL, PRODUCTIVE MEETINGS

There's a difference between facilitating a conversation and managing a meeting from a soapbox. When managers stand on a soapbox, the consequences of preaching are severe, since they're the only one participating in the meeting. The solution? Shift to a team coaching model to avoid the stale, monotonous meetings and reinvigorate them to create the engagement, buy-in, alignment, and accountability you need to achieve greater results.

THE MUNDANE MEETING

A common theme I hear from managers is frustration with their team. In fact, this is the topic that the majority of managers want to discuss at the beginning of our coaching relationship.

Like most managers, it's inevitable that you're going to be in front of your team conducting meeting after meeting. Regardless of the topic, the typical modus operandi of most managers is to lead the meeting with their agenda, share the context of the meeting, and then proceed on presenting to the team what needs to be done, by who, and when it needs to be completed.

As you can imagine, the manager expects the team to understand, agree, and get it done. While some managers end the meeting by offering to answer any questions, what typically ensues is silence from the team, so the manager concludes the meeting, thinking the objective was clear, and the team knows what to do.

Then comes the shock to the system. While some team members honor the manager's objectives and the tasks that need to be completed, either the task is not done as effectively as it needs to be, or it's simply not done at all. The manager then assesses results and reacts, thinking, "What is wrong with these people? I was clear what needed to be done. So why can't they just do it?"

GET OFF YOUR SOAPBOX

What does it even sound like if you're no longer standing on your soapbox preaching to everyone? What does it mean to *facilitate* a meeting?

If you look up the definition of *facilitate*, it's: "Making an action or process easy or easier." Building off this, the word, *facilitator* is defined as: "Someone who engages in the activity of facilitation. They help a group of people understand their common objectives and how to achieve them. In doing so, the *facilitator* remains neutral, meaning he or she does not take a particular position in the discussion."

Managers need to facilitate more than they pontificate. When a manager gets in front of their team during a meeting and does most of the talking, they're engaging in what I refer to as *soapbox management.* To produce break-through results during every meeting, the manager must stop engaging in soapbox management or preaching to their people. When managers point fingers and tell people what to do, how to do it, or what they're doing wrong, people's defenses are heightened. Consequently, they stop listening and their level of buy-in and engagement diminishes. This is your opportunity to get off your soapbox and start leading with questions that uncover other people's opinions and what's important to them regarding a topic, instead of preaching from the tower about what's important to you, what should be done, and how to do it.

RESET THE EXPECTATIONS OF YOUR MEETINGS

To create a *culture of collaboration and coaching* rather than a *culture of control and competition*, what follows is a bulletproof team coaching strategy, along with the questions to successfully facilitate your next meeting. While you may feel the following initial enrollment conversation to set new expectations is a bit wordy, I do this purposely, so you have more content to work with. Keep in mind, every template, coaching question, and coach track that I share throughout this book has been tested, proven, and validated. So make every coach track your own, while keeping the spirit of the message intact.

Here's the first step to magnificent meetings. Reset the expectation of your meetings and how they will be structured. The following enrollment conversation resets expectations, creates alignment and buy-in, and demonstrates the value realized from taking more of a team coaching approach.

> What I want for each person on the team is to feel that every meeting is highly productive. I want to ensure you leave feeling inspired, heard, and supported, and that you had an opportunity to contribute and shine.
>
> After reflecting on our prior meetings, I realize that I could have done a better job making them more collaborative and valuable for you. I apologize for this, and if I've offended you in any way based on my directive approach.
>
> I truly value you and your opinions. Besides, you're the expert in your position and I want to start leveraging your talents and experiences more frequently, since I don't always have the answers. Just like in sports, it takes a team to win the game.
>
> I realize it's going to be a change for all of us, since I'm going through this learning curve myself. That's why I'll be asking for your feedback on how I can improve as a coach and facilitator.

I'm committed to creating an environment that fosters trust, positive collaboration, and transparency, even when we must discuss things that may be perceived as difficult. To achieve this, I'll need your support, and so will your coworkers, as we adjust the structure of our meetings to the point where we actually look forward to them!

So, by a show of hands, how many of you are willing to help create a more valuable, collaborative, and engaging format for our meetings that will make us all more successful at our job?

Once you've reset expectations, embraced your humanity, taken ownership of the past and the new process moving forward, and shared what the benefit each person will realize from this change to create the needed buy-in, here are just a handful of questions to help facilitate your next meeting—or should I say *team coaching session*.

LEAD WITH QUESTIONS, NOT ANSWERS

Weekly, monthly, or quarterly meetings can get stale quickly. It also puts unnecessary pressure on the manager to keep the meetings engaging and worthwhile. The team coaching approach will remove the burden and stress when trying to make every meeting successful.

Instead of believing that it is solely the responsibility of the manager to run a successful meeting, you can lead the meeting with questions to tap into each person's experience, knowledge, and ideas. Fostering healthy, open, and rich collaboration can only occur when the manager steps down off their soapbox and leads (pun intended) each meeting with questions.

Once you've set the expectations of how the meeting will be structured and introduce the topic of the meeting, the questions will empower your team to open up and share their opinions and solutions. Don't feel that you need to ask all of these questions! Instead, utilize the ones that you feel would work best for the type of meeting that you are facilitating.

Here are 45 questions (in no particular order) that top leaders use to transform meetings from worthless to a worthwhile team coaching experience. These questions will energize, inspire, and invigorate your team so they feel acknowledged, valued, and part of the solution.

I've broken these questions into two groups. The first group are the coaching facilitation questions you can always use that are applicable for every meeting. The second group of questions can be used to dive deeper into a meeting topic or offsite event. There are a ton of questions here, so leverage the ones you feel are appropriate for that particular meeting.

TIP FROM THE COACH

When presenting to a group, I typically start with a few warm-up or ice-breaker questions that I ask each person to bring everyone closer together. If there are more than 20 people, it can get a bit time consuming. In this case, just ask a few people for a response. Here are a few examples of warm-up questions: How are you feeling? What is one thing that people don't know about you? What's your favorite food? If you were eating your final meal, what would it be? What's your favorite movie, hobby, music, etc.? What are you most proud of accomplishing? What's one "I bet you didn't know" or fun fact you can share around any topic?

20 Team Coaching Questions to Run Worthwhile Meetings

1. What are your expectations of the meeting? What goals or challenges would you like to address/discuss?

2. What recent success can you share with the team? (Personally, with a client, coworker, cross-functional team, etc.)

3. Who would you like to acknowledge for a job well done? (Questions two and three can also uncover additional best practices the team can adopt.)

4. What ideas do you have when working with (marketing, procurement, sales engineers, account managers, technical support, finance, cross-functional teams, etc.) that would improve collaboration, success, and help make everyone's job easier?

5. What else would make our meetings more valuable for you?

6. What do you feel is the common goal and expectation/intention for this meeting?

7. Who is willing to start this discussion and share some ideas to stimulate our conversation?

8. What is another way of looking at this?

9. That's a great idea. Who has a different opinion around what we've been discussing so far?

10. That's interesting. What else can be true?

11. I certainly have my opinion around this, and I'm happy to share it. However, before I do, I'm more interested in hearing your thoughts first, since in many ways, you're closer to this situation

than I am, and I trust you and your judgement around this. Can someone else please share you opinion around what we've been discussing?

12. What assumptions might we be making around this issue?

13. What are the facts that support your opinion/assumption? How do you know that this is the absolute truth?

14. What's another way of looking at this that would change our thinking for the better?

15. Thanks for sharing your opinion, I really appreciate it. Let's walk through the solution and approach we co-created to ensure it will achieve the results we want.

16. What would be possible if we were able to achieve these results/eliminate this challenge?

17. What concerns, if any, do you have at this point?

18. Let's spend the last few minutes summarizing the meeting, what our next steps are, and any deadlines associated with what we've discussed so that we're all clear and aligned around what each of us need to do.

19. How are you feeling about what we discussed and achieved today? What did you learn?

20. What if anything, do you see we can change to make the meetings even more valuable?

25 Additional Facilitation Questions to Use as Needed

1. Where do we all want to be at the end of this meeting? What is your expectation and what do you want to leave with?

2. What do you hope to accomplish over the next (hour, day, etc.)?

3. What preliminary information do you need from me to provide some context around this conversation?

4. What areas do you want to cover that are most important to you?

5. I'd like to hear from more of you regarding your opinions around this. Who is the next person to share some additional ideas?

6. What's the alternative to this point of view?

7. How could that impact the outcome (e.g., your relationship, the customer, your peer, your direct report, performance, etc.)?

8. What's your reaction/opinion around what you just heard?

9. Let's continue to build off that last point. Can someone else share their point of view or build upon what we've just heard?

10. Imagine if this would be possible? What would that mean to (you, the company, your clients, our business objectives, etc.)?

11. What would the process, strategy, or conversation look and sound like that would achieve our objectives? Where do we need to start?

12. At this point, what do we all agree on so far? Where are we fully aligned?

13. What part of this solution does anyone have any concerns about? Why?

14. What else might be missing that we need to look at, so we don't step over something important that can impact our desired results?

15. Let's identify the people who are willing to take some ownership around resolving this/achieving this objective?

16. What role is each of us committing to here?

17. What do you see as next steps?

18. What teams can we put together to foster healthy collaboration and get to where we need to be as efficiently as possible?

19. What is your preference in terms of how you like to be supported?

20. How can we hold each other accountable in a way that would sound supportive and not negative or offensive? What would that sound like?

21. How can we approach each other if someone doesn't follow through with their commitments? What would that sound like?

22. How do you like to be communicated to?

23. What's the best way for us to communicate with each other when it comes to resolving a challenge?

24. Does anyone have any preferred platform regarding how they like to communicate and collaborate (e.g., text, phone, in person, instant message, email, team meetings, scheduled or impromptu conversations, etc.)?

25. What are some of your takeaways from this meeting? What did you find most valuable?

MINDFUL MOMENT

If you're a manager struggling to come up with an approach, format, or topic for your next regular sales meeting or offsite event that won't be trite or redundant, then you're asking the wrong person for ideas. Ask your team instead!

Get Everyone Involved

Meetings don't have to be the dreadful experiences you and your team have come to expect. When everyone has the opportunity for their voice to be heard, your team feels inspired, and the meeting becomes more engaging. Try these two suggestions to further involve people who attend your meetings.

1. *Empower each person to run team meetings on a rotating basis.*
   When a different person runs a regularly scheduled meeting, your team is now hearing a fresh voice, which can positively change the energy and dynamic of the meeting. When everyone is sharing the their experiences they also develop a more cohesive, collaborative, and supportive team. Even if a manager runs good meetings, everyone can benefit from switching up the meeting's organizer from time to time.

   Some companies have leveraged their manager's time by creating a team leader. That is, taking a solid performer or top rep who has a passion and interest in management and helping others, and having them also provide coaching and support to the team. This complements but never replaces the manager's commitment to consistent and effective coaching.

2. *Have each person present on a topic they excel at or a discussion they feel would benefit the group.*
   Doing so will advance their own skills and help develop the future leaders of the company, while staying focused on the priorities that matter most. The added benefit is, by having other teammates run the meetings, you're uncovering additional coaching moments for them as you observe opportunities to better their best.

Abandon Absolute Thinking and Embrace Dualities

At this point, like most managers, you may be wondering, "When I'm coaching, does that mean I'm *only* asking questions and *never* sharing my experiences, ideas, observations, guidance or subject matter expertise?" It's not that you **never** share your ideas during a conversation, nor is it true that you *only drive the conversation with questions*. It's both. If coaching is your new dominant language and way of communicating, then it's ridiculous to think that, in every conversation, all you are authorized to do is ask questions!

TIP FROM THE COACH

Here's the drastic simplicity of coaching: Care enough to give less advice, be insatiably curious, and ask more questions. This is the foundation to create the healthy habit of coaching.

There's a strong chance that, as a manager, you may be a victim of what I refer to as an *absolute* or *either–or* thinker. That is, you're wired to believe things are either one way or another, black or white, right or wrong.

Consider this truth that will expand your line of vision. Instead of *either–or*, what if the option is *and*? Embrace the duality of conflicting truths that can both be true and coexist at the same time. Even if you lead every conversation with questions, you can *also* make suggestions and share your own experiences and options. It's the order in which you do this that matters; share your opinions *after* you've gathered and understand other people's point of view.

Review the L.E.A.D.S. framework. You'll notice that it identifies *when* you share your opinions or ideas: in the support step. When managers share their opinions earlier than that, they run the risk of shutting down the rest of the conversation.

As we cross the finish line on this topic, rather than standing on your soapbox telling people what to do, coach your team during your meetings to bring out their best. If you're looking to take the first step to do so, take out a hammer and destroy your soapbox. You no longer have any use for it.

Here's a coaching challenge. Before moving into the next chapter, or at the very least, during your next interaction with one of your direct reports who is looking for help, use the 60-second coaching strategy and see how effective it can be!

Finally, after you've created your personal template for team coaching, take that out for a test drive during your next meeting, and feel free to shoot me an email to let me know how it worked for you. My personal email address is KeithR@KeithRosen.com.

Tools to Manage the Coaching Process and Assess Results

I n my previous book, *Coaching Salespeople into Sales Champions*, people told me how much they appreciated and enjoyed the hands-on, tactical, and actionable approach to coaching and managing the coaching process. I still hear about how they would take just one idea and use it that very day with impressive results! It wasn't all theoretical with overengineered processes and poorly defined, vague coaching strategies that were hard to discern and implement.

That's why I've taken the same approach with this book, which is loaded with practical, actionable tools and the most robust sales coaching framework on the planet, which you can use immediately.

This chapter includes several forms and templates to help manage the coaching process, track results, and hold people accountable to their goals and commitments Whether you're reading the electronic version of this book, or the hardcover, log into this super-secret, password-protected resource section on my site at http://keithrosen.com/sales-leadership-resources/. Enter the password, *ICoachChampions12* and enjoy all the additional resources I've provided, including the forms in this chapter!

THE REVISED COACHING PREP FORM

One of the most valuable coaching tools you can use to manage the coaching process and ensure each coaching session is achieving maximum value, is what I call the Coaching Prep Form.

The intention of this document is to ensure each coachee leaves every scheduled coaching session with their expectations met, while also being held accountable. This includes setting the agenda of each meeting, as well as documenting progress and results around specific goals and commitments your coachees have made. Conversely, it also holds the coach accountable to honor the coachee's agenda and deliver on what they expect. The coaching prep forms are used in the following manner:

1. A gauge of accountability. The coachee must come prepared with a clear agenda and goal for the meeting.
2. Coach and coachee are clear around their roles and expectations.
3. Accelerates efficiency and focus of each coaching conversation.
4. Ensures the coach meets the coachee's expectations and identifies opportunities for the coach to improve.
5. Builds momentum from one coaching session to the next.
6. Tracks the history of the coachee's initial goals, challenges, as well as the wins and progress along the way.

Now, you're able to look back at each coaching prep form and see the measurable impact of coaching, while acknowledging the coachee's evolution and successes.

FROM THE SIDELINES

The agenda of every coaching session is driven by the coachee. If you need to approach someone to discuss a topic you need to address, that's what I refer to as an *enrollment conversation*. (See Chapter 7.)

Do you need a written prep form for every coaching session? This is surely the best practice to maximize and keep track of every session. Regardless, the overall intention is for the coachee to always come prepared with a specific agenda. How they come prepared may be slightly different for each coachee.

1. *Written Prep form* – The coachee prepared their agenda in writing.
2. *Oral Prep form* – The coachee prepared their agenda; however, they didn't write it down or send in a prep form.
3. *Timely situations* – The coachee comes prepared with either a written or oral prep form. However, something happened after they sent the coach their prep form, which caused a shift in focus to something timely that needs to be discussed.

CAPTURING THE MEASURABLE IMPACT OF COACHING

I typically wouldn't have had a problem with any of these options above, as long as the coachee comes prepared with an agenda for the coaching session. However, here's an experience I had early on in my coaching career that changed the way I thought about how important a written prep form was.

During the second year of managing my practice, Heather, a sales manager for a logistics company hired me to help build her personal brand and prepare her for her next position. During our first coaching onboarding session, we went through all the responsibilities and expectations of the coach and coachee.

One of the most critical components of coaching success is the preparation of the meeting, so the coach and coachee are clear about the coachee's specific topic, goal, win, challenge, and expectations.

After two months of coaching, she fired me. (It was the first time I was ever fired by a client!) When doing the post-mortem review, I found out that she felt that the calls were disjointed and unfocused, and she didn't get the value she expected. Well, that's no surprise, because she never came prepared with an agenda or a prep form. And if that's the case, it's easy to point to the coach and say, "Coaching isn't valuable. It's not me. You're not a good coach."

That was the last time I let a client off the hook for not being prepared for a scheduled one-to-one. In the rare times when this does happen, we take a minute to uncover a topic that would be valuable for them. If this isn't an option, I move to reschedule the call. For my client, it's a lesson on accountability and honoring your word.

For me, it was a lesson in taking a bigger stand for my clients, even if they don't like what I'm doing. After all, I'm not paid to be popular.

I'm paid to hold clients accountable around their goals and help them achieve exponentially better results faster than they could on their own.

The responsibility of a great leader is to share the observations coachees may not like to hear but must embrace, as these are the things that prevent them from greatness. This is what breakthroughs are made of.

As you may know, leadership is not a popularity contest. You don't get paid for being liked. Besides, it's the coach's responsibility to challenge people to not only move outside their comfort zone but also to dismiss its existence and create an entirely new comfortable, healthy, supportive, and challenging zone that accelerates growth and success.

Especially within your company, if you're looking to build a case for coaching, then capture the coachees' evolution in thinking, activity, learning, growth, and success in every prep form and acknowledge their results, progress, and wins. The additional benefit is, it answers the fundamental and most pressing question within every organization:

What's the measurable impact and value of coaching?

COACHING CONUNDRUM

One non-negotiable is for every coachee to come prepared to a one-to-one coaching session with a clear agenda. An unprepared coachee leads to coaching failure. If, before a meeting, the coachee isn't prepared with goals and an agenda, then they never have to be accountable for anything. The same problem emerges if the coachee fails to send a follow-up recap of learnings and commitments after each coaching session. When this happens, the coachee gets to blame the manager, which undermines the idea and value of coaching.

THE COACHING PREP FORM

I typically request that clients email their coaching prep form at least 24 hours in advance, so I have time to review it prior to our coaching session. What follows are two different forms for your coachee to choose from or modify at will.

In the spirit of keeping the prep forms simple to avoid complaints about more paperwork, here's the simplified version. Regardless of which template you use, the coachee saves it as a master template to complete and send to you prior to each scheduled, one-to-one coaching session.

Version One – Shorter Form

COACHING PRE-CALL PLANNING FORM

Date: _____

Name: _____

Time and date of next meeting: _____

1. Achievements: What I have accomplished since our last meeting/call (e.g., wins, actions, insights, improved attitude, personal and professional successes)?

2. Focus of this coaching session: I want to use my time with the coach to ... (List specifics.)
   - Skills to improve/develop:
   - Goals:
   - Challenges to overcome:
   - Areas/situations to discuss:

3. What, if anything, would make the coaching more valuable for you? For example, adjusting my coaching style; spending more time working through specific topics; putting more structure around training topics, such as conversations with prospects, customers, stakeholders, or coworkers.

(This opens the door for role-playing a conversation, crafting or reviewing an email, developing presentations, skill practice scenarios, and so on.)

Version Two – The Revised Executive Coaching Prep Form

As you will see, this coaching form is slightly longer. This is the one I use with my clients, as I find there's great value in going deeper into who they are, and beyond topics to discuss tangible wins or results achieved. It's essential to also identify the improvements in their thinking and attitude, specifically around fear, confidence, and personal balance/time management.

You'll also notice I have additional questions that focus on their personal commitments and accountability, roadblocks to progress, as well as what I can do as their coach to continually improve so the coaching remains valuable to the coachee.

Finally, there's a space for the coachee to include their vision statement and goals. Having this in the prep form for each coaching session keeps your eyes focused on the prize and ensures every coaching topic supports their personal vision and goals during every session.

EXECUTIVE COACHING PRE-CALL PREP FORM

Before our next executive coaching session (and prior to every coaching session), please respond to the five sections below. Be precise when completing this form. Please try to complete and send this at least two days before your scheduled meeting and send to (your email). This form will ensure you get the value you expect during the time with your coach, and keep you focused on the goals, challenges, and results that are most important to you.

During every coaching session, we will always respect your confidentiality. Please note that what is discussed during coaching will always remain between the coach and coachee, unless agreed upon otherwise.

Save this as a master and work from copies of this form each week. It will expedite your work, maximize the value of the time with your coach, and keep you focused on your coaching objectives. Your vision and goals, once created, will serve as a reminder on every prep form to ensure you're focusing on the right activities that align with them.

VISION: TBD

GOALS: TBD

1. YOUR INTENTION AND EXPECTATIONS:

    Here's what I want to achieve during my time with my coach. Please list specific and measurable outcomes, challenges, a strategy or skill to develop or improve (e.g., leadership/coaching, time management, sales, communication, relationships, personal brand, etc.), a desired shift in thinking or attitude, or a specific result you want. You can also share a situational issue regarding a specific scenario and how you handled it, so the coach can offer guidance, feedback, and what could be done, if anything, to achieve a better, more productive outcome the next time.

2. ACHIEVEMENTS:

What have you accomplished since our last meeting together as it relates to the coaching and development of your team and/or your personal growth. (Examples: commitments honored, wins, insights, improved attitude, personal or professional successes, behavioral shifts, process/strategy upgrade, an eliminated toleration, better time/self-management.)

3. FEAR/CONFIDENCE:

a. The fear that gets in my way to achieving greater results is _____.

b. What prevents me from developing the unconditional confidence of a champion is _____.

c. A toxic/negative belief that's been holding me back from living my potential is _____.

d. On a scale of 1–10, where 10 represents being 100% confident in myself, how would I rate myself this week? _____.

e. On a scale of 1–10, where 10 represents being fearless and leveraging fear as my ally, how would I rate myself this week? _____.

4. PERSONAL ACCOUNTABILITY/COMMITMENTS:

a. What I said I would complete and am proud of doing so. _____.

b. What I said I would have completed/worked on but didn't. _____.

c. How am I doing regarding honoring my vision, priorities, and values?

d. How consistently do I engage in the daily activities that I've committed to in my routine? _____.

e. Here's what I commit to accomplishing by our next call. (This can also be co-created together during the call.) _____.

f. On a scale of 1–10, where 10 represents full accountability, how would I rate myself this week? _____.

(continued)

(*continued*)

5. TAKING ACTION AND FEEDBACK FOR THE COACH:
   a. How are the actions/activities I'm engaging in moving me closer to and/or farther from my goals?
   b. What do I need to do to get out of my own way so that I can create a breakthrough?
   c. What would you like your coach to do more of/less of, if anything, during and after each meeting?

ARE YOU REVIEWING RESULTS OR PERFORMANCE?

Paul felt the anxiety build in his gut. It was performance review time. Every six months it was the company policy to sit with every direct report and deliver a six-month evaluation of their performance.

"I can't believe I have to fire another one of my managers," Paul thought. He anxiously paced back and forth in his office, worried about the fallout from this termination. Paul was responsible for the North American region, and in his territory alone he had to let three of his territory managers go due to performance issues.

Like many companies, performance reviews are not something that either the manager or their direct reports look forward to. Whether companies do performance reviews once a year, twice a year, or once a quarter, the format and topics for these meetings are typically unbalanced and almost all focused on results. But wait, performance reviews, by definition, are meant to evaluate the *performance* of each employee. However, since most managers do not take the time to effectively *observe* their people at their desk, in the field, with their team, during a meeting or phone call with a customer, or the emails they write, then the fact is, *managers have no idea what their people are doing.*

Following this line of thinking to conclusion, if you're not observing your people—how they work, sell, collaborate, prioritize, organize their day, or communicate—then it's not a performance review, because you have no idea how they perform. Instead, it's really a **result review!**

HINDSIGHT IS BLINDSIGHT

I get annoyed when I hear the expression "hindsight is 20–20." This saying implies that when you evaluate a prior experience, you can recognize what went wrong and how to correct it to consistently improve results and avoid an undesirable situation from happening again.

If this was the actual practice managers engaged in, then they would never be dealing with the same problems repeatedly, nor would a particular problem find its way into the next performance review!

When managers typically conduct a performance review, they tell the person what they need to do more of, change, or improve. Subsequently, the manager assumes their direct report knows exactly what to do. Inevitably, due to the daily demands of business, the performance review gets filed, only to be dusted off and compared to the next review to see what changed for the better. What if the manager invested their time leveraging what was discussed in the performance review and then aligned it with something most managers don't use that makes coaching, training, and goal attainment exponentially faster and easier a Coaching Action Plan.

For example, if you identify a performance issue, the longer you wait, the longer the problem festers, metastasizes, and becomes so large that it's often too late to remedy. If only the manager had leveraged these as coaching moments and opportunities for development, they could have saved an up-and-coming performer.

Whether you conduct reviews quarterly, twice a year, or once a year, why wait that long to tell people what they need to do to improve, when development, growth, and coaching happen every day? You wouldn't exercise twice a year and expect to be in the best shape of your life. The same holds true for how you build a championship team, and why question-based leadership never stops. To develop a healthy coaching regimen that will identify goals, measure progress and results, and ensure you build a bench of champions, enter the Coaching Action Plan.

ENTER THE COACHING ACTION PLAN

While I've developed several renditions of this CAP (Coaching Action Plan), brevity is key, and overengineering processes and solutions breed mediocrity and stagnation of adoption.

What follows is a brief document that managers use as a starting point for the coaching process by outlining the coachee's goals, commitments, milestones, and due dates.

Once this step is completed, this now becomes a debrief and accountability form that the coachee updates and sends to the coach after every coaching session. Remember that debrief form we talked about in Chapter 2 when we walked through the L.E.A.D.S. framework? This is it!

COACHING ACTION PLAN

Name: _____

Date of this coaching session: _____

Date of next coaching session: _____

Goal/Task or Action Items and Milestone Dates: What is the specific and measurable goal you are looking to achieve and by when?	Results Achieved During Today's Coaching Session: In thinking, skill, knowledge, self-awareness, insights, activity, communication, behavior, and so on.	Commitments to Honor Prior to Next Coaching Session: Results, skill development, opportunities and activities that were agreed upon during the current coaching session.
1.		
2.		
3.		
4.		
5.		
6.		
7.		

Coachee Feedback/Comments: List any feedback/comments and requests you have for your coach about the coaching session or about the coaching in general.

Coach Feedback/Comments: List any feedback/comments and requests you have for your coachee about the coaching session or about the coaching in general.

Now everyone is clear regarding what was discussed, the value of the coaching session, the coachee's commitments, what's been completed to date, and what tasks or results need to be achieved by a certain deadline. The coach and coachee can also include additional comments about each coaching session.

Do not lose sight that this CAP can also be used to schedule and assess observation sessions (during a customer visit, telephone call, deskside observation, during a meeting, and so on.), since observation is a non-negotiable arm of coaching and leadership. Chapter 11 will ensure you position observation so the coachee sees the benefit, while setting up the guidelines, rules of engagement, and cadence for observation up front via the enrollment process.

Once the coachee sets their own goals for coaching, they would write them in the CAP. From there, prior to each coaching session, the coachee would send you the prep form (their agenda for the meeting). Finally, within the timeline you both designate, whether it's one hour, one day, or one week, the coachee would complete the CAP and send it to the coach as a recap of the coaching session, and what they've committed to accomplishing by the next coaching session.

TIP FROM THE COACH

Be mindful of what the coachee is committing to achieving within a certain timeframe. If you sense they are overcommitting due to an unrealistic deadline, therein lies yet another coaching moment!

COACHING CONUNDRUM

Performance reviews are an HR-compliant tool designed to protect the company more than its people. Contrary to public opinion, the initial objective of a performance/result review is not to develop the employee. These reviews are a documentation of behavior or performance that companies lean on as a justification for either termination, or they mistakenly view these performance reviews as a twisted replacement for coaching. This breeds fear in the hearts and minds of employees. Who, then, would ever want to be coached? It's been blacklisted, and the company doesn't even realize it.

Here's a thought: Observe your people perform so that you can actually transform this result review into an authentic performance review so you can make this a positive and supportive coaching and career-development conversation.

Transforming Critical Conversations into Positive Change and Measurable Results

THE HARD TRUTH

In the spirit of supporting you unconditionally, I'm going to deliver a tough message.

If you're a manager, when you feel angry, impatient, frustrated, and disappointed with your employees and their performance, don't blame them. It's always your fault. I'm sorry if it stings a little, but you know it's true. Avalanches roll downhill. How can you expect your people to be 100 percent accountable if the manager is not?

The power of personal accountability and change starts with you. If you take responsibility and ownership of this and every problem 100 percent of the time, you're modeling greatness. And that's the great news! Because it's entirely in your power to become the leader you want to be and create the team you dream of. You're reading this book so that you can become a titan of coaching and leadership. The by-product is that you and your team win bigger than ever before.

COACH AND BE HAPPY

As you focus on your employees and their coaching needs, don't lose sight of how coaching will also impact you, the manager. Not only will you develop champions, you will also improve your quality of life. More effective coaching equates to more job fulfillment, peace of mind, and joy. When you have less work, less stress, and fewer problems, you gain time to devote to many of the issues that shouldn't be there in the first place!

This point became piercingly clear to me during a coaching session I had with Anna, the regional vice president for a medical device company located in Sao Paolo, Brazil. During our coaching session, she reluctantly and sadly confirmed, "You know Keith, I can see how the coaching and observation is moving the needle of performance with my team. But because they rely on me so much, I'm always on the road traveling from one region to the next. I would often leave my house on a Tuesday and not get home until Friday evening. This takes me away from my family, whom I want to spend more time with"

I could sense the stress, the inner conflict, and the struggle of balancing personal and work-related responsibilities.

At the beginning of our coaching relationship, Anna informed me that she was not coaching her remote team. The only conversations she had, whether on the phone, via text, instant messaging, video conferencing, or email were focused on the problems that needed resolution or quota attainment. When these situations blew up to the point that required more hands-on attention, she would travel from region to region, so she could be onsite to handle the challenges that each region was faced with assuming they need her in the field to get things done.

During one of our first coaching session, Anna shared something that sent a shooting pain into my heart. "I'm working so hard and traveling so much. I'm so tired of watching my young children grow up through pictures." Regrettably, Anna's story is not uncommon. But when managers start letting people do their own jobs and create the habit of consistent coaching, whether face-to-face or remotely, the light of possibility to create a healthy, balanced life that honors your priorities begins to shine brighter every day

The lesson here is, coaching will improve the quality of life for both the coach and the coachee.

MINDFUL MOMENT

Success is often fleeting, where regret lasts forever. The exciting news is, the power of change rests in your hands. It all starts with developing a new habit of speaking the language of coaching in your native tongue, so that you can deliver consistent, measurable value in every conversation, while letting your people do their jobs.

RESIGN AS CHIEF PROBLEM SOLVER

We've reinforced the importance of asking well-crafted, sequential coaching questions to help your people further develop their problem-solving skills, create their own solutions, become more strategic thinkers, and amplify their self-awareness and personal accountability. Leading every conversation with questions rather than solutions also helps you, the coach, resign from your role as the chief problem solver.

COACHING CONUNDRUM

A leadership paradox: Managers create the very problems they want to avoid.

I have yet to find a manager on the planet who does not want to develop a team of independent, accountable, self-driven, strategic-thinking, top performers. And yet, when playing the role of chief problem solver, you're creating the antithesis, the very outcome you want to avoid. Let's walk through this line of thinking and why this is true.

When those we coach or manage approach us because they are looking for some guidance or a solution, we often default to what we know. That is, we provide the answer and direction we feel is best, often based on our past experiences, believing that is the most effective way to assist others. Paradoxically, this approach creates the very thing that every manager wants to avoid. Rather than build a team of independent, accountable people, managers wind up developing a team of people that are dependent on them because the underlying message managers are sending is, "If you have a problem, come to me and I'll fix it for you. So, don't worry about doing your job, since I'm around to help. And yes, I'll do all of your thinking for you."

Not only does this make people mentally lazy and less motivated to perform or engage in the activities they're accountable for, but it also prevents them from sharpening their own problem-solving skills and becoming strategic thinkers. And the irony is that managers then get angry and frustrated when employees don't do their own jobs. If the leader came up with the solution, it's their idea, not the coachee's. When leaders create solutions, they inadvertently take ownership of the problems. Then, when a leader's solution doesn't work, it's the leader's fault. If direct reports didn't come up with the answer, they are free from personal accountability and instead have license to blame the leader for their failures! Unfortunately, most leaders operate as the chief problem solver for their teams, which creates more work for the leader, stifles team success, hampers individual growth, and gives people permission to resign from accountability.

COACHING CONUNDRUM

Once you attempt to solve someone else's problem, you've adopted that problem and made it your own, relinquishing ownership rights from the person who brought this gift to you, which you kindly accepted.

This begs the question, "Why does the manager feel they *must* provide the answer?"

To answer this question on a deeper level, let's peek inside a manager's mind to understand why they feel they can't let go of control and let their people do their job.

The Manager's Mindset

1. Giving the answer is giving value. If I don't, then what good am I to my team?

2. This is my job and why I was hired. I'm a good problem solver.

3. My team expects me to have the answer.
4. I like to showcase my expertise and experience so that I can look good.
5. They already know what they need to do, so why ask them? This way, I know they'll perform, and then I look good.
6. This is how I was managed.
7. It's just faster to tell them what to do.
8. I don't always know the answer, so I avoid asking the question.
9. I'm not a good coach but I am a great problem solver.
10. I don't want to be found out. What if I fail as a coach?
11. What if I ask a question and they don't know the answer?
12. What if I ask a question that I don't know the answer to?
13. Why should I praise and acknowledge people for doing their job?

An interesting set of beliefs. All of which need to be abandoned, since this mindset will sabotage your leadership and coaching efforts. Now, let's look at how a coachee may feel about having a chief problem solver for a boss.

The Coachee's Quiet, Internal Reaction

1. Great! I don't have to do the work or think for myself. My boss is going to do it for me!
2. I guess they don't have the confidence in me to do my job.
3. If they keep enabling me then maybe it's because they feel I'm not a fit.
4. If they keep helping me out by guiding me with prescriptive solutions, maybe it's because they care and think I'm doing a great job!
5. Clearly, they don't trust me. Am I on the road to termination?
6. If they can't give me the gift of their undivided attention, curiosity, and listening, I guess they don't care and have no interest in helping me succeed.
7. My manager doesn't want to take the time to coach or develop me. They only spend time with the people they like.
8. I guess I'm not a priority.
9. Since they keep telling me what to do rather than asking me what I feel is best, they must think I'm incompetent, and that their solutions will always be better than mine.

TIP FROM THE COACH

Honor the three fundamental principles of coaching.

1. Let your people do their job.
2. Let your people do their job.
3. See principles one and two.

In Chapter 4, we discussed how anyone can coach in ten minutes or less. To take it even further, I shared my bulletproof, 60-second coaching strategy that refutes the myth that the vital lesson here is, *you can't scale dependency*.

Sure, you need to hit your numbers and achieve the business objectives that you're responsible for, but that's the by-product of every manager's primary objective, which, as we discussed in Chapter 1 is to *make your people more valuable every day*. After all, you're not going to achieve your goals if you're not continually developing your team to their fullest potential.

If this isn't enough of a reason to resign from the role of chief problem solver, here's a lesson on time management: Coaching makes your people independent. Feeding them all the answers they want makes them dependent. If you keep feeding them the answers now, you'll be feeding them forever, just like a child who was never taught how to use utensils.

People respond in amazing ways when you give them the space and support to work through a challenge on their own. This builds confidence and translates into better results. If you're a sales manager, you weren't hired to be the super salesperson but instead to make your people more valuable and develop future leaders. This can only be achieved through the artful and strategic use of masterful coaching questions.

TIP FROM THE COACH

You don't always need to have the answer. Be mindful of the fact that they may develop a different solution or have a new idea that you never thought of on your own, which, shockingly, could be better than yours!

CONTROL FREAK? A CASE FOR LETTING GO

I'm sure at some point in your career, you've been in a position where you were not able to respond to your voice mails, texts, and emails as quickly as you normally do. This could be with a friend or family member, peer, partner, vendor, boss, or anyone who you manage. Maybe it's because you were in a meeting. Maybe you were with a client or working with one of your peers or direct reports. Maybe you were offsite at a training event, conference, or company retreat.

Regardless, after an hour or so, you have an opportunity to take a quick break. Of course, you immediately grab your phone to see all the calls, texts, and emails you missed. While scrolling through your emails, you notice one was marked, "Urgent." It was from one of your salespeople who was in the process of closing a deal. She had what seemed to be a pressing question that only the infinite wisdom of a manager could answer. When you finally responded to her email, the response you received read, "Thanks, I didn't realize you were in a meeting. Don't worry. I took care of this issue myself."

Has this ever happened to you? If so, what's the lesson?

> *You're reactively jumping in way too soon to solve everyone's problems when your people are fully capable to do the job you hired them to do!*

PERFORMANCE COACH OR CHIEF PROBLEM SOLVER? YOU DECIDE

Chris is a senior sales director at an advertising agency responsible for all international clients in Southern Europe. Tomar is one of his regional sales managers who manages a team of 20 territory sales managers based in that region. What follows are two distinct conversations around the topic of departmental silos and costly assumptions when selling.

The first conversation illustrates the cost of taking on the dysfunctional role of chief problem solver. Notice how easy it is for Chris to take on the problem presented by Tomar. In the second conversation, you'll observe what happens when you shift the dialogue to a coaching conversation. An entirely different and more productive outcome will be created.

The Directive Chief Problem Solver

Note: This conversation between the manager and direct report took approximately *three minutes.*

> **Tomar**: Hey Chris, before the pricing team calls you to say that I didn't follow their messed-up processes, I want to explain my side of the story and why I am just going to get the deal signed.
>
> **Chris**: Okay, what's going on?

Tomar: I need to close this business with this Acme Bank to hit my quota. I have a meeting with them next week and it would be great to be able to present a solution and pricing structure that meets their needs. Their spend dropped last year, so we need to prove our products work. I ran the rates past the pricing team and they said that they were too low. They just don't get the pressure I'm under.

Chris: Did you tell them about the time crunch? Do they understand the revenue opportunity?

Tomar: I think so. They are concerned that, because the spend level is dropping, the customer doesn't deserve below-floor discounts, even though we'll lose millions from this client.

Chris: And you sold our value proposition?

Tomar: Sure did. I'm telling you, *I've tried everything.*

Chris: Hmmm. Did you escalate this to Marissa, the manager of that pricing team?

Tomar: Yes! She agreed with my original strategy.

Chris: This could be huge for our region, not to mention the quota attainment that you would get, rather than asking for quota relief! Let me give Marissa's manager, Laura, a call and see what I can do.

Tomar: Great! I really appreciate it.

Chris: No problem. Whatever we need to do to get this deal done.

Chief Problem Solver Debrief

So, what did you hear? What did you notice? Let's see:

1. Did the manager learn why this is happening?
2. Did the manager deliver value with their response?
3. Did the manager identify the gap, coaching moment, or root cause?
4. Did Chris challenge the assumption when Tomar said, "I've tried everything."
5. Did Chris ask Tomar exactly how he presented the value proposition?
6. Finally, did this exchange instill accountability or result in a positive behavioral change?

Of course, the answer to all these questions is *no*. And I'm sure Marissa will be very happy knowing Chris skipped over her and went directly to her boss, Laura. While the manager asked a few questions, most were closed ended. In addition, the end of the conversation demonstrated how the manager, as chief problem solver, took the responsibility to resolve this issue, rather than empowering Tomar to self-reflect, think through, and create his own solution.

Chris successfully put more work on his plate, then wonders why he has no time. It's because, like most managers, he's in this constant state of reaction, jumping from one problem to the next.

Coaching in the Same Scenario

Now, let's listen in on what a coaching conversation could sound like using the same scenario. Notice how Chris learns more about the situation, suspends assumptions, and uncovers new possibilities using powerful questions that build accountability and empower people to think on their own. One final point to be mindful of: As you read through this dialogue, notice how I've also included the steps in the L.E.A.D.S. Coaching Model throughout the conversation to provide you with greater context and insight into how the coaching framework will flow naturally in any conversation, rather than feel formulaic—that is, if you allow it.

An Eight-Minute Coaching Conversation

Note: This conversation between the manager and direct report took approximately *eight minutes*.

Learn

> **Tomar**: Hey Chris, before the pricing team calls to say that I didn't follow their messed-up processes, I want to explain my side of the story and why I'm just going to get the deal signed.
>
> **Chris**: Thanks for bringing this to my attention. I'm sensing you're really frustrated about this. Is that a fair observation?
>
> **Tomar**: Definitely. I feel I can't do my job and they're just making this deal more complicated. Then, we're always at risk of losing a customer.
>
> **Chris**: Looking back on some prior deals, you and I have worked through this type of situation before. Is that correct?
>
> **Tomar**: Yeah, well, it's getting obvious to me that the only way I can get my job done is to spend my time on dozens of emails,

pushing them or escalating this problem. Can you give Marissa or her manager a call to see what you can do?

Chris: I'm here to help you any way I can, Tomar. The fact is, you are much closer to this situation than I am, and I trust you and your judgment, which is why I would need to know more about this situation to best assist you.

Tomar: Thanks. I get it.

Enroll

Chris: What I want for you is to have a plan to win this sale, as well as resolve and prevent the issues you're experiencing with the pricing team so this doesn't happen again. Would you be open to discussing this so we can come up with a better approach for getting pricing approval, which will avoid these headaches and enable you to close more deals faster?

Tomar: Sure, sounds good to me.

Assess

Chris: You mentioned you tried to get the pricing team involved. How did you approach them?

Tomar: Like I always do. I emailed them and asked for the below-floor discount.

Chris: Okay, let's get specific. What exactly did the email say? May I see it?

Tomar: Sure. The last one read, "I have an upcoming meeting at Acme Bank on this highly strategic project where we are trying to win more business from them. Looking for a below-floor discount. Thanks!"

Chris: Okay, and what was their response?

Tomar: Michael, who works on Marissa's team, responded that the drop-in spend last year means that a below-floor discount wasn't justified.

Chris: I see. And how did you respond?

Tomar: I told him that I would love to get a high-price commitment as much as he would, but they aren't going to commit until they see better results. Besides, I know that they have more budget.

Chris: How did Michael respond?

Tomar: He suggested that I offer a different set of products and more audience offerings to make it a better deal for him.

Chris: Okay, what did you do next?

Tomar: I sent them another email asking for an update, but it was like having the same conversation all over again. They keep wasting my time.

Chris: Then what happened?

Tomar: Nothing. Last week, I had a pre-meeting with my team to prepare for next week's meeting with this customer. That's when I escalated this to Marissa via email, who leads the pricing team, because I needed her input.

Chris: What does *better deal* mean to Michael and the pricing team?

Tomar: (Pause) Actually, other than him wanting me to have an actual spend commitment, I'm not 100 percent sure. I would just assume that we're both on the same page when we say "better deal."

Define

Chris: Why else do you think he responded this way?

Tomar: Because he doesn't get our business.

Chris: How do you know that's true?

Tomar: I don't know. It's what I feel based on my interactions with him. I'm just frustrated. Maybe he does get our business and just doesn't want to help.

Chris: I'm curious, if you couldn't use that reason anymore as to why you feel the pricing team won't help you, how would you resolve this?

Tomar: (Pause) I guess I'd have to go talk with them.

Chris: Okay. And if you did, what else could you uncover that may also be true?

Tomar: That he doesn't understand the pressure we are under. And I probably don't understand the pressure he's under either.

Chris: That's an interesting observation. Let's explore that from his perspective for a moment. What could this situation look like through Michael's eyes?

Tomar: (Pausing to process.) Probably that I don't understand his role and the pressure he's under. Wow! Plus, if the overall spend is going down, why would I think the discount is justified? I get that, but aside from the obvious quota consideration, I really believe that if we start delivering on their performance metrics, they will increase their spend with us. I know there's more budget if we just deliver on this one thing.

Chris: Let's back up here for a second. Tell me more about your thinking around why you feel this is the best place to begin?

Tomar: Well, I guess it's the path of least resistance. I think that the prices are too high myself, so I didn't push back on the customer and risk losing the sale when we need to close it ASAP.

Chris: How far above floor price did you start the negotiation?

Tomar: Above floor? Ha! As I said, our prices are already too high, so I started at the floor price and now they want discounts on top of that.

Chris: Is that what your customer told you regarding your pricing model?

Tomar: Not exactly, but I've been doing this long enough to know that's their biggest concern when making a decision. Most of the time, it always comes down to price.

Chris: Why do you feel that's always true?

Tomar: Well, not every time.

Chris: Okay, what else could be true?

Tomar: There could be a bunch of things, especially considering that I haven't heard back from them. Maybe they're busy. Maybe they're dealing with another priority. Maybe they're still evaluating what we proposed. Maybe they need to get internal approval before getting back to me. Maybe they're just seeing how much of a discount they can squeeze out of me and plan on buying anyway. I guess it could be more than just price.

Chris: Thanks for sharing that, Tomar. I appreciate your insights. If I'm capturing this accurately, what I'm hearing is you felt that by offering this client a discount, we would win their business, which could be the deal that helps you attain quota. So, you called the pricing team who told you they couldn't discount further, especially since you were already at floor pricing. I also heard that we just uncovered a disconnect between you and the pricing team regarding what a *better deal* is, and that price may not be the reason that's stalling the sale. Is that correct?

Tomar: That's pretty much it.

Chris: Got it. What assumptions might you be making here?

Tomar: Given what I just said and heard, several! I need to be more mindful of these things, rather than assume that it always comes down to price with customers, or the pricing team is my enemy! This reminds me that I need to go deeper into what the customer perceives as value and how they make purchasing decisions. Just on that alone, I can see how I could have missed a handful of qualifying questions.

Chris: How much more business could we expect from Acme if we get these discounts for them?

Tomar: I haven't really confirmed that either. Again, I just assumed that this would close the deal.

Chris: Based on what we've uncovered, what are you hearing?

Tomar: (Pause) I guess the deal is not *fully* qualified.

Support

Chris: I appreciate and admire your ability to reflect on this and find the opportunities for you to improve. Let's take a moment and think about this from the pricing team's perspective. If you were Michael, how would you respond in this situation?

Tomar: (Pause) I guess I'd probably react the same way. I see your point. I really can't fault him for wanting to do his job. I just know we have a great opportunity here and I don't want to blow it. And if I couldn't get the discount approved, I just assumed that you would back me up. Jeez, another assumption. If you did, we would have made this situation worse and we still wouldn't have earned Acme's business!

Chris: I understand how important this deal is to you. And I certainly want to provide you with the support you need to win this business. However, given what we've discussed, what do you feel the best approach would be to resolve this when you call the pricing team?

Tomar: For one, start with an apology. They deserve that. Then, get a better understanding of what they define as a *good* deal and the parameters around that, so I can understand their ideal client profile and what they're looking for the next time. And it would probably be better to have a conversation like this over the phone rather than email, since that's the easiest way to create time-consuming miscommunications. It would also help if I had a better understanding of their role and the best way to work together. With an approach like this, I feel better already!

Chris: I admire your commitment to resolve this. How else was our conversation valuable for you?

Tomar: I need to do a better job keeping my assumptions at bay and recognize the difference *between a customer's objection and ones that I may create in my head*! I can't always assume it's price because when I do, I stop asking other questions around building and confirming value. And I can't assume that everyone knows the responsibilities of my role either. Finally, I need to be more sensitive to other people's responsibilities and agenda and not just my own.

Chris: It sounds like you have some new ideas around what you can do to avoid the frustration you've experienced and generate the results you want.

Tomar: I certainly do, Chris. Thanks!

Chris: You mentioned earlier about missing some qualifying questions. What questions are you currently asking?

Tomar: (Lists a few basic questions but clearly missed the deeper, more challenging questions that would have avoided the situation he's in.)

Chris: Thanks, Tomar. That's helpful. Can I share an observation that would also help you avoid these pricing issues?

Tomar: Of course!

Chris: As you mentioned, there are probably some additional questions you need to ask every prospect. How about we schedule another time to write out everything you need to know about every customer you work with. Then, you can craft the questions that would give you the essential information you need to ensure they're a fit. What do you think?

Tomar: I love it.

Chris: Great! We uncovered another valuable topic for our next meeting. For now, let's take a few minutes to recap what we've discussed and ensure we're aligned around next steps.

Tomar: First, I need to refine my message in a more collaborative way and empathize with their role and priorities, instead of always assuming no one will ever understand what I'm going through. I also want to make sure I do a better job explaining why this is a good opportunity for everyone, and give the pricing team a reason to approve this particular discount, rather than just telling them it's important to me.

Chris: That sounds spot on. Let's start now with taking the approach you shared and writing it down, so you have a positive, compelling message when you approach the pricing team. Then, we can role play that conversation. This way, you can practice on me and not them, which, as you know, is a lot safer! What do you think?

Tomar: I'm ready! Thanks again for taking the time to work with me on this! It's really helpful.

Chris: I'm glad you feel that you have a strategy you're comfortable with and are ready to write out what you want to say when approaching the pricing team

Tomar: Let's do it!

The Coaching Recap

What a totally different conversation! Notice how many coaching opportunities were uncovered here when the manager used the L.E.A.D.S. coaching model to facilitate this conversation with questions, rather than leading it with answers. The entire conversation, as well as the outcome, was entirely different, and succeeded in identifying the root cause and the gaps that prevented Tomar from collaborating effectively with the pricing team.

Notice how much deeper Chris went in this conversation by challenging Tomar's assumptions. Chris also ensured alignment around certain words and phrases (i.e., *better deal*), and asked the expansion questions in both the assess and define steps to ensure he gathered all the facts and uncovered the root cause, rather than make his own assumptions. Some of these questions include:

- Then what happened?
- What else can be true?
- How did they respond?
- And?
- What exactly did you write in the email?
- What did you do next?

In addition, Chris coached Tomar to recognize all the assumptions he made about his coworkers and customers, which contributed to the constant price objection and confrontational relationship with the pricing team. If you're wondering how your direct reports may react to being coached, the example shows one possibility. It seems that Tomar was pumped up and excited about how valuable the conversation was and made it a point to let Chris know how much he appreciated his time!

This conversation also illustrates an issue that managers struggle with. That is, how many gaps do you need to uncover and coach to during one conversation? Notice Chris identified several gaps in this conversation. There were assumptions, toxic communication, and several holes in Tomar's qualifying process.

However, during this conversation, Chris focused only on creating the talk track for Tomar to use with the pricing team. He specifically suggested to work through his qualifying questions in a separate meeting to be scheduled at the end of this conversation. This all ensures they both honor the coaching cadence needed. When you find yourself in a similar position, remember to stay hyperfocused in order to create measurable change. Coach one gap at a time through to completion, which is what Chris exemplified here.

Finally, there was a clear path to further develop Tomar and what he needed to refine in his approach and messaging when communicating with his coworkers and qualifying his prospects and customers.

I trust this second dialogue provided you with some new ideas about how to coach in these types of situations by leading with questions rather than answers.

Furthermore, you're leaving this conversation with a great exercise you can do with your sales team when it comes to crafting essential qualifying questions!

I timed these conversations to demonstrate that you *always* have time for coaching! Is it worth investing three, five, or even ten additional minutes in every conversation to resolve a situation completely, instead of having the same conversation for the rest of that person's career? You do the math and stop arguing with yourself over investing a few extra minutes in what is probably one of the most important conversations you'll have that day. Instead, rethink and realize this coaching time is a sound investment that will pay back massive dividends, including improved team performance and more time for you.

MINDFUL MOMENT

Coach more, work less.

CHAPTER

7

Creating Unity, Trust, and Buy-In: The Art of Enrollment

Managers are certainly a directive bunch. Given the pressure they're under at work and at home, who can blame them? They have valid reasons for being this way. As someone who is extremely overprotective of the leadership community and my clients, I get it. On top of personal responsibilities, managers are also competing with countless meetings, reports, forecasts, project deadlines, business plans, performance reviews, joint sales calls, unsupportive bosses, time to coach, and other departments vying for their time. There are also monthly team scorecards to evaluate and goals to achieve.

When you consider all of these responsibilities, it's no surprise why managers are so stressed out and feel the time pressure to get everything done *now*. Unfortunately, this often comes at a cost.

As we discussed in Chapter 4, great managers lead with questions, rather than with answers; that's the premise of coaching. Whether you're coaching someone around an agenda they bring to you or you initiate the discussion (your agenda), it's an occupational hazard to default to *directive mode*.

Before we dive into the steps to conduct an enrollment conversation, let's recap what enrollment is, what it sounds like, and why it's essential for every leader to master this communication strategy if you want to create alignment, consensus, trust, and a unified front that is focused on one core objective and shared vision.

FROM THE SIDELINES

People are motivated by what *they* want, not what *you* want.

TIP FROM THE COACH

If you ever experience pushback to coaching, change, or any requests you make, then there's a breakdown in your enrollment process, or the person simply isn't a fit. That was easy.

WHAT IS ENROLLMENT?

Typically, when we hear the word *enroll*, we think about school or health plans. However, the word enrollment is also synonymous with acceptance, permission, appreciation, commitment, perspective, and observation. Each of these words could be integrated into the definition of enrollment. If we were to capture a brief definition of enrollment, like coaching, it's the language of great leaders.

However, where coaching is *always* about the coachee, here's the massive difference: Enrollment is about setting *your* expectations and clarifying *your* intentions in a conversation, while aligning *your* agenda with each person's personal and professional goals. Enrollment is the language that inspires change, collaboration, engagement, unity, and people wanting to be part of a shared cause that can be bigger than them or about them.

In any conversation that you initiate, where you need someone to do something, buy into something or change something, people immediately want to know what's in it for them. If they don't see the *why* behind the *what*, your request, or the value that's in it for them, resistance is imminent.

If you want to know about the effectiveness of your enrollment strategy, your ability to gain consensus, and you positive influence of others, it's quite simple. Is the person open to having the conversation with you or not? Are they embracing what could be perceived as a difficult conversation or are they resisting it? So, look in the mirror, go to a peer or your coach, and ask for some coaching and feedback to find the missing pieces in your enrollment process.

The enrollment conversation to set intentions and create alignment isn't limited between a manager and their direct report. It can be used to enroll *anyone*. By leveraging the art of enrollment, you can start a conversation with partners, vendors, peers, salespeople, customers, the boss, cross-functional teams, and even strangers, family, and friends.

Enrollment sets the intention of the conversation and creates alignment around a mutual goal. In any situation where you need to find a common ground, create consensus, have people align with your ideas, share an observation that may be difficult for someone to hear, or initiate what you may perceive as a difficult conversation, leveraging the power of enrollment is what will make you a world-class leader and strategic communicator.

Now let's get personal. Enrollment can be leveraged for the masses, for the few, and even for the one. Here are just a few important conversations that a manager would typically initiate and where enrollment would be used to successfully open up the conversation.

- Asking for coaching or enrolling others in being coached
- A change in company policy
- Taking full ownership around individual goals and commitments
- Adopting a new process, such as a revised sales, recruiting, or procurement process
- Effectively using your CRM and complying to company policies
- Addressing negative behavior and a toxic attitude
- A performance issue or opportunity (improving the performance of your A, B, and C players)
- Improving or resetting relationships
- Rebuilding trust
- Improving efficiency and time management
- Uncovering people's motivations and core values
- Positive collaboration with cross-functional departments
- Approaching your boss regarding (a promotion, a raise, more consistent coaching, a difficult observation, coaching up, discussing a challenge, asking for help, asking for permission to make an important decision)
- Observation (e.g., customer visits, deskside observation, time management, written communication, phone calls, etc.)
- Accepting feedback that results in behavioral changes
- Building a personal brand
- Holding people accountable

- Developing or improving an essential skill or competency.
- Making a purchasing decision
- Territory management
- Compensation change
- Change in roles and responsibilities
- Creating realistic expectations around an individual's career trajectory

Imagine for a moment that I'm holding both of my arms out straight in front of me so they are parallel with each other. In one hand, I'm holding a person's job responsibilities and business objectives. In the other hand, I'm holding their personal goals and dreams. Now, think about what would be possible if you can align these two things so each person on your team is not only working toward achieving a shared goal, but also seeing how reaching their business goals will help them achieve their personal goals. Now you have a united team working together toward a mutual goal, while respecting each person's individuality and personal goals.

Now you've successfully aligned what your people want personally with the changes and results they are responsible for in their role and what they need to do to get there. And you did so in an empowering way.

MINDFUL MOMENT

It's one thing to think strategically. It's another skill set to leverage the art of enrollment to become a strategic communicator.

Of course, many managers continue to play the power card that would sound like this.

Manager: You all need to focus on inputting the accurate information we need about every customer into our CRM.

Direct: But why? I mean, I have a system that works. I've been using it for years before you rolled out this CRM. It's cumbersome, time consuming, and I don't see the value in it. Besides, it's just another way for management to micromanage us. So, why do we have to do this?

Manager: Because I told you to and it's part of your job.

The discussion has now concluded. This manager effectively shut down this conversation, using their position of seniority to bully people into submission. For those managers who are doing this, how's this working for you? I'd bet you're having many redundant conversations. This is the typical modus operandi of managers when they feel they need to sell people on agreeing with or doing something. Leveraging your position to get people to do things through fear or intimidation pushes people into doing something where they don't see the value and the benefit for them. Therefore, whatever you ask of them, whether it's to do something, try something, or change something, they may do it because it's part of their job, but any buy-in and alignment that potentially existed is short lived.

Now, imagine if they see the benefits of achieving their business goals in relation to their personal goals. They know if they achieve what they need to at work, the personal reward will be waiting for them.

COACHING CONUNDRUM

Enrollment or soapbox management? Choose, preacher man.

When you realize you can take a step back, take a breath, and choose how to conduct an effective conversation, you will soon be communicating like a powerful, influential, and respected leader, while eliminating confrontation—permanently. Speaking of confrontation, have you ever had a difficult conversation? That's why it's time for you to discover how to eliminate difficult conversations permanently.

EVERYONE LOVES CONFRONTATION

I want to work on improving my communication, especially with my peers, boss, sales team, and my customers. I find it challenging to talk with some people or have those difficult conversations, based on their personality or my experience with them. That's an insightful statement to make if you're one who embraces continued growth, personal evolution, and the journey of lifelong learning and self-development. But wait. Put your coaching hat on. Now, get in the habit of keeping it on. Did you immediately read the first paragraph and think, "Coaching moment"? If so, props to you. Now, what's the first question you thought to ask? *Why? Why do you feel you need to/want to improve your communication? Why do you find it challenging to talk with certain people? How would you define difficult conversation? Why are these conversations difficult?*

It's time to start a journey of exploration to uncover the root cause.

I often schedule days at a time to go onsite and provide coaching hours to employees. In one session with the senior leadership team and with Amhad, the CEO of Marble, a multi-billion-dollar telecommunications company based in Kuala Lumpur, Malaysia, I posed this very question. His response, which I hear quite often was, "I need to be better at handling disagreement and conflict. I tend to either erupt like a volcano or avoid these types of conversations. I hate confrontation or having difficult conversations with people."

I asked Amhad exactly how he defines *confrontation*. He said, "Combative. You know, an argument."

"Say more," I requested.

"Well, I know it's confrontational when it erupts into an argument or I get pushback from the other person around my comments, opinions, or ideas. I also get emotionally charged when someone reacts negatively to what I say or approaches me with an aggressive posture—and vice versa. I notice a variation in my tone, I raise my voice, and my body language and posture change.

"Confrontation to me is also disagreement. Then, people often wind up throwing jabs at each other like, 'Look what happened the last time you tried that' or, 'You're wrong' or, 'Do you really think that's going to work?' or, 'Do you really believe that's the reason why you didn't hit your sales targets this quarter?' or 'You may want to spend more one-to-one time with your reps to figure out why your team's performance is slipping.' These are the ingredients for a brewing, imminent conflict about to bubble to the top that often leads to an explosive ending."

THERE'S NO SUCH THING AS A DIFFICULT CONVERSATION

I then introduced him to an alternative way of thinking by using a contrarian question. "What if there was no such thing as a difficult conversation?"

"That's ridiculous," Amhad said. "Of course, there are. I can name a bunch of conversations that are tough to have." Amhad then shared his list of challenging topics. Here are a few that he mentioned:

1. Dealing with an underperformer or behavioral issues
2. Performance reviews or not hitting sales objectives
3. Compensation changes
4. Internal policy changes

5. Customer service issues

6. Not meeting customer expectations

7. Disagreement or having different points of view around sales process, strategies, how to handle certain situations, and so on

8. Managing someone who is having a strong emotional reaction to something that happened or tends to become overly sensitive

9. Strained interpersonal relationships between team members, especially if someone wronged the other person

10. Trying to get the sales veterans on the team to try something new

11. When the other person thinks they're right but they are flat out wrong

12. Coaching people who I perceive are more skilled at their job than me

13. Keeping promises made by others that my direct reports expect me to honor

14. A salesperson who is struggling to close a difficult deal by quarter end

15. A person who has little to no self-awareness

"These are clearly difficult and often awkward conversations to have," Amhad stated with great certainty.

Managers and salespeople continually experience the fight or flight syndrome when faced with conflict or challenging situations like the ones mentioned here. Rather than approach these conversations like a charging rhinoceros or sticking your head in the sand to avoid them, hoping these problems magically disappear, what if the real conflict was all conjured up in your mind?

STOP CREATING THINGS THAT AREN'T THERE

Think of a turbulent or challenging conversation you've had. Now, rewind the tape of that conversation in your mind. What made that conversation so difficult? The root cause will always go back to any of these five things:

1. Your approach

2. The current assumptions you perceive to be the truth

3. Your mindset going into the conversation

4. Your expectation of the outcome

5. Your experiences surrounding the situation, including your past experiences in dealing with similar situations or people, your relationship with that person, or the role they are in

We think to ourselves, "Well, I remember the last time I had to have a tough and candid talk with someone about their performance. Let's just say it didn't go very well."

Then, the next time we're faced with a similar scenario, we create the hypothetical outcome in our mind, and react based on our experience and the assumption of the truth. The by-product of this thinking is, you continue to re-create the same experiences you've had in the past based on your reactive approach. The self-fulfilling prophecy gets validated and, as such, these *difficult conversations* will continue to appear in your life!

The perception you hold regarding how people are going to react, and how strong of a position you take around your beliefs, influences how you choose to engage with others. In essence, you are choosing to communicate and react based on things that may not even be true! This only continues to exasperate unproductive interactions and enforces your expectation of an undesirable outcome, rather than create a new and better possibility.

When you shift the way you communicate through enrollment, you change the way people listen, engage with you, and how they feel. In every conversation, you create the environment that determines whether people shut down or open up and communicate honestly in a productive, collaborative way. That's all in your power, so rather than surrender your power, harness it.

TIP FROM THE COACH

It's not the other person's responsibility to communicate the way you like to communicate. The best leaders align their communication style with the way other people like to communicate.

THE SIX STEPS OF ENROLLMENT

Since you're initiating the conversation, before you begin, it's critical to ensure the timing is right for the person. After all, you're approaching them. However, if you ask one of your direct reports if they have a minute to talk, there are not many who are likely to say no. Rather than instill fear in their hearts, try this approach.

Step 1. Assess the timing of the conversation.

"I wanted to talk to you about a few things I've observed that, if we can work on together, would make you even more successful and eliminate some of the challenges and additional work on your plate. Do you have a few minutes now or are you in the middle of something?"

Step 2. Demonstrate support of their goal.

What I want for you …

Example: "*What I want for you* is to achieve the success and satisfaction you want in your career."

"*What I want for you*" is a statement supporting their goals and what is most important to them. This is when you take a stand for what they want, their priorities, not what you want. What you want shows up in the next step.

MINDFUL MOMENT

If you haven't yet taken the time to sit down and uncover what motivates each person on your team, keep this in mind before you make assumptions around what you think they want. Rather than assume what drives each person, use a general enrollment statement, one that can be used for every enrollment conversation. As you can see in step two, you're having them define what success and fulfillment mean to them, not to you. Once you take the time to uncover what specifically motivates and inspires each individual, along with their core values, you can then customize your *wanting for* statement around their specific goals to make it personal (what I want for you is to be able to afford that new home), rather than saying the same thing to each person you need to enroll.

Step 3. State your intention.

Here's what we're doing.

Example: "During the last customer meeting we had together, I noticed a few things in terms of how you were engaging with the customer and the discovery questions you used that I'd like to discuss with you, which I believe is the cause of the dip in performance."

Step 4. Clarify the *why*.

Here's why we are doing this and *what's in it for you.*

Example: "You have my commitment to work on this with you, so you can close more business faster, without the additional stress or pressure you told me you're feeling."

Step 5. Confirm engagement.

This is one of a few times where you need to ask a closed-ended question to affirm if they're open to having the conversation or not.

Example: "Are you open to discussing how we can achieve this together?"

In the rare instances they say *no*, that becomes another coaching moment, led with one of the most powerful coaching questions known: *Why?*

Step 6. Coach!

Enrollment is the communication strategy to initiate and set the intention of the conversation. Then, once you have that alignment, the coaching can begin! The only difference between enrollment and coaching is dependent upon the person who initiates the conversation, the coach or the coachee. If you initiate the conversation as a manager, then enrollment is the additional step that precedes the coaching that follows.

IT'S WHAT *THEY* WANT, NOT WHAT *YOU* WANT

The *wanting for* statement is always meant to be positioned in a positive way that articulates what is most important to the individual you're enrolling. Therefore, while you are bringing your agenda to this conversation, this initial part of enrollment, steps one and two, are about them.

It's easy to tarnish the purity and impact of the *wanting for* statement. So please, stay away from toxic assumptions that will sabotage your enrollment efforts and actually make the situation even worse. Here are a few examples of statements to avoid.

1. "What I want for you is to still have job by the end of the quarter." Ouch. This is a negatively positioned, fear-based statement.

2. *"What I want for you is to hit your sales goals this month."* This is all about your agenda. The first step in enrollment is using the wanting for statement to take a stand around supporting them around what *they* want. Once that's achieved, it's then followed by your agenda to create that alignment between the two, not the other way around. Of course, if this is something they said is important to them, then this statement would be appropriate.

3. *"What I want from you is to improve your relationships with your clients to increase retention revenue."* There are two potential challenges in this statement. The first is if the manager didn't confirm this as the root cause. The second is that the manager is assuming that if this person improves client relationships, it would improve retention. Now the manager is combining their agenda with assumptions!

My hope is that you see how essential it is to develop this habit of enrollment and feel confident in your ability to do so, especially now that you have this beautiful, newly refined enrollment strategy!

And yet, managers still struggle with recognizing when the situation is more of an enrollment conversation or a coaching conversation. Let's clear this up once and for all.

COACHING VERSUS ENROLLMENT: THE DIFFERENCE AND SYNERGY

I pride myself on learning different languages when traveling. Certain phrases I can say in over 20 different languages. And while one can say they speak a language fluently, it doesn't mean it always translates the same way throughout every region of the world.

When spending time in Egypt, I picked up a few words in Arabic. Following my time in Egypt, I jumped on a plane to Riyadh, Saudi Arabia, to work with a team of Microsoft managers.

Developing deep connections with people is a core value of mine. That's why when I travel to other countries, I feel it's a demonstration of respect for other countries and cultures when you honor their customs and at least try to speak their language. After all, I'm in their home. Inevitably, people appreciate your efforts and it fosters a deeper, mutually respectful connection with every person I meet. While delivering my program in Riyadh, I tried out the Arabic that I learned while in Egypt. Clearly, I failed miserably, as each person in the room looked at me as if I were speaking another language other than Arabic or English, both of which everyone in the room spoke fluently

With blatant curiosity, one manager quickly asked, "Where did you learn your Arabic?"

"Egypt," I said. The manager smiled as if this wasn't the first time he's had this conversation. "There's a difference between Egyptian Arabic and Saudi Arabic, just like you'll find hundreds of different dialects across Africa and India." This certainly makes it more challenging to master another language. Of course, we all had a good laugh at my expense. And I did learn the proper Arabic to use while in Saudi Arabia.

THE RELATIONSHIP BETWEEN COACHING AND ENROLLMENT

The Differences and Similarities Between Coaching and Enrollment
The topics of impromptu, situational coaching and scheduled coaching sessions are *always* initiated and developed by the coachee.
The topic of an enrollment conversation is initiated by the coach or manager, not the coachee. Here's when you approach an individual or a group with your agenda, observations or a topic you want to discuss.

L.E.A.D.S. = Coaching Framework	E.L.A.D.S. = Enrollment Framework
The Five-Step L.E.A.D.S. Coaching Framework	The Six-Step Enrollment Framework to set intentions and create buy-in. (Step one: Assess the timing of the conversation.)
They come to you for coaching, guidance, and assistance around their goal or challenge.	You approach them with your agenda, goal, challenge, or the observation you want to discuss. **Then coach!**
The objective of the enroll step in the L.E.A.D.S. Coaching Framework is to confirm they're ready for coaching, while ensuring there's enough time for an effective coaching conversation.	The Enrollment Framework sets your expectations, agenda, and what the benefit is for them, while ensuring the timing of the conversation works for them, rather than direct or push. **Then coach!**
Coaching is *always* about the coachee, *their* expectations, goals, and agenda.	Enrollment is about getting permission to share *your* expectations, goal, agenda, or observations that need to be discussed. **Then coach!**
Although *they* initiate the conversation, honor the primary objective of leadership: to make your people more valuable.	Although *you* initiate the conversation, honor the primary objective of leadership: to make your people more valuable.

FIGURE 7.1 Differentiating Between Coaching and Enrollment.

This experience runs parallel to the scenario I find myself in when discussing the differences between an enrollment conversation and a coaching conversation, as there is a symbiotic relationship between the two. The subtleties in language can destroy or make a positive, exponential impact on the meaning behind the words you choose, especially when some of the same words hold a different meaning in the same language! After discussing the difference between coaching and enrollment, managers are inevitably confused. What's the difference between the *enroll* E in the L.E.A.D.S. coaching model and the *independent* E in the separate enrollment model?

Figure 7.1 illustrates the two types of conversations, their differences and similarities, and when to have them. To further clarify the difference, if you look at the L.E.A.D.S. coaching model, all we're making are two minor changes. First, we're changing the order of the *learn* and *enroll* steps, and second, the person who initiates the conversation. If we put this in acronym form this is what it would look like:

L.E.A.D.S. (coaching) vs. E.L.A.D.S. (enrollment, then coach!).

Once you've positioned your intention and set the expectations of the conversation using the six steps of enrollment, the conversation will naturally evolve into a coaching conversation! Remember, the language of leadership, regardless of who initiates the conversation, *is* coaching.

TIP FROM THE COACH

Whether coaching or enrolling, regardless of whose agenda it is, always honor the ABCs and *always be coaching*. The only difference between coachees coming to you with an agenda, and you going to them with your agenda is, when enrolling someone, your coaching begins *after* you've enrolled them. Just move the E to begin the conversation, so the model is first *enroll*, then coach: E.L.A.D.S.

To Bring or Not to Bring Your Agenda When Coaching

"But if they would just do it my way, everything would work out perfectly and they would be successful!" As you can imagine, I've never heard this from sales managers before. It doesn't matter where I deliver my management coach training program. Whether it's in the United States or on the other side of the world, there is still some confusion (and even resistance) around when it's appropriate to bring your agenda, prescriptive advice and guidance, or observation into a conversation and when to park it at the conversational doorway, then pick it up when you're done.

From the time I wrote my first coaching book until today, I still attest that the most challenging thing for a manager, salesperson, and every human being to do every day—especially when delivering authentic, effective coaching—is to *detach from the outcome* during a conversation in order to create a new possibility. While doing this may sound practically impossible to some, it is not. To be straight on, if you don't learn how to be present and detach from the outcome during every conversation, then you're creating a ton of collateral damage you might mistakenly label as typical business issues. I'm certainly not suggesting this is easy. Just like learning anything new, it's initially challenging to do! And I'll readily admit that, as an external executive sales coach for any client, it's much easier to detach from the outcome when I'm coaching executives and salespeople who don't work for me! After all, you, as the manager, have goals and quotas to reach. Similar to a sports coach, your success, as well as your reputation and career, is tied directly to the success and performance of your team. Like it or not, your team is a reflection of you. That includes their behavior and how they *show up* to the world, especially at the end of every quarter or during a playoff game. But at this moment, it isn't about your direct reports. It's about *you and the message you send to your team regarding who you are and what you do*

BREAK THE PATTERN

What makes direct reports think a manager is a bit unfocused, unpredictable, and maybe even a little unstable at times is that the manager is not being consistent with their approach. So, the coachee has no idea who's showing up every day! Sometimes you're genuinely coaching people with patience and unconditional support. Yet, often the situation, time of day, pressure felt from the top, other commitments, deadlines, or a poor attitude can squash coaching and, consequently, trust, in an instant.

It's ironic. *What managers do to their people is the very thing managers don't want done to them!* Here's how to distinguish between the two general types of conversations you have and why it's essential to do so.

> **You have an agenda.** That is, there's something you need your team to do, or change, or try. Maybe there's been a change that's been sanctioned from the top. Maybe a new policy, technology or new compensation structure is being rolled out. Maybe there's a need to conduct a specific customer, pipeline, or forecast review. It's also possible for you to want and expect your people to improve upon their attitude, skills, and execution of your sales methodology and process. Or maybe you're dealing with an underperformer and, given their responsibilities and the expectations in their position, mediocre or average performance is not an acceptable option.

> Clearly, you have an agenda and a defined goal or objective in these conversations. And that is okay! But do yourself a favor. Don't label this type of conversation as a *coaching conversation*. Call it anything but coaching (even though you are), because they aren't initiating the conversation! You can call it a strategy session, win session, meeting, brainstorming session, morning huddle, even an enrollment conversation!

This is an *enrollment conversation*. This is where you *enroll* that individual or your team to create buy-in around your agenda, goal, vision, or idea and create deeper alignment and engagement around what you need them to do or change, to the point they *want* to. Not because their boss told them they must, but because you took the time to align their personal goals with your objectives. Subsequently, they see what is now in it for them, and how they can benefit from working to achieve this mutually aligned goal.

Rather than going from *what* they need to do to *how* they need to do it, weave in the *why*. Now the conversation sounds like this: "*Here's what we're doing, here's why we're doing it, and here's what's in it for you.*"

HOW TO DESTROY TRUST AND ISOLATE YOUR TEAM

Imagine that you have a scheduled coaching session with one of your direct reports; keyword here being *coaching*. They drive the agenda and you are there to support them in achieving their goals. Because this is a scheduled coaching session, you also have the time to focus on skill development, or do a deep dive into what you've observed during a joint sales call.

If this is the expectation you have set, here's how to sabotage coaching and trust. Say something like this: "*I know you mentioned that you wanted to use this coaching session to talk about the next step in your career and how you can get there. However, before we do that, I have a few concerns about your performance and sales numbers that I think we should address first, starting with your biggest account that is on the verge of going to a competitor.*"

COACHING CONUNDRUM

Never violate the sanctity of a coaching session. If you collapse a coaching session with your agenda, without setting the expectations and parameters of these meetings, your coachee won't know what to expect, trust is violated, and the experience, reputation, and value of authentic coaching is compromised.

You just blindsided them. If you engage in this tactic, it is a surefire strategy to erode the fabric of trust, as well as the commitment to their job and to the company that each manager is desperately looking to create within their team. Now, at the end of the next coaching session with that person, you're going to feel that your direct report was simply telling you what they think you want to hear!

Trust is gone, because the coach violated the core principles of coaching. Keep it always about the coachee and don't change the rules midgame, or you will tarnish the experience and sanctity of coaching. *That's why I created the six-step enrollment strategy for you to have strategic conversations that you initiate!*

When managers say they're coaching, and then focus on their own objectives or become directive, prescriptive, even defensive, impatient, or reactive, they dilute the essence of what coaching is all about. You've eroded what is meant to be a positive, valuable, empowering experience for the person being coached. And this is all a result of muddying the pure coaching water.

WHAT MANAGERS STRUGGLE WITH MOST

During what has been identified by you and your direct report as a verified coaching session, the direct report drives the agenda. That's the value of coaching. They get to focus on what they want and what's important to them, not what you want them to do.

Coaching is not meant to be a performance review. That's a separate conversation, so treat it and schedule it as such. Coaching is *always* about the coachee and never about you.

I know the intense pressures managers are faced with every day. But what time commitment are we really talking about here when it comes to giving one or two hours each month for a scheduled coaching session, whether face to face or remotely? Stop doing the math. Remember, the more you coach, the more time you have to coach.

Providing each person time that is just about them and what they want is a gift you give. And as a manager, if you don't get this yourself, then it's probably difficult for you to see how important and impactful it is for others and how needed it is.

Ideally, you're scheduling a one-to-one with each person on your team each week, but I can sleep well knowing you're having a scheduled coaching session with each person you coach twice a month. (Keep in mind that impromptu, situational coaching and observation is always happening.) Imagine how you would feel if your boss created this type of consistent, safe, and trusting environment for you?

MINDFUL MOMENT

Does coaching and enrollment ever stop? When communicating across any platform, does verbal, auditory, physical, emotional, and written communication ever stop, regardless of the topic of conversation? Do the world's top athletes ever stop practicing? Therefore, neither does enrollment and coaching if you want to maintain the champion status of your company and sales athletes.

To add to this confusion, even though at times you, as the manager, may have a specific agenda that you need to address—whether it's during a deal review, forecast review, compensation review, or when there are other changes sanctioned from HR or from the top—it doesn't mean you won't be coaching them.

As a reminder, coaching is simply a more powerful way to communicate. This richer form of engagement begins by asking better, well-crafted questions that focus not solely on the result but on the process as well. And this can happen during every conversation you have.

Then again, you're always coaching or simply communicating in a more engaging way. So, while the topics, people, situations, objectives, and conversations may change, the foundation—that is, the coaching and enrollment frameworks—remains consistent, never changes, and never falters.

Here's an example to drive this point home. During a training event in London, a director of one of the top five automotive companies made a powerful observation. She said:

> Keith, there are times I have to get other people who don't report to me to work with me or collaborate on a project or shared goal. These can be other managers, departments, stakeholders, partners, customers, even my boss. But it's not like I will actually tell them I'm coaching them.
>
> Instead, I'm just going to make sure I understand their expectations of every meeting, and ask them better, more strategic questions to drive deeper engagement, alignment, and buy-in. I'm going to get away from my agenda for a moment and take the time to better understand and respect their point of view, and then together, collaborate on a new possibility we can both create together that would support our shared goals.

That was the *aha* moment for this director, when she shared her definitions of coaching and enrollment, said in a different and equally effective way.

Remember, you don't *do* coaching to someone nor is it an event. You're not running around telling people you're putting your coaching hat on, because the fact is, you're always wearing it.

THE COST OF NOT ENROLLING

Although every conversation presents you with an opportunity to ask better, open-ended coaching questions, it's imperative you draw a very clear line between a coaching session, a strategy session, a deal review, an enrollment conversation or a performance review. If you continue to muddy the waters by poorly defining the boundaries around these distinct types of conversations and what to expect, you are not only eroding trust but you're leaving it up to people, especially your direct reports, to decipher what your *real* intentions are.

That's when they'll start looking at you funny and wondering if you're Dr. Jekyll or Mr. Hyde. (Example: "Is my manager going to coach and support me now, or is this going to turn into a directive, one-way conversation where I'm reminded about my goals and that my performance needs to improve?") Even if you're coming from a place of care and support, if you do not prepare your people for change, set clear intentions, and let them know what you're doing, why, and what's in it for them, like everyone on the planet, *their default mindset will be rooted in fear*.

Let me explain. If, out of the blue, you ask one of your employees if they *have a minute to talk*, they immediately move into a reactionary, fear-based mode and freak out! After all, if your boss did this to you, chances are, you'd have the same reaction!

COACHING CONUNDRUM

If you make changes without telling your team/coachees, or if people don't know your intentions and what's in it for them, every human being will default to fear-based thinking.

Here's a great example of a reaction you may have experienced when reading the subject line in the following email from your boss.

Subject Line: Please Call Me ASAP!

What's your visceral reaction? *"Oh, shit." "What did I do wrong?" "Am I in trouble?" "Did I fail to deliver on something?" "What is my manager's hidden agenda here?" "Why are they asking me to do this?" "Am I getting fired, demoted, or a pay cut?"*

When you finally connect with your boss, you come to realize they only wanted to know about the status of your latest project. You never hear people react with, *"My boss wants to tell me how awesome I am!"* Our default file will always be fear, not pleasure, when it comes to the unknown, until you retrain your brain and create a healthier habit of thinking. With emails like these, managers then wonder why their team won't open up to them!

And for those of you who feel you can split the one-hour one-on-one coaching session with each direct into 30 minutes of their agenda and 30 minutes of your agenda, you're once again diluting the value of coaching along with trust in the minds of your people. This typically happens when you say, in so many words, "This is where the coaching portion of the conversation stops, and I get to be directive."

Failure to set and manage expectations is the leading cause of the problems and communication breakdowns you deal with every day! Here's the good news. All resistance around coaching or to making changes can be resolved simply by setting new expectations, while focusing on what the other person wants. That's the real secret to creating buy-in and company-wide alignment.

TIP FROM THE COACH

If you don't have trust, you have nothing. The great news is, you can always enroll and re-enroll people to build or rebuild trust or every relationship.

MANAGE EXPECTATIONS WITH PRECISION: A DIFFERENT KIND OF CONVERSATION

The best managers are very clear about their intentions and expectations in every conversation and realize the collateral damage that can be caused when they continue to change the rules throughout the game. If you want to eliminate most of the challenges and communication breakdowns throughout each day, while continuing to build the trust you need in every relationship, be mindful of how you approach every conversation, and how effectively you manage expectations. To maintain full alignment with goals and coaching, and to maintain your team's trust, always:

1. Define the parameters of coaching with the coachees. It's about them.
2. Honor the six steps enrollment when you have an agenda. You're initiating the conversation that will help them and open the door to coaching.
3. Exemplify what good coaching looks and feels like.
4. Have the coachee establish the objective of every coaching session.

Seven Essential Enrollment Conversations That Create Companywide Alignment

Q uick check-in. So far, we've covered:

1. How to define your ideal corporate culture and an assessment to prepare for this cultural evolution

2. A proven, globally adopted and newly revised L.E.A.D.S. coaching framework and methodology used by managers in over 50 percent of the Fortune 5000 companies

3. The L.E.A.D.S. Coaching Model in action

4. The revised six steps to an enrollment conversation and how they complement your coaching efforts while also creating a unified team, buy-in around change, address any topic, and stimulate positive change an innovation

Is it safe to start coaching? Yes ... and no. You can use many of the strategies we've discussed immediately, including the 60-second coaching strategy in Chapter 4. But for conscious, intentional enrollment conversations that manage the expectations around your transformation, the shift in your daily communication as a coach and how you lead the enrollment conversations are non-negotiable. Here are all the coach tracks you need to get your people on board with coaching, and the additional changes needed to generate exponentially healthier results, fast.

PREPARE YOUR PEOPLE FOR CHANGE

"Keith, when I go back to my team tomorrow, where do I start in terms of introducing coaching as this new way of working together and how my style of management is going to change for the better?" This is always the question on every manager's mind at the end of participating in my leadership coaching program.

There is a proven best practice when it comes to the sequential steps when introducing coaching to your team or company. While I've included a template of what this would look like in the appendix, what follows are the most eloquently scripted conversations and best practice coach tracks you can use immediately that will be the conduit to creating the culture you want.

CREATING ALIGNMENT AND BUY-IN AROUND COACHING

What are your options here when introducing or reintroducing coaching to your team? Some managers start with an email, then schedule a team meeting to introduce the coaching idea to their entire team, knowing that a one-to-one conversation will follow. Other managers prefer having this initial conversation about coaching in private, one-to-one meetings. This could also include the reset coaching conversation for those managers who thought they were coaching but realized after attending my management coach training program that they weren't or were coaching to some degree, but after being formally trained, realized they needed to make some drastic changes in their approach to make their coaching more effective and valuable for their direct reports.

Regardless of how you introduce or reintroduce coaching to your team, clarifying your intentions and what's in it for them will save you hours of having to handle the collateral damage that ensues when you leave it up to your team to decipher what your agenda really is. This will foster a strong, healthy relationship that you can build upon right from the start, creating the positive, trusting, collaborative, and open environment that will enable you to earn your direct report's deeper respect, trust, and commitment to their objectives, even in the face of change.

Conversation #1: Email to Prepare for Positive Change

You have the option to send this companywide or just to your team. As you'll see in the second conversation that follows, you can quickly cover this in your next team meeting, whether remote or face to face. Here's a template you can tweak when introducing the changes coming. This is best sent from the top. Feel free to edit accordingly including the subject line. It's wordy, so you have a lot to work with!

Email Subject Line: Creating Greater Success for You, Your Team, and [company name]

> Good day!
>
> As you may have noticed, we are making some positive changes that will impact each of us in a positive way. Along with any change may come a degree of discomfort as we stretch outside our comfort zone to do something new, unknown, or unproven. One thing is for certain: We are all going through these changes together and each of you can count on the support you need from the leadership team and from each other throughout this transformation.
>
> To keep our competitive edge, change is the only constant. So, how do we leverage everyone's passion, strengths, natural talents, and personal goals in a way that fosters deeper trust, engagement, and collaboration among each person within the company, as well as with our clients? How do we continue to deliver our exemplary customer experience? How do we successfully build the future leaders of the company?
>
> One way is by changing the way we all communicate with, support, and develop one another, and that will improve through the skill and language of *performance coaching*. After all, every professional athlete in the world has a coach, so it only makes sense that we, as the greatest business athletes within our industry, do the same. Through coaching, each person will have the opportunity to truly live their fullest potential, while designing a career they are passionate about.

I am truly excited about the new standards we are setting in our company. As our company grows, it is critical that each member of our team make a conscious choice to want to grow with us. After observing other companies going through a similar transformation, we all need to make a fundamental shift from *competing* to *collaborating* with one another. And we understand for a company to change, it must start from the top. And that change will start with me and how I communicate, support, and engage with each of you.

Over the next several weeks, you can expect your manager to schedule a time with each of you to discuss why we are doing this, where we are today, and where we will be tomorrow. Then together, you will work with your manager on designing a coaching strategy that will best support you to achieve your goals as a team, as well as your individual goals, so that they know how you want to be coached to attain what matters most to you, personally and professionally. *And expect your manager to be open to your coaching and feedback as well.*

With your support, we are confident that during this transformation, we will all contribute to the company to bring about healthy change that everyone can be a part of. These changes will enable you to make a positive impact on our organization, our customers, your career, and each person within the company.

Positive changes are coming, and we can't do this without you, your talents and contributions, and our 100 percent unified, collaborative efforts. We will be there to support you during this process every step of the way and will be going through this journey together.

Thank you again for your support, commitment, openness, and assistance. If you have any questions or concerns around this, please don't hesitate to contact me or discuss with your manager anytime. We look forward to creating greater success for each person within [**COMPANY NAME!**]

Sincere regards,

FROM THE SIDELINES

Enrollment is the conduit that drives a successfully executed strategy.

Conversation #2: Team Enrollment in Coaching and Setting Expectations

As mentioned when we discussed the danger of not preparing people for change, if you were the chief problem solver yesterday, disappear for a few days when participating in this program, and then show up a few days later transformed into a best-in-class coach, how do you think your direct reports are going to respond if you don't prepare them for this change? Questions will replace your directives and answers. That's certainly a big shift. And they'll still be the same as they were before you went through this program!

If you're changing the rules, it's essential you set new expectations so that your people know what your intentions are and what's in it for them. Otherwise, a blanket of fear will cover you, your team, and your coaching efforts.

While introducing coaching in a team environment has its benefits, some managers would rather skip the team introduction to coaching and just have that conversation one to one. Alternatively, other managers want to deliver a blanket message across their team at one meeting so everyone knows what to expect. Whether you choose to introduce coaching in a team meeting or during a one-to-one conversation with each person on your team, the one-to-one deeper dive meeting is an essential, non-negotiable step in this process.

This is when you have an opportunity to discuss coaching and what it is, their perception of coaching, their expectations of coaching, the parameters surrounding coaching, and finally, their concerns about being coached. This type of in-depth exploration is better left for a one-to-one conversation where your people are more apt to share their real concerns and goals in a private, confidential setting. Here is an example of what the group introduction might look like:

Manager: What I want for each of you is to achieve your team/ department goals, as well as your personal/career goals and support each other in doing so. Quite frankly, when it comes to preparing you for your next role and further developing you in your current role, I feel I've let you down. For that, please accept my apology. I'm fully committed to be the best manager and coach to make you as successful as possible here.

I attended this master leadership coaching course and have some great ideas on how to coach everyone that deliver tons of value for you. Granted, this is a journey we're going through together, and I'm counting on learning from you as well, so coaching becomes something that will help all of us live our potential, just like world-class athletes.

That's why I'm asking for your help. Together we can become a unified team that achieves all our goals. But coaching is the only way this can happen. So, is everyone open to resetting the expectations around coaching, how I can best support you and the way we work together, and what we need to do to make coaching a win for everyone?

Team: Absolutely! Woo-hoo! [Maybe they won't be that enthusiastic, but it would be pretty cool!]

Manager: Thanks everyone. I appreciate your support around this. The next step would be for me to send each of you a meeting invitation for a one-on-one meeting so we can align our efforts and discuss what I can do to be the best manager, coach, and resource for you so that you can achieve your career and personal goals.

Conversation #3: Schedule a One-to-One Meeting for Individual Enrollment

Here's the template you can use for your one-on-one conversations to introduce coaching to each direct report. Notice this template also honors the six steps of enrollment.

I'd like to share this experience I had going through this two-day course, which will help all of us become even more successful. Do you have a few minutes now to discuss this or are you in the middle of something? What I want for you is to experience the level of fulfillment and success that you really want in your career. After completing this leadership coaching program, I learned that, just like technology continues to evolve, so does the way managers engage with their team in order to maximize each person's true potential. Think about sports. The coach is there to make sure each player is always at the top of their game. I learned how I can be a better manager and coach for you so I can support you in a way that would make you even more successful.

Keep in mind, this learning curve is something that we're both going through together, so I may not get it perfect the first time, which is why I'll be looking for some feedback and coaching from you as well. What's most important is you understand my intentions here. That's why I'd like to take some time to talk about what your perception of coaching is so we can come up with a mutually agreed upon understanding and definition of coaching, set some measurable expectations and parameters around our coaching, and what I can do to make this the most valuable experience that I can for you.

How do you feel about discussing this? (Or if you prefer: Are you open to discussing this to ensure the coaching I provide helps you become more successful?)

Now, the manager can move into a series of coaching questions to achieve what the enrollment template intended. Again, use the questions you want; however, I've italicized those questions that are essential to ask. And you've just completed the E in the E.L.A.D.S. enrollment model!

1. First, how would you define what my role is, as a manager?
2. What responsibility do you feel I have in making you as successful as possible in your role, and what activities would that include?
3. *How would you define what coaching is?*
4. *Have you ever been coached before? What was your experience like?*
5. *If you could redefine the parameters and definition of what coaching is so it's a valuable experience for you, what, if anything, would it be?*
6. *What would your expectations be of me from our coaching?*
7. *If you could design the structure of these one-on-one meetings, how would you want it to be?*
8. *What would you like to accomplish or ensure we cover during our coaching sessions that would be important and valuable to you?*
9. *What concerns, if any, do you have about our coaching and what we discuss?*
10. Would you like to have check-in touch points between our regularly scheduled coaching meetings to ensure you have the resources you need to stay focused?
11. What is one thing that I should be mindful of when coaching you? What would you like me to do/not to do regarding how I coach you? (They may not know until after they have experienced good coaching firsthand.)
12. What is one thing you'd like to accomplish or cover during every coaching session? (They may not know until after they have experienced good coaching firsthand.)

Once you've had this conversation, you can discuss your style of coaching and make any needed refinements to ensure it fits for each person.

Can I share with you how I envision coaching you and my style, so that you know what to expect and ensure it's aligned with your expectations?

Before you conclude this conversation, schedule your first coaching session. You can position this using the following dialog.

Let's take a moment and schedule our next coaching session so we can focus specifically on a coaching action plan, your goals, and any timely challenges you are having. I'll also share a useful and brief coaching prep form and Coaching Action Plan for our coaching sessions that would help set your expectations for each coaching session to ensure you get the value from each meeting we have.

Conversation #4: Coach Up! Schedule a One-on-One Meeting with Your Manager

When discussing the reasons why coaching will not work, the common assumptive response I hear is, "My boss. Knowing what great coaching is, my boss is not coaching me in a way I find valuable and I don't think she would be supportive if I were to approach her about this. Besides, at the end of the day, I'm evaluated on results, and so is my boss."

I get it, but that's not why you're reading this book. (Otherwise, you'd keep doing what you did yesterday.) Regardless of your position or tenure, as a direct report or manager at any level, most of us have someone to answer to. You might wonder: "But isn't it my manager's responsibility to approach me, to find out how they can best manage and coach me instead of me telling them what I need? This whole book talks about the how the manager is the one responsible for creating the culture they want on their team." You'll find no argument here. Unfortunately, everyone doesn't have the same level of self-awareness. There are still managers who have yet to get the memo on the importance of the topics in this book.

The unfortunate truth is, if your boss doesn't take the time to listen deeply, give you their undivided attention, patience, and focus to effectively coach you, then it's hard for the manager to see the value in doing so for others and how important it is as a leader to do so. After all, if you don't know what good coaching looks and feels like, then how do you know what to model when it comes to emulating best coaching practices? World-class leaders have a presence, communication style, and disposition that sets them apart. If you've had a bad coaching experience, it may hinder your desire to coach! That's why some managers don't recognize your needs and how important it is to give you the attention you need. So, you can either wait around and hope that your manager recognizes your needs and how you want to be coached and managed or be proactive and initiate these critical conversations.

If your manager doesn't take the first step, then it's up to you to do so. Otherwise, you may be waiting your entire career for them to approach you.

TIP FROM THE COACH

Your boss isn't clairvoyant. Sometimes you have to tell them what you need, because it's hard for people to recognize the needs of others when it's something you don't get yourself.

If you're fully committed to creating a coaching ecosystem on your team and across the company where everyone is coaching each other, then it's also each employee's responsibility to seek out the coaching from your boss, peers, and direct reports, and that includes how you want to be coached, managed, supported, and held accountable. Unfortunately, many believe approaching their boss in a way that would open them to change in how they communicate, manage you, or deliver more positive, constructive feedback is a daunting and difficult task. Some even feel it's an impossible undertaking, or one that would make them vulnerable, put them in harm's way, expose their weaknesses, or assume, "My boss isn't going to change, and if I want to keep my job, I'll have to tolerate this."

No one wants to feel like they're going to be punished for being honest, whether they're sharing a developmental opportunity, facing a personal challenge, providing an observation that could help your boss or team improve, or making a request for something to change for the betterment of all. But what if you could approach your boss and have these conversations in a way that doesn't put you in the firing line and creates the opportunity to reset expectations with your manager around your job, responsibilities, expectations in your role, learning moments as well as how you like to communicate, collaborate, and be coached? How receptive they are depends solely on your approach.

MINDFUL MOMENT

Rather than assume the worst or avoid what you perceive may be a difficult conversation, change your thinking from making it initially about you and what you need, to making it about your manager and what you can do to best support them.

What follows are two distinct coach tracks to approach and enroll your manager on how you want to be coached, while ensuring you're meeting your boss's expectations. If these expectations of performance are not clarified, you run the risk of having your manager continually move the goal post on you, change your responsibilities, and change their expectations of you in the middle of the game—often setting you up for failure.

You could address both topics in one conversation or, depending on your situation, break them up into two distinct meetings. Modify these templates to fit your personal style of communicating, while maintaining the integrity of the message.

MINDFUL MOMENT

Coaching is a gift you give and one you get yourself because it's a reflection of how much you care about people.

Coaching Up—Enrollment Talk, Track One: Aligning Your Role with Management's Expectations and Priorities

Hey William, what I want for you and the company is to ensure the work I'm doing is aligned with the company goals, priorities, and your expectations. While I'm confident in my role and responsibilities, I would find it helpful to carve out some time to ensure I'm moving my team toward achieving your objectives and priorities and uncover anything I need to do to course correct. And that includes how I can best support you and make your job easier.

One thing I see I can improve upon is leveraging our CRM, scorecard, and reports to uncover coaching and developmental moments for the team.

Although there are no glaring issues now, I'd rather be proactive around this. It would be very helpful for me to have a better understanding of your expectations of me so that I'm doing everything in my power to continually achieve our goals.

Would you be open to sharing some observations around what I can do more of or do better so that I'm maximizing the value I can deliver and ensure we're collaborating effectively?

Here are some questions you can use to manage this conversation:

1. Outside of my job description, what are your expectations of me? (Results, activity, responsibilities, deadlines, behavior, etc.)

2. How would you score me around (performance, coaching, efficiency, collaboration, brand, and so on)?

3. What opportunities for development have you observed that would help me be more successful in my role?

4. How can I make your job easier?

5. Have any of the top priorities of the company changed? To reconfirm, given the projects I'm working on now, can we review them to ensure I have them listed in order of priority?

6. Where do you see the greatest opportunities are for improvement within the company?

7. How else can I support you?

Coaching Up—Enrollment Talk, Track Two: Establishing Expectations of Coaching with Your Boss

If your manager isn't taking the lead on creating a coaching culture on your team, you can enroll them around how you plan on coaching your team, while also using this as an opportunity to set expectations around how you like to be coached, managed, and supported:

> (Boss), I really value your opinion and support, and not only appreciate your willingness to coach me but I'm excited about it. To ensure we generate worthwhile results from coaching, it's important I have a better understanding of your definition of coaching and coaching approach so that I can make sure I'm leveraging every coaching opportunity I have with you and my team that would help achieve our business objectives.

> I'd like to work with you to identify the coaching and management style that works best for me to help maximize my productivity, and the coaching I plan on doing with my team, so I can leverage the ideas you have and ensure that we're both clear about what we can expect from each other. Would you be open to discussing the parameters around our coaching so we can achieve this?

Conversation #5: You Don't Know Your People: Uncover Their Individuality and Motivation

Before sharing the coach track for this conversation, I wanted to illustrate the importance of this conversation. Here's yet another true story of a salesperson who turned down a $5,000.00 bonus.

During a leadership program I was facilitating in Milan, Italy, we were talking about how managers try to motivate people using bonuses or incentives. The frustration quickly rose as the managers shared how much they struggle with finding a way to continually motivate each person on their team to perform consistently, especially in the face of change or difficult times.

All of these managers admitted to, at one time or another, designing an incentive program for their team. I asked them, "Have these programs or bonuses you've offered achieved the results you want?" There was a consensus that the bonus programs they've put in place don't work.

"Why?" I inquired.

One manager explained, "Well, Keith, in the past, when I've designed a bonus program for the team, I would typically position it so that the top salesperson for the quarter or for the month would get some sort of additional monetary compensation."

My follow up question, "And how has that been working for you?"

"You can probably guess what happens. The top performer always wins."

I reaffirmed, "So basically, managers with good intentions put together some type of bonus structure in place where the top person wins something, typically some amount of money.

"Now, envision this. You have your top performer or A player lined up at the starting line next to your average or B player. And next to them is your underperformer or your C player. Then the starting gun goes off. What happens to the C player? What do they do?"

One manager said, "The C player looks at the A player and the B player next to them and thinks, 'I'm not going to even try because I don't have a chance.' So, they check out immediately."

The very incentive plan the manager had put together had now become a disincentive for their lower performers!

Now, the B player looks at the A player and thinks, "Okay, I have a chance here. I'm going to give this a shot and do my best." However, at some point during the race, they see the vast lead the A player has and, just like the C player, the B player now checks out and gives up. So, who wins?

"The A player. The same person who always wins." The managers nodded in consensus. It's evident to these well-intentioned managers that the bonuses they set up were structured for the A player to win, while the rest of the team looks at them feeling doomed to fail from the start. The overarching question was apparent. One manager asked, "So what do we do to get everyone engaged and motivated? And to add to this, given our company policy and resources, we don't always have the ability to keep offering our team additional money to perform."

It was during this conversation that I was reminded of a story where in one financial institution, the manager was going to give out a $5,000.00 (USD) bonus to the person who outperformed the rest of the team for that quarter.

Well, at the end of the quarter, to no surprise, this manager's top performer won.

When the quarter ended and all the sales for that quarter were confirmed, the manager called into her office the salesperson who won. She handed a $5,000.00 check to this high performer and said, "Congratulations on winning. Here's a check for $5000,00. Well done! You deserve it."

"Thanks," the salesperson replied with a lack of enthusiasm. The manager was surprised by such an unenthusiastic reaction.

Puzzled, she responded to this salesperson by saying, "I just handed you a check for $5,000.00. I would think you would be more excited! What did I miss here?"

And that's when she heard the unexpected comment that shocked this manager into a new way of thinking. The salesperson looked at her manager and said, "To be completely honest, I'd hand this check back to you right now and would feel more rewarded and motivated if you announced to everyone on our sales team that I am the best salesperson on the team."

What a surprise! Her reaction totally blindsided this manager.

Some of you may be thinking, "Are you kidding me? I would take the money!" However, there are always people in the room who feel differently and would rather receive that kind of acknowledgment. The reality is, most managers truly don't know what inspires and motivates each individual person on their team to perform. Instead, they make two general assumptions. The first assumption is, "Salespeople are coin operated and only motivated by money." Clearly, this story refuted that assumption. The second dangerous assumption that managers make is when they're coaching in their own image. That would sound like, "Well, I know what motivates me. So, I bet it's going to be the same for the people on my team." Then, managers wonder why people aren't responding positively to what you perceived would motivate them to push harder so they can perform better.

How to Inspire Each Individual on Your Team

Managers spend so much time anguishing over what the perfect bonus program would be that would exponentially motivate their people. Well, if you're struggling to come up with the answer, then chances are you're asking the wrong person—you! Instead of trying to come up with what you perceive will motivate your people to better their best and go the proverbial extra mile, what if you let them design their own incentive?

Keep in mind, it's not always about the money. All of your rewards don't have to be tangible to spark inspiration and drive. So, if you're concerned that effective bonuses require some type of monetary compensation, consider there are other ways to reward people that they would deeply appreciate and work even harder to attain. Here are just a few:

1. Time off.

2. Mornings or afternoons where they can leave work early to pick up their children or drop them off at school/daycare.

3. Time to play golf or spend time with their family or what they like to do during their down time.

4. Lunch with their manager. (Yes, some of your people do want to spend time with you!)

5. Half-day workdays, for example on Friday, or permission to work remotely from home.

6. Authentic acknowledgment in private or in front of the team. (Don't assume what they like or what makes them uncomfortable. Ask them how they like to be acknowledged!)

7. Rewarding them with a new or specific account.

8. Providing them with a certain type of lead or client to manage.

9. Giving them more time to craft their career trajectory and personal brand.

10. Empowering them with more responsibility (e.g., team leader, running meetings).

11. Providing additional administrative support for a certain period of time.

12. A company T-shirt, jacket, or hat. (Yes, people do go crazy for this stuff!)

TIP FROM THE COACH

Rather than banging your head against the wall figuring out what will motivate your team to push themselves out of their comfort zone and achieve more—just ask them!

Notice that most of these incentives don't cost you a dime. And, ultimately, it's what your people want most, aside from a monetary reward. But the only way you can assess what they want, rather than what you think they want, is by taking the time to sit down with each person and have a one-to-one conversation around what truly inspires them to come to work every day.

Taking the time to uncover what makes them feel most fulfilled and satisfied, along with what would push them to go the extra mile becomes the impetus to peak performance, especially if they know that what they wanted most was waiting for them at the finish line.

The questions I'm about to share are also good for facilitating a follow-up coaching session after you've set up the expectations and parameters of coaching. Remember, you need to enroll them in this type of conversation to set expectations as to *what* you are doing, *how* you are doing it, and *why* you're doing it so they clearly see what's in it for *them*.

The Conversation to Uncover Motivation, Drive, and Personal Goals and Objectives:

> What *I want for you* is to feel that as your manager, I'm a valuable resource who can contribute to your success by aligning what your personal goals are with the objectives you have at work. For me to best understand how I can do so, I'd love to learn more about what is most important to you in your job, as well as how I can best support and manage you in a way that you find valuable. I'd like to ask you some questions so that I can get to know you better (*and feel free to ask me any of the same questions as well!*). Are you open to exploring this with me now?

Once you get confirmation they are open to having the conversation, continue with the following questions to guide the conversation.

1. What do you want to achieve six months from now? One year from now? Two years?
2. What is most important to you in your career?
3. What motivates you to come to work each day?
4. What are the things that you enjoy most about your job?
5. What do you love most about your job/position?
6. What gives you a sense of accomplishment at the end of each day?
7. If you could design your perfect day, what would it look like?
8. If you didn't have to work, what would you do with your time?
9. What would you love to change about your job if you could?
10. What would make your job even more exciting and fulfilling?
11. How do you like to be rewarded/acknowledged for a job well done?
12. What do you want to achieve in the short and long term?

To build accountability and a path to help them get what they want:

1. What's your action plan to achieve (this task, project, goal)? How does this break down and get scheduled into your daily routine and activity?
2. What concerns do you have or barriers you need to be mindful of that could get in the way of reaching these goals?
3. *How can I best support you to achieve these goals? (How do you like to be managed?)*
4. *What type of reward or incentive would drive you to achieve even more?*
5. *How can I hold you accountable and be your accountability partner in a way that will sound supportive rather than negative?* (How can we ensure accountability in a way that's positive and works for you?)
6. *How do you want me to approach you if you don't follow through with the commitments you make? What would be a good way to bring this up?*

Conversation #6: Identify Their Priorities and Values

Keep in mind, this conversation is meant to complement Conversation #5 and can be had during the same meeting. While the questions I just shared would stimulate a thought-provoking conversation, the reality is, most people have never been asked these questions, so they may not have an immediate answer. Here's an additional tool to leverage to ensure alignment with the responses they shared regarding what truly motivates them. But you must enroll them first:

What I *want for you* and for each person on our team is to feel that the work you are doing each day is in alignment with what is most important in your life so that you can achieve your personal goals as well. I found this great tool to help uncover a person's individual motivation. Basically, it's a list of about 50 different items that inspire or motivate us at work, which provides more purpose, focus, and fulfillment from our job, or the personal goals and values we treasure most that get us out of bed each day.

I found the exercise very useful when I completed it and thought it would be worthwhile for you to do. Just review the chart and circle the top five items that jump out to you as most important. Then we can schedule a time to review it together, and I'd be happy to share my results if you'd like. When the work you do is in alignment with your values and priorities, your career becomes the vehicle for you to get what you want most. Then, I can better support you around achieving your goals. So, how would you feel about scheduling a time to review this together?

Exercise: Identifying Your Priorities and Values

Use Figure 8.1 to identify your top five values and priorities.

Conversation #7: Discussing the Motivation Exercise

Fast forward to your follow-up meeting. What would that sound like? What questions would you use to facilitate this debrief? How can you leverage this as a coaching conversation?

Once they complete the exercise, use the following coaching questions during your follow-up meeting to better understand who each person is, their values, and their motivations.

1. What did you learn about yourself from going through this process of identifying your priorities and values?

2. In what way was this exercise valuable to you?

WHAT ARE YOUR TOP PRIORITIES, MOTIVATORS, AND VALUES?

Mentoring Others · Learning/New Experiences · CREATIVITY · Faith · Affecting Change · Vacation Time · FAMILY · Strong Personal Brand · New Technology · Variety · Philanthropic Work/Charity · Responsibility · Buying a Home · Job Security · Following Process · Recognition · Joy · Freedom/Flexibility · Saving for Children's Education · Leading Teams/Developing/Helping Others · Acknowledgment · Project Management · Solving Problems · Toys/Shopping · Promotions · Independent Contributions · Go-To Person · Money · Collaboration · Making a Difference/Impact · Contributing to Others · Subject Matter Expert · Community Service · Teamwork · Fun · Client Interaction · Respect · My Children · Retirement Security/Tomorrow · Travel · Being the Best/Top of Class · Lifelong Learning · Peace of Mind · Interacting with Management · Relationships with Coworkers · Career Growth · Financial Security/Today · Eradicating Pressure From Others · Buying a Car · Getting Results · Getting out of the House · Intellectual Challenges

FIGURE 8.1 Top Five Values and Priorities.

3. *If you were to put these in order of priority what would they be?*

4. How close are you from living these values and honoring or focusing on these priorities?

5. What has to happen/change for you to achieve what matters most to you?

6. How do these things align with your current job, goals, and business objectives?

7. What's the cost or implication for you if you don't achieve these things?

8. If you were able to achieve these things and honor your core values, how would that impact you, your performance, your attitude, your life?

9. How can I best support you around your efforts to create these things that matter most to you?

10. How can I coach and be your accountability partner for creating what you have identified as most important to you?

FROM THE SIDELINES

Now that you know for certain what their core values, priorities, and motivations are, weave what they value and want most into every enrollment conversation, using the, *"What I want for you ..."* statement. Now, every *what I want for you* statement becomes personalized and specific for each person to reflect what's most important to them, rather than using a generic wanting for statement.

A SUBTLE DISTINCTION

There's a lot of personal joy and satisfaction I feel when inspiring people about what's possible for them. When I talk with sales managers and they tell me they manage a team of salespeople, the truth is, they're managing a team of individuals who happen to share the same title, job function, and responsibilities. It's a subtle yet important distinction. One leads to the manager coaching in their own image and pushing conformity. The other promotes individuality by focusing on who each person is and not just a number on a spreadsheet. Maybe that's why managers shy away from certain conversations, simply because they don't know how to coach to them. Well, you know I always have your back. Let me show you how in the next chapter.

CHAPTER

Coach Tracks: Turn Difficult Situations into Coaching Wins

D
o you find yourself butting heads with some coworkers or clients? Are you stressed and frustrated because they prevent you from getting your job done? Do you resist having what you may perceive as a difficult conversation? (See Chapter 7 to debunk the myth that there are difficult conversations.) These issues stagnate growth, productivity, and revenue. There's no reason to tolerate toxic relationships or stressful situations when all it takes is a conversation to repair and reinvent them.

Here are six coach tracks for common situations historically perceived as *unfixable* that will make every manager's job easier and more enjoyable, improve collaboration and performance, reduce conflict and contention, so you can be the person everyone loves working with.

CONVERSATION #1: ELIMINATING DEPARTMENTAL AND INTERPERSONAL SILOS

Imagine what would be possible if everyone in your company was unconditionally supportive of each other and was accountable for developing healthy, empowering relationships—without the drama. Working within the confines of your team is one thing. However, marketing needs to play nicely with sales. Sales and every department need to play nicely with each other, whether operations, finance, engineers, IT, HR, or customer support. People lose sight of the fact that working toward a shared vision helps everyone win.

What is the root cause of this isolation and competing responsibilities that prevents unified collaboration and the ability to focus on the overarching company vision, values, and shared goals?

THE CAUSE OF DEPARTMENTAL SILOS AND HOW TO CREATE UNITY

The answer is simple. *Everyone has their own agenda and employees aren't respecting other people's role and goals.*

Here's a common scenario: A salesperson in the field needs an internal resource to close a deal or serve a customer. The typical modus operandi is to contact the person who can help them. However, their focus is typically around what they need in the moment rather than what they can give. Moreover, they're not considering that your request isn't the only request they get every day! It's as if they're just sitting around waiting for you to call so they can respond immediately.

This creates pressure and strains every relationship. Departmental silos shut down collaboration, cause dissention (the vindictive sabotaging of others), and compromise the results each person is looking to achieve. The irony is that everyone is focused on the same goal: to deeply serve your external customers and coworkers.

The solution to breaking down these silos to foster profitable collaboration instead of competing with other departments is a simple enrollment conversation. Here's an approach you can use to begin the process.

> Hey Jan. When would you have some time to discuss some ways that would help reinvent our relationship for the better and allow me to best support you in your role, so we can collaborate toward our common goal, while respecting your priorities and agenda?

Once you hear a confirmed *yes* or schedule a time for this conversion, here's the coach track to use:

> What I want for you is to feel that I'm a trusted resource who supports you to achieve your goals. Since we're in different departments (roles) and are evaluated by different metrics, scorecards, and key

performance indicators, I know we haven't always seen eye to eye when relying on each other to get our jobs done. We all have different priorities and points of view, and I may not have always given yours the attention or respect it deserves. So, I'm asking for your forgiveness, as I was guilty of doing this.

That's why I'd love to hit the reset button on our relationship and with your help, redesign how (our departments/we) interact and work together so we can support each other to achieve our goals.

I know there may be some things that were said or done that created the tension and disconnect between us and our (departments/role). That's why I want to better understand your role, challenges, how you're evaluated and your business objectives, so I can support you (and your department), while aligning our collective efforts to achieve our mutual goals.

So, let's work together to redesign our relationship, clarify the best process for us to collaborate, and the most effective way to communicate, even when working through a timely challenge.

Setting these clear expectations will be beneficial for everyone and help our company achieve our common goal and shared vision.

Are you open to discussing how we can remove these barriers between (us/our departments) so we can all achieve more by collaborating rather than competing with one another?

Great! To start, may I ask some questions about your role? Feel free to ask me the same questions as well.

26 QUESTIONS THAT CREATE UNIFIED, SUPPORTIVE RELATIONSHIPS

Once you have buy-in around having this conversation, here are the questions that will achieve your objective. You don't have to use all of them, so choose the ones you feel are most relevant.

1. I'd love to learn more about your role and responsibilities. Would you mind sharing your job description, so I can be more respectful of your role?

2. How are you measured? By what criteria?

3. Do you have your own scorecard and a defined set of key performance indicators?

4. Can you help me understand the expectations the company and your manager have of you?

5. What part of your role or the work we collaborate on is most difficult/stressful/frustrating for you?

6. What do you see that's working?

7. In your opinion, what's not working that we need to address?

8. What's your biggest concern regarding the immediate, timely requests I make?

9. Ideally, if we can redesign the way we work together, what would that look like? (What do we need to do to work together in the most productive way?)

10. How do you like to collaborate?

11. What's your expectations or definition of exemplary, five-star customer service?

12. What is your approach to dealing with a customer issue?

13. If I need you, what's your response time so I can avoid putting more pressure on you?

14. How do you typically like to communicate? (e.g., face to face, phone, instant message, text, email, etc.)

15. If there's a challenge that needs to be handled/addressed, what's the best way for us to resolve it? How would you like me to approach you, so we can work together in the most productive way?

16. Other than you, who else would you want me to contact in case of a timely need or challenge if I'm unable to contact you, without overstepping you and your role?

17. If we don't agree on something, what approach works best for us to create alignment or a resolution?

18. How can I best support you in your role?

19. What else do I need to know about you that I need to be mindful of and would improve our relationship?

20. What are your thoughts on scheduling a meeting where you and I connect once a week to ensure we're aligned in our approach and objectives so we can avoid potential problems?

21. What can I do to maintain our positive relationship?

22. What would compromise our relationship?

23. What would it look and sound like if we both committed to holding each other accountable for our commitments in a supportive way?

24. If we notice we're dropping the ball on our commitments or reverting to toxic behavior, how can we communicate this without offending each other? What would be a good way to bring this up?

25. What concerns, if any, do you have at this point?

26. Given our conversation, what strategy can we put in place to ensure we're achieving our goals?

   Jan, I appreciate your time and willingness to create a plan that would enable us to work successfully as a team and maintain a positive relationship. I'll send you an email recapping what we've discussed to ensure alignment and capture next steps. What else, if anything, would you like to discuss before we wrap up this conversation?

STOP COMPLAINING AND START REPAIRING—RECIPROCITY STARTS WITH YOU

The next step is up to you. When you focus on helping others first, in turn, they will want to help you. That's the law of reciprocity. But know that any change in activity, thinking, communication, collaboration, or behavior that you want to be reciprocated starts with you. This includes trust, coachability, respect, observation, embracing feedback, transparency, support, positivity, accountability, work ethic, and so on.

This is how you're going to be remembered and this is a powerful step to building a well-respected personal brand. After all, when you change the conversation, you change the outcome, which will make everyone's job easier and more enjoyable.

CONVERSATION #2: INHERITING AN EXISTING TEAM

If you're a manager who has the luxury of building a team from scratch, following these strategies I share throughout this book will ensure you develop a champion team.

However, what happens if you inherit a team from a prior manager? What follows are two coach tracks for two distinct situations to set and reset expectations with your new team.

   What I want for you is to feel that you have a manager you trust who will always be there to support you, have your back, and help you achieve your goals. With our aggressive business objectives, there has been a lot of changes within our company and in people's roles. If we don't manage change well, it can create uncertainty and fear, become a distraction, and derail the focus on our goals. I know I've felt that way in the past when a new manager inherited my boss's position.

As your new manager, I'm not going to assume what kind of relationship or experience you had with any prior managers, how you like to be managed, your perception of me and my role, or how you want me to support and coach you.

That's why I would love to understand how I can be the best manager for you, address your concerns, if any, and ensure we are aligned to achieve our goals together. We have an opportunity to create a positive relationship from the beginning that would be mutually supportive.

Also, I'd love to learn how you do things, and the best practices you use to achieve results, so that I can learn from you as much as you can from me. Regardless of your experiences with prior managers, are you open to designing our relationship so expectations are clear, and we can support each other in a positive way that would lead to greater success?

Now coach!

Since we covered this in Chapter 7, you know that once you enroll someone in the conversation you want to have with them, the next step is to shift your energy and focus to coaching them.

Questions That Seek to Understand People's Point of View and How They Want to Be Managed

- Can we start by sharing a little about ourselves, background of our current roles, and how we would like to work with each other? (How would you define your role? How would you define my role?)
- To avoid sounding redundant, what do you already know about me? What else would you like to know about me?
- How have you been managed before?
- How would you describe your prior boss's management style?
- How often did you meet with your manager for one-to-one coaching sessions?
- What did you find most valuable in terms of how your manager supported you? (Least valuable?)
- How did their approach align with your expectations around how you like to be managed?

- What new expectations, if any, do you have that would make you feel I'm being the best manager I can be for you?
- What's the best way for us to (work together, communicate, handle problems, and so on)?
- Were there any additional goals that were discussed with your prior manager or promises made outside of your job responsibilities that I need to be mindful of? (A career promotion, a failure to honor a commitment, a change in compensation, role or territory, and so on.)
- What, if anything, would you like me to change in the way I lead that would align with how you like to be managed? (Effective, consistent coaching; observation; interactive team meetings; team collaboration; incentive programs; positivity; and so on).

TIP FROM THE COACH

Here are two valuable exercises worth doing with your new team. First, have them write out their ideal job description. Then, meet with them to compare it to their current job description to see how aligned they are, while uncovering what's most important to them. And since you didn't build this team from scratch, it's your responsibility to uncover what motivates them, so use the motivation exercise we discussed in Chapter 8.

From here, you can focus on more tactical, job-related questions. Here are a few examples:

- Can you walk through the process of (how you best manage your accounts and your customer's expectations, prospect, sell, plan your day, work with cross-functional teams, manage projects, and so on)?
- How would you describe the dynamic, environment, or health of the team?
- What ideas do you have to improve operations, strategies, and collaboration to achieve our business goals? (What systems do you feel need to be refined/created?)
- What challenges, if any, have you been faced with that need to be resolved? (How has it been handled so far?)
- What's going well right now for you and the team?
- What is your biggest challenge as it relates to (how you were being managed, working with your peers and customers, prospecting,

selling, working with other departments or teams, time management, your key performance indicators [KPIs] and scorecard, servicing your accounts)?

- What systems have been working well regarding your productivity, how you work with the team, and how you navigate through the various departments to get your job done?
- How do you like to (collaborate, be managed, coached, motivated, held accountable, and so on) that would continually strengthen our relationship? (See Chapter 8 for a more detailed strategy.)

CONVERSATION #3: PEER YESTERDAY, BOSS TODAY: CHANGING ROLES FROM PEER TO BOSS

To avoid redundancy, the coach track used to set expectations when inheriting an existing team, and the coach track you would use to reset expectations as you transition roles from their peer to their boss is virtually the same, with one minor tweak. I've adjusted only the first two sentences in this coach track, as the rest of the template will apply in either situation. You can use this coach track to prepare your team for your role change from peer to their manager.

> What I want for you is to feel that you have a manager you trust who will always there to support you, have your back, and help you achieve your goals. Maybe you're excited about the change. Maybe it feels a little awkward, since yesterday we were peers and today, I'm now your boss. It's certainly a big adjustment for me! With our aggressive business objectives …

Now, simply follow the rest of the template and questions under the preceding "Inheriting an Existing Team" section.

CONVERSATION #4: THE REVISED 30-DAY TURNAROUND STRATEGY FOR UNDERPERFORMERS

Chapter 12 of *Coaching Salespeople into Sales Champions* was the first time I introduced the strategy to turn around an underperformer in 30 days or less, or collect the evidence that they're not a fit. The goal is to avoid having to write people up, put them on warning, or get involved in HR compliance issues and put them on a performance improvement plan (PIP). I've renamed this acronym to more accurately reflect what this plan really is.

- P.O.P. – The Pushing Out Plan
- R.I.P. – The Rest in Peace Plan

My reason for this is that, by the time an employee is put on a PIP, they and the majority of managers have checked out, given up, and the HR-compliant process is simply to avoid any future litigation.

While you may push back and say the PIP has worked before, statistically speaking, the success rate is less than a conservative 20 percent, especially if you consider that, ultimately, a high percentage of these employees leave or get terminated after successfully completing a PIP. They revert back to their self-sabotaging behavior because fear-driven, motivational management tactics are always short lived, which is why I created this strategy. Let's first review a revised enrollment conversation when approaching the underperformer in question, and the objectives of the 30-Day Turnaround Strategy.

30-DAY TURNAROUND STRATEGY: THE ENROLLMENT COACH TRACK

What I want for you is to achieve the level of success you want in your career and start performing at that level. I'm fully committed to supporting you and giving you the attention you need. However, what's more important is your commitment to your own success. Here's what I'm proposing. Let's look at what you are committed to doing, set some *measurable parameters, activities, skills to improve (quality of activity), and results* to achieve, and work on a plan to turn around your performance.

At the end of a four-week period, we will assess progress and, based on what we find, determine what the best course of action is for you. Whether that means staying in your current position, finding a new position within the company that's a better fit for you, or bowing out of your position gracefully because after the next four weeks, you'll be able to determine whether this position is a good fit for you.

So, if you are truly committed to your success here, how do you feel about this plan? Is this strategy something you are willing to commit to?

At this point, you'll hear one of these common responses.

- I'm in! I appreciate the support!
- Forget it. Four weeks of this and then a PIP? (They leave on their own.)
- This sounds like a PIP. It smells like a PIP. And it looks like a PIP. Is this a PIP?

Responses one and two are fantastic! They've self-selected in or out. If you hear the third response, use this clarifying *wanting for* statement.

"What I want for you is to avoid the PIP."

or

"What I *don't* want for you is to feel overwhelmed or stressed/worried about being placed on a PIP. That's one of the objectives here, to avoid the PIP."

THE FIVE CORE OBJECTIVES TO ACHIEVE IN THIS 30-DAY STRATEGY

Here are some final objectives to keep top of mind when it comes to using this strategy.

1. Instead of repositioning the performance improvement plan (engrained negativity), introduce the new turnaround strategy as a positive solution for them.

2. The objective is to collect *evidence of change* in activity, quality, attitude, self-awareness, and results. This gives you certainty rather than being seduced by their potential ("I know they can do it if they try!").

3. The person self-selects in or out. They are always at choice to engage or disengage at any time. It's ultimately their decision to honor the commitments they've made. That's why they're either firing or hiring themselves.

4. You've succeeded in taking an *unconditional* stand for your people, modeling and reinforcing the positive environment and trusting culture you want among your team. Remember, everyone is always watching you.

5. Finally, this program must be positioned as an *organic*, four-week intensive coaching program. Do *not* institutionalize this, or make it an HR-compliance policy. This strategy is meant to mirror the

coaching that's always happening, but with a more consistent cadence. Never use this against the coachee, *unless this is agreed upon up front* that if performance drops, or the person does not achieve committed objectives, this will become an HR issue. Leave this option entirely up to them. Otherwise, you may as well just call it a PIP, rather than a coaching strategy to avoid a PIP.

But the primary reason I did a refresher on this strategy is to prepare you for how you can now leverage it for your A and B performers!

CONVERSATION #5: THE EVOLUTION OF THE 30-DAY TURNAROUND STRATEGY: THE SUCCESS ACCELERATION PROGRAM

Since writing *Coaching Salespeople into Sales Champions*, I've heard countless managers tell me how much this 30-day turnaround strategy eliminated the stress of dealing with an underperformer, saved them time and money, and kept the integrity of the team's culture and attitude in place.

But what about those A or B performers who can achieve their next level of success? Or, what about the top performer who may need an attitude adjustment? Do you just continue to coach them, or is there some strategy that can be put in place for this population of your team?

Here's an opportunity to rebrand the turnaround strategy and transform it into the 30-Day Success Acceleration Program! This is simply an accelerated four-week coaching strategy and can be used to coach your A and B players to achieve greater success. Just like training for a marathon, you want your coach to push your limits. Here is an example of how to position this plan:

> What I want for you is to achieve your goals and perform at the level that would give you a strong sense of satisfaction and purpose with the work you do. Even though the performance expectations and our personal quotas continue to increase, we have some great opportunities to grow our business, and I want to ensure I'm supporting you the best way I can when it comes to hitting your goals here.
>
> The fact is, you're doing amazing. You're at quota, a great team player, demonstrate a healthy attitude, and have a respected personal brand.

Now, consider this. What if every professional athlete stopped practicing? Stopped trying to better themselves? Do you think that player would be playing in the pros? And think about how this could impact the team? These athletes also want to leave a brand and legacy they're proud of. That's why athletes practice daily to achieve more than they thought possible. That's exciting, that's new, that's purpose.

Here's what I was thinking. What if we carved out some time to focus on what you want to achieve, and together create a plan to shorten the time to attain your goals and the role you'd like me to play in supporting you around this?

We would meet each week over a four-week period to identify any challenges, as well as opportunities to achieve more. Together, we'll ensure you're doing what you love best, maximize every opportunity, and if you want, work on positioning you for your next role.

How do you feel about discussing this to see if this is something you could benefit from?

MINDFUL MOMENT

Enrollment conversations are always best had in person. Video conference or telephone is still effective. In addition, if you're doing this face to face, take the opportunity to have the conversation outside of the workplace, where people tend to be more comfortable, loosen up, and share more than they typically would.

This Success Acceleration (Coaching) Program will move the needle of productivity on your team and with each person. And if you prefer to name it the Success Accelerator or Success Acceleration Program instead of calling it a turnaround strategy when working with an underperformer, then feel free to do so! While many of the core issues or gaps you can work on with your team are often performance-, activity-, or skill-based, there's always a limiting thought or belief attached to them, creating a mental roadblock to success. So, how adept are you at coaching the inner game of champions?

Mindful Coaching: The Inner Game of Coaching Champions

L earning about other cultures and religions throughout the world fascinates me and honors one of my core values of honoring and respecting individuality, making a deeper, authentic human connection.

Needless to say, I've experienced many cultures and, I must admit, before traveling the world, I too had many cultural assumptions! Which is exactly the topic we're going to explore here. That is, how to identify and eradicate costly assumptions from your life.

I remember while working with Pfizer in Moscow, Russia, one manager shared an experience she had when calling on a customer in Britain. The customer said she wanted to *table this discussion*. Well, if you're from the United States, Russia, and many other countries, *tabling a discussion* means putting it off until another time. However, in the United Kingdom, *tabling a discussion* means to put it on the table and talk about it now. Imagine the confusion!

Assumptions happen not only geographically or across cultural borders but within our own country, company, team, family, and virtually every conversation you have, especially when coaching.

ASSUMPTIONS IN COMMUNICATION

If you're leveraging the questions in the L.E.A.D.S. coaching framework, you may notice how assumptions run rampant when coaching, and are quite often the root cause to many of the challenges, miscommunications, eroded relationships, lost sales, or roadblocks people face in pursuit of their goals. In fact, assumptions run so deep in our daily thinking we don't recognize them because all we see, if not challenged, are assumptions disguised as facts that we believe to be true!

Since I don't want to *assume* you and I share the same definition of what an assumption is, here's my definition: "An assumption is something you believe to be true, often based on past experiences and projected as a future expectation, without the facts to support it." Following this line of thinking, assumptions continually show up in the way we communicate; whether spoken, written, or in our disposition and body language.

Because this is such a widespread problem, we don't realize how deeply assumptions run in how we're wired, think, communicate, engage with others, and in our decision-making process. To help quell this catastrophic practice when coaching and communicating, I've identified several ways to uncover assumptions that can change the course of the conversation, the value of coaching, and the decisions made. Ultimately, assumptions will be the determining factor between a successful coaching conversation or one that crashes in flames.

FACT OR FICTION? CHALLENGE THESE ASSUMPTIVE TRIGGER WORDS

Over the years, I've noticed managers struggle with recognizing what an assumption is and what it is not. However, there are certain trigger words that need to be challenged to assess if what the coachee is sharing is a fact or an assumption. Here are 33 assumptive words that can help you separate fact from fiction.

33 Assumptive Driven Words to Challenge

1. They/I implied
2. They/I suppose
3. They/I presume
4. They/I presuppose
5. They/I think
6. They/I guess/surmise
7. They/I imagine

8. They know me
9. I find that
10. They/I take for granted
11. They/I believe
12. Given my experience
13. Based on what happened before
14. Since I know them
15. I know them and what they want, so
16. I assume
17. I've been working with them for so long that
18. They/I probably
19. They must have
20. They/I feel
21. Given the situation
22. In this economy/market, it's hard to
23. The only thing customers want is
24. Since all customers want
25. With what happened in the past
26. Their email suggests/sounds like
27. They/I/or the situation implies
28. They/I always
29. They/I never
30. From what I've seen
31. If you look online
32. Ask anyone
33. This worked the last time I dealt with a similar situation, so

TIP FROM THE COACH

Get your head out of your assumptions.

Once you keep assumptions top of mind, you'll start recognizing how many assumptions you and every person on this planet makes in every conversation, and how many coaching moments will either be missed or rise to the top of the conversation so they can be recognized and addressed.

COACH THE WIN

A salesperson closes a big deal. They're excited and can't wait to share this win with their manager. And when they do, the manager's first visceral response is, "Great job! *But* what about the other deals in your pipeline that aren't closing this quarter? Let's focus on those."

While the manager's intentions may be to help their direct report, herein lies a defining moment for any manager. In that very instance, this manager missed a powerful coaching opportunity to further develop talent and reinforce best practices, thinking, and strategies that makes their team successful!

It's the occupational hazard of being a chief problem solver—you actually seek out problems you can fix. If managers are always focused on the problems and what's not working, then how do your people recognize the things they do that are working? Think about how this affects the disposition, morale, and focus of your team. If you're always focusing on the negative, what's going wrong, what needs to change, or what's not good enough, think about what you are modeling for your team.

Subsequently, what do you think your people are going to be primarily focused on when speaking with you, their peers, and customers? The solution or the problem? The greater cost here is that you missed an opportunity to consider how this impacts the culture and environment you want to develop.

SHIFT YOUR QUESTIONS TO FOCUS ON WHAT'S RIGHT

The only way you'll be able to reinforce the positive behaviors you want your direct reports to continually practice and refine is if the manager places the wins in their line of vision.

Here's an example of eight questions you can use today in a conversation when coaching a win.

1. Congratulations on that sale you just made. Great work here. Before we move on to discuss what's next on our agenda for this meeting, I'd love to hear more about it. Can you walk me through what happened when you first talked to or met with that prospect?

2. You mentioned that they initially pushed back hard. How did you turn them around? What did you do differently this time?

3. What did you do well that you're proud of?

4. How did you respond when the customer said they were happy with their current vendor and weren't interested in talking with you?

5. What questions did you ask that you may not have typically asked before?

6. How was your disposition and state of mind at the time?

7. What (best practices, conversations, questions, activities, etc.) can we identify and embed into your sales process to ensure you use them during every customer interaction to consistently achieve the results you want?

8. How did you acknowledge yourself for a job well done?

To build a world-class sales team and reinforce the behaviors you want them to engage in, turn your binoculars around and start magnifying and focusing on what they're doing right more often than what they're doing wrong. And what you perceive as *wrong* may simply be another way to achieve the same or better results. Consider that there is no wrong. There are only learning opportunities that lead to coaching moments and the creation of champions.

MINDFUL MOMENT

If you're always focused on what your people are not doing well, then when are you taking the time to reinforce what they are doing great? In every conversation and interaction you have, you are either building trust and confidence, or you're eroding it. The choice is yours.

PHRASEOLOGY: ONE WORD AWAY FROM A COACHING BREAKTHROUGH

Did you ever have someone tell you, "I tried to *call* the customer. They didn't respond." Or, how about, "I *spoke* with them. They're not interested." Depending upon the generation you grew up in, what does *call* mean to you? What does *spoke with* mean? Does it mean communication via the telephone, mobile phone, a face-to-face office visit, pinging someone via social media, text, instant message? I had one salesperson tell me they connected with their prospect through Xbox Live!

These are powerfully specific examples of how assumptions overshadow our ability to effectively align on common ground and communicate with each other, as well as seek out and listen for that moment to coach the meaning behind the words.

We know that leadership is about keeping people focused on the shared vision, as well as providing guidance, coaching, direction, autonomy, and support, while developing future leaders.

To achieve this, it needs to be effectively and masterfully communicated throughout the organization in a way that creates clear understanding and buy in. The language of leadership used to achieve every manager's primary objective is coaching, and that also includes enrollment. And these are both languages to be learned, just like any other, whether it's Spanish, Italian, Hebrew, Hindi, Mandarin, or Arabic.

COACHING CONUNDRUM

Just because we speak the same language doesn't mean we speak the same language! Clarify how people define words to ensure you're both speaking the same language and to uncover more coaching moments.

Challenging communication assumptions = mastering phraseology, the study and understanding of words.

When coaching clients, I spend a significant portion of time helping leaders refine their message when communicating with their team, coworkers and customers. Whether it's via email, text, instant message, the phone, face to face, or facilitating a team meeting, leaders must realize that every word used must be chosen carefully and strategically, with surgical precision.

Otherwise, you run the risk of delivering a message that can be misinterpreted, lands on people in a way you did not intend that causes a negative reaction, which consequently creates the distrust, assumptions, strained relationships, and communication breakdowns that cost you time, peace of mind, and productivity. This is where phraseology comes into play so you can ensure understanding and agreement around the definitions people have around the words they use.

As you read through the following story, be mindful of how a failure to align and understand definitions around key words and phrases can lead to more problems and breakdowns, whereas listening for, clarifying, and going deeper around the meaning behind certain words can create a breakthrough coaching moment.

TIP FROM THE COACH

Don't assume you know what people mean, what they do, or how they do it. Challenge all adjectives, jargon, and colloquialisms to understand the intended message behind the words they use.

Assumptions in Action

During our first live coaching session in Berlin, Germany, Hans provided an assessment of his team, where they stood regarding performance, and what his approach was in developing them and uncovering the areas they need to work on. Since Hans and his management and sales team worked remotely, his coaching was done over the phone.

"I've been working with two of my frontline sales managers," Hans began. "There's a lot of diversity within my team. One is fairly new and doing well. I still have a lot of work to do in getting him up to speed with his team. As with many salespeople who move into management, this new manager was trying to avoid doing the job of their salespeople out of fear they'd screw up a sale or make a mistake with a customer."

Hans continued to share the landscape of his team. "Now Sven, this other manager I'm working with, is a more tenured manager who's been with the company for 18 years. I've only recently inherited this team, so I'm still assessing where I can deliver the most value.

"With the conversations I've had with Sven, it's clear he has his own way of doing things. He's hitting his numbers and getting results. However, I know if he became more strategic in his thinking and in his approach, he would be more successful."

"Strategic," I thought to myself. I have my own definition of what strategic means but wasn't sure if my definition was aligned with Hans's. Since I didn't want to make any assumptions that could derail our conversation, I asked, "Hans, when you say you'd like Sven to be more *strategic*, how do you mean?"

Hans clarified. "Well, I mean that if Sven had a documented strategy and consistent process regarding how he will effectively manage his direct reports, work with each customer, and manage his team, it would help him focus on what he needs to do consistently, instead of his ad hoc, inconsistent approach that produces sporadic results.

COACHING CONUNDRUM

Some people are successful despite themselves. It's up to the coach to assess if this is an anomaly due to working in a thriving territory, or if they truly have the right skills to perform like a champion in both good and challenging times. That's when the true essence of a person's character, courage, trust, skill, commitment, integrity, attitude, and perseverance become apparent.

"It's frustrating that he doesn't see value in developing a path to success and a longer-term strategy, albeit he's successful now. I'm tired of having the same conversation every week. I've acknowledged him for hitting most of the KPIs [key performance indicators] on his scorecard, but told him that a more defined strategy would make him more efficient, productive, and successful. His typical response is, 'I'm not micromanaging my team.' That's why he doesn't want to put a strategy in place."

"Okay let's explore why he may be so resistant to creating a strategy." I asked Hans, "How do you define the word *strategy*?"

Hans replied, "It's an executable plan. You have a goal and a defined path, steps to follow and activities and tasks to complete in order to achieve it."

"Did you ask Sven how he defines the word *strategy*?"

"Actually, I didn't."

"You shared with me that when you asked Sven to become more strategic, he said he didn't want to *micromanage* his team." I paused. "What did he mean when he told you he didn't want to *micromanage* his team?"

Hans took a second to reflect, then replied, "Maybe that he doesn't want to stalk them or be on top of them every moment, challenging everything they do and have his hands in every decision or account. He wants to give them the autonomy to do their job."

"This sounds like your definition of *micromanaging*," I observed.

"Correct."

I followed with, "Is his definition of *micromanaging* the same as yours?"

"I'm not sure."

"How about his definition of *strategy*?" I continued. "When you asked him to be more strategic, how clear were you to ensure you were both aligned with the definition?"

"I just assumed that if you're a manager for a certain period, you better be clear about the difference between micromanagement and being a strategic thinker. It sounds like I made a stupid assumption. I think he may be collapsing the definition of strategy with micromanaging his team. Since I never asked, I just assumed we'd be aligned with what I mean. Probably not the best idea, considering the situation I'm in now."

"And?" I inquired.

"It sounds like I need to have a reset conversation with Sven. I need to be more mindful around the words people use to ensure their definitions align with mine."

I asked, "If you don't have this conversation, how can this impact you?"

"More time-consuming problems, conversations, miscommunications, and conflict."

"So, the next time you approach Sven, what would it sound like?"

Hans said, "For starters, I need to enroll him in having this conversation."

"And what would that sound like?"

"Probably something along the lines of, 'Sven, I was reflecting on our last conversation, and I owe you an apology. As we were talking, I never took the time to clarify what I meant by becoming more strategic, nor did I ask what your perception of what micromanaging is, which is why I feel there was a disconnect. I hope you can accept my apology, so we can reset this conversation and arrive at a better solution. Are you open to this?'"

"Well done!," I told him. "Your enrollment was spot on and you even followed the enrollment model! When will you have an opportunity to have this conversation with Sven?"

"I'll email Sven after our session to get something on the calendar today and explain the intention of the meeting, so we can better understand each other and come up with a mutual definition of what it means to be strategic, set a course of action, and create some questions to avoid this from happening again."

"What ideas are surfacing?" I inquired.

"I can start with these questions":

1. When I suggested for you to become more strategic, how did you interpret that?
2. What's your definition of *strategy*? Of *micromanagement*?
3. Can I share my definitions with you to see how closely aligned we are?
4. I see where the breakdown occurred and what we need to do to create more alignment and a mutual definition when we use words like, *strategy* and *micromanagement*. This way, when we talk about these things, or any other topic, there's no confusion and we can work more efficiently and successfully together. Does that work for you?

TIP FROM THE COACH

Insatiable curiosity is the fuel for crafting better questions.

"It sounds like you did some great self-coaching!" I acknowledged. "When can I expect an email recap of our conversation and the conversation you're going to have with Sven?"

"How about by the end of the week to ensure we had time to schedule the conversation?"

"That works! How are you feeling about our conversation?"

"Very enlightening!" Hans said with great excitement. "Thanks for pointing out a blind spot I didn't see! I look forward to reconnecting and sharing the results of my conversation with Sven!"

MINDFUL MOMENT

By becoming insatiably curious and mindful of phraseology, you are going to ask more and better questions that seek to understand the other person's point of view, while avoiding assumptions that you all speak the same language.

PHRASEOLOGY = COACHING MOMENTS

Proactive, intentional listeners are masters at the *art of phraseology*. They suspend assumptions regarding the mutual interpretation of words to paradoxically create moments to coach assumptions!

Consider these words and phrases:

1. Success
2. Satisfied
3. Frustrated
4. Value
5. Stressed
6. Overwhelmed
7. Difficult
8. Unhappy
9. Sell value
10. Qualify
11. Affordable
12. Quality
13. Great service
14. Coaching
15. Call
16. Organized

17. Persistent
18. No budget
19. Wants a bigger discount
20. Not a fit
21. Great fit
22. Competition is offering a better deal and product

They often hold different definitions for each individual and can be interpreted in a variety of ways. That's why proactive listeners ask the critical questions others don't. Think about your visceral reaction when you hear a comment like: "I'm feeling stressed and overwhelmed with my difficult workload." You may assume you know what this person means based on a previous experience, when they used words like *stressed*, *overwhelmed*, and *difficult*. Because you have an answer ready, you don't take the time to look behind the words and validate what the statement and the words she used mean to her. Consequently, you just blurt out your response before truly understanding her message.

SPRINGBOARD QUESTIONS

A better approach would be to use what I call a Springboard Question, also known as a Clarifying Question. Here's your opportunity to explore deeper into what she wants or needs most. Notice a Springboard Question simply builds off what the person shared (an adverb, noun, adjective, etc.), adding clarity to ambiguity in order to prevent costly assumptions. Here are a few examples:

1. When you say, "*stressed and overwhelmed*" how do you mean?
2. Can you go into more depth regarding what you mean when you say *difficult workload*?
3. When you heard, "the customer is pushing back," can you say more about that?
4. How do you know that to be a fact?
5. What are the facts that support (your position, how the customer feels, etc.)?
6. What does being overwhelmed look and feel like for you?
7. When you say you want to build your brand, become more successful here, and make more money, can we break each of those goals down so we're clear about what the end result is you want to achieve? What would that look like once you've achieved this? What would be present for you?

8. What's your definition of (coaching, observation, success, failure, stress, collaboration, difficult customer, assumptions, exemplary customer service, confidence, fear, etc.)?

9. I hear that you expect the help desk to be more responsive to your requests. What would that look like for you? Can you share some specific examples that would make you feel they're being more responsive

10. How exactly did you go about selling value to that customer?

Questions that focus on the phraseology of communication allow you to clarify what you've heard or go into a topic in more depth, so you can become clear with what they are really saying. Moreover, questions will challenge your core assumptions and turn off your automatic, passive listening and responses in every conversation.

COACH THE WRITTEN MESSAGE

If countless studies have confirmed that employees, especially salespeople, spend more than 60 percent of their day reading, writing, and responding to texts, social media, and emails, then why do some of the smartest, most successful people find it so difficult to put together an intelligent, well-crafted written message? Here's the scary part: Your team, your communication, and how you collaborate and engage with people is a reflection of you, your product, and your entire organization. Before people buy, you've already created the perception of value in the prospect's mind that you and your company can deliver.

A HIDDEN OPPORTUNITY

Whether you do this during your interview process to assess a candidate's competencies or during a meeting to assess your team's writing skills, evaluating people's written skills is a missed opportunity and something managers need to do more consistently.

Unfortunately, most managers don't have a process to successfully assess someone's writing aptitude. To compound this challenge, what if the person who is doing the hiring also struggles with written communication? Who can objectively and effectively evaluate a candidate's writing acumen?

Here's a make-or-break exercise you can add as another step in your interviewing process to ensure you are hiring someone who is an all-around engaging, collaborative, and effective communicator that would only enhance your company's brand. It also makes for a great exercise for your team meetings.

Here's what you do. Look at your email archives. If you're using this on a potential hire, find a few emails that contain the entire written conversation thread to provide background and context that would be most relevant for the position you're looking to fill. Make sure there are three distinct situations from three different people.

The emails don't all have to be from customers. Depending upon the role you're hiring for, the email could be from a prospect, peer, boss, customer support, or if you're looking to hire a manager, it could be from their hypothetical direct report. Any relevant scenario could work. Here are some examples.

1. Service issue
2. Creating a value proposition
3. Upselling issue
4. Irate customer
5. Competitive situation
6. Renewal/contract terms
7. Getting to the decision maker
8. Competitive situation
9. Several pricing objections from the prospect
10. Discount issue/procurement issue
11. Internal employee/peer issue
12. Help desk issue/compliance issue
13. Sales needs to communicate with support
14. Relationship issue/cross-functional team
15. Working on a project with a cross-functional team
16. Performance issue
17. Follow up after a sale
18. Follow up to renew a customer's membership

Remove the names of the people from the original emails and conversation threads or any other sensitive information you need to omit to protect privacy, intellectual property, or if you have any internal compliance guidelines to follow.

Once done, schedule a meeting with the candidate (phone or in person) and forward these three emails to them. Each candidate will then be asked to craft a response to each email, which they will then send to you to be evaluated. Make sure you explain the intention and objective of this simulation. Here's one simple way to do so:

> Let's imagine for a moment that you have been hired for this position and are now the acting director of business development. You have just received these three emails from three different people. You can gather the details of each scenario in the email thread. As the acting director of business development, how would you respond to each email?

Provide them with enough time to craft an intelligent response. Within the next 20 minutes or so, you will receive three email responses written by these candidates, making this simulation as real, relevant, and as timely as possible.

Most important, you have just assessed whether you would feel comfortable with how this person communicates in writing, how they represent your company, and how well they work under pressure and tight timelines.

Can they cheat? Sure. That's why I suggest scheduling this exercise with them on the telephone or in person and have them complete it within 20 minutes. They don't have time to hire a professional copywriter, sales veteran, or find a template online.

The added benefit and insight you get from this is observing how they react to the exercise where they are purposely put under pressure to perform within a limited amount of time. Do they do so with poise and professionalism or stress and overwhelm?

And what about your current employees? It's never too late! You can do this as a team or an individual coaching exercise to uncover opportunities to strengthen their written communication skills and, ultimately, their personal brand. When it comes to making the right hiring decision, this can be the difference between hiring a champion or a mistake.

A Real-World Success Story and How To Evaluate the Written Message

Here's how one manager leveraged this exercise to make the right hiring decision.

Aside from the typical corporations, I've worked with dozens of professional sports teams in the NHL, NBA, MLB, NFL, and MLS. Brian was the VP of ticket sales for Manchester United Football Club. He was looking to hire a new director of hospitality. He narrowed it down to two candidates. He felt both were a perfect fit and that he couldn't really make a bad decision, but he couldn't decide. I suggested this exercise, which he did.

After reviewing the emails each candidate had written, Brian reported back that it was this exercise that secured his decision.

Throughout the interviewing process, Brian said that both candidates were very articulate, polished, and experienced. On the telephone and face to face, each person presented and communicated very well.

They also had successful track records and stellar references. However, when comparing their writing acumen—their expertise, style, professionalism, clarity and brevity of message, spelling, grammar, etiquette, closing statement, and vocabulary—one candidate clearly rose above the other.

When you effectively evaluate all the core communication and writing competencies that every person needs in order to be successful in their role, you'll move away from hiring fast to hiring right.

COACHING THE ELUSIVE TOPIC OF TIME MANAGEMENT AND PERSONAL PRODUCTIVITY

Time management and life balance are topics that elude leaders when it comes to coaching, because everyone struggles with them! That's why my last book, *Own Your Day*, tackled this global conundrum of time mismanagement, so people can design their ideal career and life, making each day a gift filled with joy, meaning, balance, productivity, and self-care, while honoring the priorities and values they hold in their hearts.

This isn't a lesson on time management, but on how to make time management a coaching moment, which I know managers do not do. It's still your responsibility to help others design their ideal career and life, which in turn, helps everyone win.

When was the last time you evaluated each person's daily calendar to ensure it's a reflection of all the activities that would move them to their goals in an effective and balanced way without burnout?

Since you're initiating this conversation, start by enrolling them to set expectations, your intentions, and what's in it for them.

COACHING PERSONAL PRODUCTIVITY AND TIME MANAGEMENT USING THE E.L.A.D.S. AND L.E.A.D.S. FRAMEWORKS

Enroll:

Mary, what I want for you is to feel that you are as productive and efficient as you can be each day, so that at the end of every day, you can experience a greater sense of accomplishment and feel good about what you've achieved, while honoring your personal priorities.

I have some great tools and ideas around time management that will allow you to achieve this, and it's also something I'm working on myself. This way, I can support you and learn from you as well, so we can achieve what's most important to both of us. Would you be open to having a conversation around this so that I can best support you to create the lifestyle and career balance you want while achieving your business objectives, without the overwhelm and stress?

Learn:

Coachee: Yes.

Assess:

1. Can you please walk me through how you manage your day? (You need to have their calendar in front of you to coach effectively.)

2. How do you determine what tasks or projects are priorities? (Example: by your boss, the time commitment to complete the project, importance, the person who's asking for something, resources available, things you want to do versus those you have to do, your comfort level around performing that task, and so on.)

3. What does time-blocking mean to you?

4. How do you typically make time to focus on your priorities?

5. How do you currently time block all the activities and appointments in your calendar?

6. How effective are you at adhering to your time blocks and your calendar?

7. When have you noticed you're most productive? Least productive?

8. How do the time blocks you have in your calendar align with your priorities and goals?

9. How would you define *routine*?

10. What if you were to come up with a healthy and attractive definition of what a routine is? What would that sound like?

11. How much of your calendar includes all the daily tasks and priority activities you engage in each day?

12. How do you define *life balance*?

13. What would you like to have more time to do each day, personally and professionally?

14. What would you like to spend less time on so that you can focus on the peak productive activities that will most impact your success?

Define:

1. To recap, what I'm hearing is ...

2. Why do you feel life balance is so difficult/easy?

3. What else could be true?

4. If life balance was truly possible and not difficult to create, what would your ideal life look like?

5. What would need to happen for you to create the ideal, balanced life you want?

6. What would it mean if you had a routine that was flexible, doubled your productivity, and provided more life balance for you?

7. How do you feel about creating a more systemized and realistic routine that accomplishes this?

8. Imagine if your routine was the answer to eliminating stress, overwhelm, and the missed deadlines, tasks, or commitments that can fall through the cracks.

9. What could get in the way of consistently honoring your calendar and commitments?

10. What needs to change so that you can honor your commitments and priorities?

Support:

1. In your opinion, what are the steps you need to take to achieve the balance and lifestyle you want?

2. What are you willing to commit to completing by our next conversation? By when?

3. When should we schedule a quick check-in to ensure you're moving toward greater efficiency and success?

4. How can I best support you and become your accountability partner to ensure you're adhering to your routine so that you can achieve what matters most to you (e.g., through observation)?

5. Can I share some ideas that would simplify this process so that it's not so overwhelming?

6. How are you feeling about our conversation? What did you learn?

7. What, if anything, would you like me to change regarding how I'm coaching and supporting you?

8. Let's schedule our next coaching session and let me know when I can expect the recap of our conversation.

Let's be real. You can't be a great coach, salesperson, or leader if you don't own your day.

I'm sure you notice the relationship between effective coaching, self-management, and your team's personal productivity. This is another opportunity to observe your people in the workplace to get a realistic sense of what they're doing and how they manage each day so they're positioned to win.

COACHING A TOP PRODUCER TO CHANGE THEIR TOXIC ATTITUDE AND BEHAVIOR

I was in Norway coaching several managers, as well as the rest of their advisors who work in that branch of JPMorgan Chase, when this lesson appeared that I'm compelled to share with you.

Before we dive into this last coach track for what was once considered a difficult conversation, be mindful how this is formatted.

First, I honored the six steps and shared the positioning enrollment statement (E) to open the conversation. Then, notice the coaching strategy that follows is broken down into each step of the E.L.A.D.S. enrollment framework, so you can see the alignment between enrollment and coaching.

The objective is to discuss Frank's visible and vocal frustration and behavior, and how Joanne, his manager, can coach him from toxic to terrific, so he's positioned for the promotion he wants.

Notice the shift Frank will make when he's more self-aware of his attitude and the impact his behavior has on the team, himself, and his personal brand. As with every template I've shared, take the questions you like, as the rest you can leave at the question buffet.

Enroll:

Joanne: Frank, what I want for you is to maintain your personal brand and status as a high-potential employee, and also the relationships you have, which will mean you're positioned for the promotion you want, while eliminating some challenges and stresses you mentioned.

Because of your commitment to the company and your role, I noticed there are times when the way you come across, even with your good intentions, can have a negative impact on performance and on your relationships with coworkers.

That's why I'd like to discuss what I've observed to ensure you're positioned for continued success, have an awesome personal brand, strong and trusting relationships, and make your job a little easier. Are you open to exploring how we can achieve this together?

Learn:

Frank: Sure, I'm open.

Assess:

1. How are you feeling about your performance and your potential for advancement within the company?
2. You shared with me on a few occasions how you've been frustrated at work. When you say *frustration*, can you define that further?
3. What are your main sources of your frustration?
4. If you were to ask your coworkers (and customers) how you're perceived, what do you think they would say about you? (How would they describe you? How would you describe yourself?)
5. How do you want to be known? (What is your ideal personal brand?) What do you want people to say about you?
6. What's changed from the last successful quarter to now, where you're behind on a few KPIs on your scorecard?
7. What were you doing differently when you were meeting your goals?
8. Where do you want to rank in terms of maintaining top producer status? (How important is this to you?)

Define:

1. So, if I'm hearing you correctly … Is that accurate?
2. Why do you think this is happening? What are the trigger points that cause you to react this way?

3. What assumptions could you be making about your coworkers and their role in supporting you?

4. What else could be true?

5. If you were to self-reflect for a moment, on a scale of 1 to 10, where 10 means you're performing like a champion and portray a consistent positive attitude, collaborate effectively with coworkers when dealing with problems, have great working relationships with each department, and 1 means the antithesis, where would you score yourself?

6. If you were to observe yourself, what do you feel needs to change to make this a 10?

7. How does your attitude impact your relationships with employees/peers and with your customers?

8. How does it impact your performance?

9. If you don't improve your performance, attitude, and how you work within a team environment, how can that impact your personal and career goals, as well as your personal brand (in addition to family, income, lifestyle, peace of mind, career, relationships, etc.)?

10. What would it mean if you got this promotion?

11. How would it impact you if you didn't?

12. What would happen if you were able to improve your attitude and how you're known within the company?

Support:

1. What's your opinion on how to create a consistent, positive attitude?

2. What do you feel needs to happen to repair or reset any damaged relationships?

3. When you get promoted into management, how would you handle this situation if the roles were reversed?

4. Are you ready to collaborate on creating some new habits and conversation coach tracks that would allow you to continue to voice your concerns in a constructive manner, while at the same time raising your value within the company? (This is mini-enrollment, gaining permission.)

5. Great. Then let's walk through your ideas together to ensure they achieve the results you want, okay?

6. If gaps need to be filled, ask: May I share some observations that will ensure your strategy will achieve what's most important to you?

7. How can I be your accountability partner to ensure you make these positive changes a habit?

8. How do you want me to let you know when you revert to displaying a negative or poor attitude (e.g., verbally, email, text, hand signal, code word)?

9. What is one thing you are willing to commit to doing this week? By when?

10. If you don't follow through with your commitments, how do you want me to bring this up in a way you'd be open to discussing?

Joanne: Great work, Frank. I admire your openness to have this conversation and your commitment to continually develop into the leader I know you can be. I look forward to our coaching session next week to discuss your progress and how I can continually support you.

A Quick Recap

Let's see what Joanne accomplished here:

1. Honored the E.L.A.D.S. Enrollment Coaching Model using a strong enrollment positioning statement that opened Frank up to the coaching conversation.

2. Asked objective versus loaded or leading questions.

3. Had Frank assess the impact of his current attitude.

4. Amplified the awareness of how his behavior impacts his personal brand and career goals.

5. Frank articulated the benefits of change.

6. Frank articulated the cost of not changing.

7. Discussed what could be perceived as a difficult observation to share.

8. She suspended assumptions and judgment.

9. Had Frank define next steps and how he wants to be held accountable.

We've now done several deep dives into the critical conversations managers have around the most importation scenarios you're faced with in your role. You now have the coaching and enrollment frameworks, as well as the language, coach tracks, and questions that will make you a masterful coach.

CAN YOU COACH FEAR AND CONFIDENCE?

Notice that the topics discussed in this chapter are not easily identified as coaching moments, which are typically identified as either problems to fix, or skills that need to be worked on. Managers simply have no idea how to approach these conversations or developmental opportunities.

Don't lose sight of the fact that many of the coaching topics in this chapter fall more under our EQ rather than our IQ (e.g., self-awareness, compassion, attitude, assumptions). So, be mindful of the opportunities to coach the inner game.

Two other coaching topics worth putting in your line of vision are *confidence* and *fear*. Every manager I've met has a hard time approaching these topics, which is why you'll find related tools and coaching strategies when you sign into the resource section of my website at http://keithrosen .com/sales-leadership-resources. Enter the password, *ICoachChampions12* and enjoy all the additional resources.

With all the new strategies, ways of thinking, coaching approaches, and methodologies introduced in this book, why would a coach stand on the sidelines observing their players during practice and the big game? To quickly assess what needs to be refined in order to ensure their athletes perform like champions.

So, how much consistent observation are you doing, and is it resulting in immediate behavioral changes? If not, you'll thank me for what's to be unearthed in Chapter 11.

11

Know Your Players: Transforming Talent Through Observation and Feedback

D uring any program I deliver, eventually, managers talk about their top performers and underperformers. I'd ask these managers, "How do you determine the root cause as to why someone is a top performer and why someone is underperforming?"

The most common response: *"I look at their numbers. I look at their activity. I look at their results. I look at their business plan. I review the data and key performance indicators."*

Is this the best place to look to uncover that *perfect* coaching moment? How do you recognize where your direct reports need coaching and could benefit from it most?

TIP FROM THE COACH

Great leaders and top performers don't always do different things. They just do things differently.

THREE WAYS TO UNCOVER THE GAP

Uncovering *what* you can coach someone on, from a tactical perspective, is the easy part. Managers are good at recognizing problems, needed strategies, and desired outcomes by looking at a report. However, uncovering the *why* (the *real* root core of the issue) and the *who* or the often very elusive and limiting thinking, assumptions, values, or outlooks that drive people's actions and behavior, takes more conscious intention, which no report can provide. We discussed how to coach through some of these topics in Chapter 10.

Therefore, there's a high probability that the solutions managers offer up either fail or are not fully developed, and as such, become a fleeting solution.

When coaching, you're looking to identify the gap, root cause, coaching moment, or an observation to share around their thinking, skill, strategy, or behavior that the coachee can't see on their own. To build upon this, there are three primary ways you can identify the gap. This gets you to the root cause, so you can create the *a-ha* moment, rather than continually treat the symptoms

1. **Through Evaluation and Inspection.**

   While data, reports, forecasts, activity, results, and performance metrics are essential components to evaluate market trends and identify areas that require attention to maintain organizational growth and profitability, many managers hide behind and rely too heavily on diagnosing problems through inspection and the analysis of reports, spreadsheets, and data. When it comes to developing champions, it is the least effective of these three strategies to uncover the gap. Even conducting peer-to-peer or customer interviews to gain further insight about your direct report, while immensely valuable, still only provide you with a portion of the story with some potentially twisted facts. However, when used in conjunction with the other two strategies, this becomes another complimentary and critical component to identify deficiencies in certain activities, results, and performance.

2. **Through Conversation.**

   Whether it's the telephone, text, instant messaging, social media, face to face, video conferencing, or email, the core coaching opportunity can also be identified in every interaction you have. Creating the safe space allows people the time to process their thoughts, challenges, and feelings on their own. This encourages a deeper level of self-awareness and a more accurate self-diagnosis, while strengthening their problem-solving skills. Sure, there are certain strategic opportunities, skill gaps, assumptions, or misconceptions that can be identified through conversation. In addition, keep in mind that any great coaching must be complemented with observation, so you have firsthand evidence of what is really going on with the person you are coaching without relying solely on other sources of intel.

3. **Through Observation.**

To clarify what is meant by observation, I'm referring to you, the manager, seeing, hearing, or reading firsthand what your people are doing throughout their day on the job or when engaging with customers, peers, partners, or prospects. For salespeople, observation can include listening to a conversation over the phone, sitting next to the person's desk (deskside observation) to observe how they manage their day and activity, reviewing their weekly calendar or the emails they send, or shadowing a face-to-face joint sales call to observe how they present and interact with customers and prospects.

If managers don't consistently observe, they will fail their team. They run the risk of relying solely on what they read in weekly reports or hear from customers, the coachee, and coworkers. While it may be *a* truth, it's only a subjective or partial truth or piece of the puzzle based what *others* see solely through *their* eyes. Observation helps sports coaches on the sidelines identify the blind spots that every athlete has in order to get a full panoramic view of the objective truth and what is really going on. Yes, another root cause and coaching moment uncovered.

MINDFUL MOMENT

Like professional athletes, salespeople cannot self-diagnose when they are in the middle of the game. That's why you need the coach to observe the things the players can't see on their own. If you don't observe, you and your team are making assumptions and you have no clue what your people are actually doing each day and how they do it.

COACH THE PERSON, NOT THE SPREADSHEET

Keep in mind, data and reports show you *what* people are doing in activity and results, but that is only one-third of the story. Metrics don't tell you *why* or *how* people perform the way they do. As such, observation and coaching conversations must also be leveraged to gather all the factual information.

Data doesn't assess skill set, acumen, core competencies, best practices, knowledge, communication, attitude, consistent execution of your sales process, and, ultimately, how effective and skilled each direct report is when engaging in the activities they need to achieve their goals.

That's the real difference between the champion performer and the underperformer. Yet, when managers evaluate only the data, they struggle with uncovering the root cause of certain problems and performance issues.

Sure, you can guess and hypothesize as to why some people don't hit their goals. But when managers take the time to observe their people in the trenches, the truth is (often painfully) apparent.

Granted, managers are often left in a state of shock when they see firsthand what their people do and how they're doing it.

However, the upside of observation is, managers now know the real reasons why their people aren't performing, have strained relationships, aren't closing more sales, and what the manager must provide (e.g., additional coaching, training, resources, strategies, templates, and so on) to help reinforce and embed changes that will improve performance.

Just think about sports and the top athletes in the world. Where is the coach during a game? On the sidelines. What if a coach never observed his athletes play? How could they identify opportunities for refinement? Winning or losing a game only shows the result, just like winning or losing a sale. The result doesn't tell you why or how it happened. That's why observation, like coaching, never stops.

FROM THE SIDELINES

When it comes to holding on to the chief problem solver role, consider this: You never see an athletic coach run onto the field to play for his players. Neither should you. Stop jumping into the roles and responsibilities of your direct reports and taking over their positions. Instead, coach them to do it masterfully on their own.

OBSERVATION RELUCTANCE

If observation is the missing ingredient to quickly assess talent gaps that, once filled, create a team of sales champions, then why is there such resistance around engaging in this activity?

While managers complain that they don't have the time for observation, the real cause of their reluctance has to do with the fact that they feel:

- Observation is hard, even confrontational and uncomfortable at times.
- They either assume or have firsthand experience that their direct reports simply do not want to be observed, especially their top performers.
- Managers assume what their people are doing based on results, activity, or conversations with their direct reports. As such, instead of gathering the facts, they're replacing the facts with costly assumptions.
- The team is remote, and as such, makes it difficult to find the time to travel and observe them.

Observation is only difficult because most managers have never been shown how to observe and deliver feedback in a way that people are not only open to, but results in a positive change in behavior.

SOLVING THE WRONG PROBLEMS

What makes matters worse is when managers rely solely on the results or their direct report's activity to assess the root cause of the problem or the gap in someone's performance. Consequently, they often wind up inaccurately assessing what's really at the core, addressing the wrong gap, and ultimately, providing a solution for the *wrong problem*.

Here's a common scenario: You're a salesperson and your manager shares the following advice to help you become more successful: "Listen, we both know you have to improve your performance to hit your quota. Looking at your activity, it seems you're behind on the number of calls to make and the number of appointments you need to book each week. So, just make more calls and schedule more meetings with key decision makers."

Can you envision that salesperson leaving the meeting, reading that email, or hanging up the phone after hearing this sage advice, feeling inspired and empowered to make the specific changes they need to succeed? That is a prime example of hollow advice and empty coaching.

If you're a manager who may have delivered a similar message, do you really believe that your direct report is thinking, "*Now* I know what I need to do to solve all my problems. I just need to make *more* calls!" Not likely.

And for those direct reports who might take the worldly wisdom of their manager into consideration and make more calls, we all know that if they don't have the right approach, strategy, mindset, and message, they will not achieve the results they need.

ENROLL PEOPLE IN OBSERVATION

Where do you begin the process of making observation part of your coaching cadence? Enrollment. If you fail to clarify intentions, you're leaving it up to the coachee to form their own conclusion, and the human default is fear. Here's a coach track to set expectations, your intentions, and the value the coachee will realize:

> What I want for you is to perform at your fullest potential, so you can experience the success you want. To do so, it's important that we have a mutual understanding of what observation is, what it means, and how it could be valuable for you. Think of any great athlete. One thing they all have in common is a coach who observes them playing, because you can't self-diagnose when you're in the middle of the game. That's why the coach is on the sidelines seeing the things that these athletes can't see on their own. The coach observes, then refines behavior to ensure players continue to perform like champions.

> The same holds true when selling or even managing. When salespeople are selling, it's hard for them to focus on their activity and at the same time self-diagnose their behavior, because when you have a certain habit or way of doing things, we can't see it in ourselves. That's why observation makes you aware of your blind spots. Otherwise, we keep engaging in behaviors that get in our own way of being more successful. Would you agree? (For example, it could be things like unknowingly cutting off the customer during a conversation, missing questions that gather the key information that you're not leveraging, your tone, the speed and inflection of your voice, missed qualifying questions, and even how you respond to your coworkers, prospects, or customers.)

> Keep in mind, I'd be open to *you observing me*, since I value your feedback. So, are you open to discussing this?

Now, the coaching kicks in! Here are a few questions to facilitate this conversation:

- What does observation mean to you?
- What has your experience been when being observed?
- What concerns, if any, do you have around having me observe you?
- How can we make impromptu and scheduled observation sessions/joint sales calls a valuable experience that support your success?
- Let's set up the rules up front so that we know what to expect as well as how to manage each customer visit that we both go into together, okay?

Fast forward. You accompanied one of your salespeople on a customer meeting. After it's over, you're at the debrief stage, based on what you've observed. Let's look at the strategy you can use to deliver feedback in a way that achieves worthwhile results.

Focus on the Solution, Not the Problem

Picture this: A manager is observing one of their salespeople during a meeting with a key account. After the meeting is over, the manager and salesperson are back in the car or at the main office. Often, this is how the manager starts the debrief conversation. (I can't make this stuff up.)

- "Here's what you did wrong."
- "Here's what you should have done."
- "Why didn't you do it this way/qualify better?"
- "What were you thinking?"
- "Now I see why you're not going to make quota this quarter!"

As you can imagine, this certainly does not do anything to stimulate an atmosphere of open and healthy collaboration. First, the salesperson may have gotten beaten up by the prospect or customer they called on, then they get their second beating by their manager!

Notice the focus of these statements and questions. They are problem focused and highlight what's wrong or why the person can't or won't achieve something.

Managers are too focused on what their people are *not* doing or what is not working, instead of what *is* working. Because of this line of thinking, they don't reinforce the positive behavior they want their team to adopt and practice. (See Chapter 10.)

Effective Feedback Starts with a Self-Assessment

Now that we've uncovered what questions and statements to avoid, what are the positive, solution-oriented questions you can ask that would co-create a new and better outcome, while encouraging the coachee to uncover their own gaps and developmental opportunities?

Managers need to provide feedback in a way that would not only be well received by their direct reports but would result in a positive behavioral change. So, how can you achieve this without people pushing back or resisting your feedback?

FROM THE SIDELINES

The ability for the manager to tailor feedback specific to each employee is a distinction of the best coaches and explains why coaching is often superior to training when it comes to changing the unique behaviors of each individual.

While counterintuitive, when delivering feedback, rather than share what you observed and what they did right or wrong, start with questions that help your direct reports self-assess so they can do a personal analysis without being tainted by your opinion.

The following questions build personal accountability, helps the coachee assess how self-aware they are, and avoids the risk of redundancy or telling the person something that they already know.

- How do you feel that call/meeting went? What did you observe?
- How did it feel when delivering your presentation? What did you sense from your prospects/clients/audience you were delivering to?
- What did you do well?
- Where do you feel you got stuck?
- What could you have done differently?

- What, if anything, do you need to improve or change to achieve better results the next time? (Was there anything you feel was stepped over or needed to be addressed that was not?)
- (When presenting with a team.) What else did you notice that would help the team work more cohesively when presenting? (What they did well, what they need to improve, and so on.)
- How would you rate yourself regarding achieving the objectives of the meeting (yours and the customer's)?

Now that you know what they observed and what they missed, here's where you deliver your feedback based on what you observed, after they've had a chance to self-diagnose. So, fill in the gap, starting with the following question:

- I want to make sure I support you the best way I can. May I share a few things I observed that would help you become more successful?

Seek to understand first, *then* provide your observations that they missed to avoid redundancy. This is the value you deliver, since you're sharing things they didn't see that were outside of their line of vision. Now, you can ask this permission-based question, since you now know what they observed and what they missed.

MINDFUL MOMENT

People cannot change what they do not see.

Once you share one or two things that you observed, continue with the following questions to confirm what they have learned, as well as their next steps to ensure you build momentum, habit, and accountability:

- What is your action plan and the changes you plan to make for the next meeting so that you can achieve the results you want?
- What's the lesson here? What did you learn from this?

- Would you be open to bringing what we discussed into our next scheduled coaching session, so we have the time to give these observations the attention they deserve?

People will now be more open to their personal development, collaborating on a better solution and critiquing themselves because they are responding to solution-driven rather than problem-focused questions, which put them on the defensive.

Furthermore, you'll be able to better uncover the gap and the coaching moment in their thinking, strategy, and approach to provide them with the coaching and an effective solution they need to fill the chasm. Figure 11.1 provides an overview this approach.

MIND THE COACHING GAP: A MATHEMATICAL EQUATION

When do you share your observations, ideas, experiences, suggestions, and feedback?

After you identify what they **know and see and what they don't**.
Redundancy turns off listening.

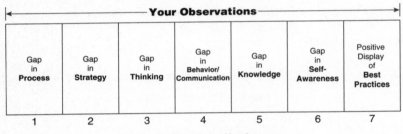

Lead with Questions, Not Answers

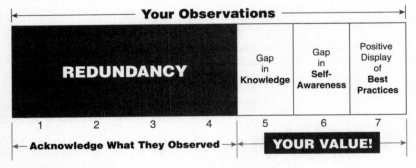

FIGURE 11.1 Identifying Gaps and Offering Observations.

TIP FROM THE COACH

When sharing your observations, don't share more than one or two depending upon how major a change they are. Save the rest for another joint sales call, or suggest bringing these topics into your next coaching session when you have time to coach, develop, and refine the skills and mindset that would help develop the habits that will make them be their very best.

What Can You Observe?

Observation is not limited to what you see (e.g., environment, body language, physical/facial gestures, the customer's or prospect's reactions, behavior, and so on) but also what you hear (e.g., what is said, how it's being said, and what is *not* being said). Whether you're a manager of salespeople, of non-salespeople, or of managers, these same guidelines still apply. Here's a short list of 22 areas to observe and keep top of mind from which coaching and developmental opportunities will emerge.

1. Written communication (presentations, emails, case studies, proposals, business plans, social media, texts, instant messages, etc.)
2. Verbal communication (face to face, telephone, video conferencing, etc.)
3. CRM usage
4. Presentations (print, over the phone, via a webinar, case study, in person)
5. Communication with teams
6. The sales process (for salespeople)
7. Team engagement, collaboration, and coaching
8. Working with other departments and coworkers
9. Team and one-on-one meetings (as the presenter and participant or coach and coachee)
10. Coaching sessions/conversations
11. Coworker interaction
12. Paperwork, reporting
13. Product knowledge
14. Time management/organization
15. Handling upsets

16. Focus on priorities
17. Listening skills
18. Disposition/appearance
19. Attitude
20. Problem solving
21. Social events, outside of workplace
22. Environment, workspace, desk, car

MINDFUL MOMENT

Observation creates coaching moments. Coaching moments create break-throughs. Therefore, observation creates breakthroughs.

Global Managers and Foreign Languages Provide Observation Opportunities

If you're a global manager, where some of your direct reports are calling on companies in certain regions of the world in which you may not speak their language, do not despair! You can still observe.

Here are five things you can observe as an international manager.

- Tone, pace, and voice inflection.
- Are they cutting off the customer when speaking with them?
- Are they talking too much?
- Are they asking more questions and listening instead of talking?
- Can you sense a change in their approach or attitude?

These are things you can observe with your ears, even if you don't speak their language. You can also ask one of your peers who speaks that language to listen in on a call with your direct report, then share what they have heard with you.

In some cases, it's legal and compliant to record calls that, for example, salespeople make. This is something you can then share with a peer who could listen to the conversation and provide feedback.

SHARING AN OBSERVATION VERSUS DEVELOPING SOMEONE: WHAT'S THE DIFFERENCE?

While managers may believe they're developing and building their team in a variety of ways, there's a major disconnect between developing someone and sharing observations. Here's what you can do to immediately accelerate performance, authentically develop your people, build their skills, and create champions. I'll never forget the conversation I had on day two of my leadership coach training course in Belgium. It all started with a simple question: "Can anyone here provide an example of when you developed someone?" A manager raised his hand and began to tell his story.

He said, "I was on a customer visit with one of my salespeople. Since the salesperson was running most of the meeting, I sat and observed positive behavior to reinforce, as well as behavior he could improve upon that would help him achieve better results in the future."

I thought, "This story sounds promising!"

The manager continued. "Well, after leaving the prospect's office, we got into his car and began to debrief on what transpired during the meeting, while it was still fresh in our minds. I asked my salesperson how he felt the meeting went. After sharing what he observed, I then jumped in and shared a few observations."

"And what did you share with him?" I inquired.

"I started by telling him that during the meeting, I observed a few things to be mindful of for his next meeting that could help improve his performance."

My curiosity peaked. "And what exactly did you share with him?"

"First, I noticed he didn't set expectations at the start of the meeting around the prospect's agenda and what the prospect hoped to learn and accomplish. I also told him he didn't ask the prospect how much time they had allocated for the meeting, nor who else, if anyone, needs to be present who would be part of the decision-making process.

"Finally, I told him that he missed several questions during his qualification process when gathering the information needed about the prospect's situation, unmet needs, current products and services used, pain points, what an ideal solution would look like, current priorities or competing initiatives, and their decision-making process, so that he could assess a fit and how he could add value. I told him that he needs to be more diligent with his questioning."

At this point, I was looking for the manager to bring his story home with how he coached and further developed this salesperson's skill set. With excitement, I asked, "Then what happened?"

"Well, that was it," the manager said. "That's where we ended the conversation."

I paused for a moment and asked, "So, at what point did you actually *develop* this salesperson?"

"I told you," the manager replied. "I helped further develop them when I shared what I had observed."

The defining moment was now apparent. I acknowledged the manager. "Thanks for sharing your story. However, I'm wondering if anyone noticed the difference between sharing an observation and developing someone, or are these two distinct behaviors being collapsed into one definition?"

Expand Their Peripheral View, Then Coach!

When you share an observation, you are sharing a general overview of *what* you heard or saw; the best practices and opportunities for improvement. When you're authentically developing someone, you're moving the conversation to a deeper and more tactical level that will cause a change in behavior and thinking. You're shifting from a general overview into the development and refinement of best practices, or what needs to change to improve performance.

This can include an upgrade or refinement in thinking, knowledge, behavior, communication or coach tracks and messaging (written, verbal and nonverbal). After all, leadership and selling are languages of coaching to master, and the most important factors that distinguish the top performers from the rest.

This is the area of opportunity where managers can positively transform people's attitude, thinking, and behavior by challenging both their inner critic and outer voice to exponentially impact performance.

MINDFUL MOMENT

The lynchpin of success will always boil down to how positively and effectively you know yourself and communicate with people. Coaching unearths your inner voice to assess the validity and health of the stories you tell yourself and others.

So, how you can you take your feedback and turn it into growth opportunities? What would the rest of that conversation sound like? This is the struggle managers go through, as they often stop a few feet before the finish line, right after sharing their observations because they assume positive behavioral change will follow.

HOW TO SHIFT FROM OBSERVATION TO COACHING

Building off my experience in Belgium, here are a couple of ideas and exercises to do with your team that will move the conversation from sharing an observation or a *nice to know* to measurably improving performance through coaching.

Coaching Scenario #1

Observation: "During your next sales call, don't you think you need to do a better job qualifying and learning about each new customer?"

Does this cause a measurable change in behavior? Absolutely not. While the observation may be relevant, it wasn't followed by *how* it needs to be done and what exactly needs to change. Now, let's look at the language that follows your observation.

Coaching and Development

Consider this approach when speaking with your salesperson: "What do you need to know about every new prospect and customer to earn their business and serve them best?"

You would then (hopefully) hear from your salesperson all the information they would ideally need to know to provide a solution that would solve their problems, save time or money, improve performance and efficiency, and be aligned with their needs and expectations of your service and results. From here, the billion-dollar developmental question would be, "What questions can you ask that would provide you with the needed information when qualifying each opportunity?" Does this develop someone's skills? Absolutely. The end product is, a salesperson who has an actionable and specific list of discovery and qualifying questions. These can become a documented best practice for the rest of your team. The best part is, this sales rep owns and embraces these questions because it was their creation.

Coaching Scenario #2

Observation: "It may be a good idea to call the CFO/CEO/CTO and explain to them why we can't provide the discount they're asking for. What do you think?" I can't come up with more of a loaded and leading question if I tried. This manager just cornered that person into the inevitable, "Yes, sure I'll do that." But do you know *how* they will approach the conversation? Not at all. In fact, because the manager failed to provide any guidance on how to change their message, chances are the salesperson will take the same approach and inevitably generate the same, less-than-favorable result as before.

Coaching and Development

Consider this approach: "What happened during the last conversation you had with the CFO? What did the CFO say? How did you respond? How are you going to approach the CFO when you call them? Let's practice. I'm the CFO. How would you approach me in a way that would best resolve and defuse this situation? What would that sound like?"

CROSS THE FINISH LINE

While many managers do a great job enrolling people in observation, sharing feedback, and having people align with what you've observed in them, they often stop right before they cross the finish line and move the feedback given into a coaching moment. If you want to build a bench of champions and future leaders, it's critical to go beyond simply sharing a passive, just-so-you-know observation and coach them around who they are—their skill, behavior, attitude, proficiency, and how they will make a measurable change in their conversation and messaging to perform like a champion. Unfortunately, most managers rely on their assumptions of what needs to change, rather than the facts. Once that happens, they become incapable of seeing what's really going on around them.

Now that you're working on getting your head out of your *assumptions*, it's time to uncover the most common of the destructive behaviors that distinguishes the ineffective leaders from the titans.

12

15 Common Coaching Killers That Sabotage Coaching Success

A s we approach the finish line of this book, what I want for you is to adopt these best-in-class practices so you can become the transformational leader and coach I know you are and will continue to become! The fact that you're at this point in the book demonstrates that you already possess the most important, core characteristic needed to become a respected leader and coach—care.

And, while we've focused on what you need to do to be the best you that you can be by continually developing and refining your skills and leadership DNA, it's just as important to be mindful of the negative thinking, behaviors, and things we do and say that will sabotage your coaching, brand, trust, and legacy. What follows are 15 common mistakes or coaching killers that leaders need to recognize, learn from, and sidestep.

TOXIC TACTIC #1: NINE PAINFULLY STUPID, DISEMPOWERING WORDS TO STOP USING

Remove any words that end with *n't*. If we know coaching is the language of leadership, then take these words out of your vocabulary, because they don't translate. As a manager and coach, you have no use for them. These words focus deeper on the problem, instead of moving toward creating a new and better solution and opportunity.

- Can't
- Won't
- Wouldn't
- Shouldn't
- Couldn't
- Aren't
- Didn't
- Isn't
- But (Negates everything stated before it. Use "And" instead.)

Managers tend to focus more on what their people are not doing and what's not working, instead of what is. As such, they don't reinforce positive behavior and best practices. Inevitably, they wonder why they deal with the same recurring problems, including lost trust, waning confidence, lackluster performance, and team disengagement.

Consequently, when managers go deeper into the problem, it reinforces undesirable behavior and the excuses as to why something can't be achieved, which moves you further away from creating a better solution.

How to avoid this trap? Here's the one habit to focus on. A simple shift in language will eradicate these venomous words. Asking, "How can/will you," is certainly more powerful than, "Why can't/won't you." One empowers people, the other deflates them, erodes accountability, and creates more dependence on you.

COACHING CONUNDRUM

There isn't any cheese down that tunnel. Said a different way: When you keep digging further into the problem, you're moving further away from the solution and what you're looking to achieve. You've already gotten to the root cause during the define step in L.E.A.D.S. Now it's time to create a new and better possibility.

AVOID THESE DAMAGING, PROBLEM-FOCUSED QUESTIONS

Notice when you use phrases such as "Why can't you ... Why aren't you ... Why won't you ...," the focus of the question is on the problem or on making others wrong, rather than on the solution or how to create a new possibility.

Negative words breed negative outcomes! Language is everything, including what we tell others, and what we tell ourselves. Notice the response you'll get to any of the following questions.

- Here's what you did wrong …
- Where do you feel the gap is in this solution and why isn't it going to work?
- Why didn't you deliver a stronger compelling case?
- Why aren't you going to make your number this quarter?
- Why didn't you close that deal?
- Why can't you improve your relationship with that (partner, customer, AE, peer, direct report, coworker, etc.)?
- Why didn't you qualify better?
- Why don't you want to make more money?

Congratulations! By using these negatively charged questions, you've given full latitude and authority to your direct report to use all the reasons and excuses as to why they can't do something. Instead of creating a coaching moment, you've given them permission to kill the coaching by suffocating it with excuses!

Don't be surprised if you hear, "Thanks boss, for providing me with the opportunity to use all the great excuses I have as to why I can't, won't, and didn't do what I need to do."

TOXIC TACTIC #2: ARE YOU COACHING PEOPLE OR CLOSING THEM?

Outcomes are often based on perspective. Here's an experience I had working with a great team of Microsoft leaders in South Africa. Let me be clear: This is something every manager struggles with. As you read through the following dialog, notice the two contrasting points of view.

THE MANAGER'S VIEWPOINT

They just don't get it. I start with great intentions. I'm paying attention to the questions I ask. But once I feel I've given them enough questions and they still don't know what to do, I lose *patience* and go right into problem-solving mode. I get impatient because they're not coming up with any ideas, nor are they self-reflecting fast enough to recognize opportunities for their own development. As a result, the coaching stops and the prescriptive me overshadows all coaching efforts.

I've tried everything to work with this person so they can improve their performance, but nothing seems to work, and I truly do want to help them.

While this manager has good intentions, when patience is lost, coaching stops. And the reason why patience is lost is because *you're living in the future, pushing for the result you want in that conversation.*

If you were living in the present, moment by moment, you'd be more patient and able to recognize opportunities for growth or improvement that typically go unnoticed. Otherwise, you shift to telling people what to do or you ask leading, closing questions hoping to rapidly push the person to where you want them to be. If you're wondering how this impacts the coachee, take a look.

The Salesperson's Viewpoint

My boss knows I want to be better and I am open to coaching! But I'm still learning about the company, policies, products, and sales process—and how to navigate through the company when I need something.

"Between the complex sales cycle and extensive product line, I was told many times it could take up to a year to start performing at the level the company expects. I'm fully committed to being coached to be the best I can be. Yet, when I ask my manager for help, the conversations start well, but degrade to the point where my manager loses patience and tells me what to do.

Then the conversation ends with, "Let's just stop. Here's what I need you to do." As you can imagine, this approach makes me feel inadequate and robs me of my motivation and energy.

"I'm becoming more hesitant to approach her for help. I'm trying to get up to speed and I love the company. I want to build a career here. I realize I'm still learning. So, when my boss tells me, "You learned all of this during your onboarding and initial training," it makes me feel like an idiot.

"I feel like my boss doesn't trust me or value my work. Without her confidence in me, I see my own confidence starting to deteriorate, along with the belief that I'm capable of succeeding at this job.

"It seems she gave up on trying to coach me, and instead, pushed me in a certain direction with the questions she asked. And when that stops, she just tells me what to do. I don't feel like I'm being coached anymore.

"Her directive approach makes me feel I'm being manipulated, because the questions she asks aren't questions to better understand me. And the questions certainly don't create a safe space for me to reflect and walk through the situation and possible solutions on my own. They're questions that guide me to the outcome she wants in the conversation. If coaching is manipulation, then I'm not interested in being coached.

"For now, I'll rely on my peers for coaching and what I can do on my own to learn and perform, since it's clear that my manager doesn't trust me or my abilities. And if that's the case, then maybe this position isn't for me.

A Coaching Culture or Closing Culture?

Closing is not something you do when you're *coaching* someone. Unfortunately, when managers collapse closing with coaching, the results can be catastrophic. To make matters worse, if you're a sales manager who used to be a salesperson, it's in your DNA to ask rapid-fire questions to quickly drive the person to the answer you want to hear.

Managers who transition from the role of independent contributor to sales manager have a hard time letting go of old sales habits. After all, when they're selling, traditional sales wisdom suggests you ask questions that guide the person toward the natural conclusion of the sales process. If done well, you've now earned the right to ask for the order and close the sale.

While this behavior can win more business, it can simultaneously destroy your coaching efforts and relationships, even with your best intentions. That is, instead of coaching people to create a new possibility, managers wind up closing them instead.

Manipulative Management Tactics

Here's how to recognize whether you're *coaching* or *closing* someone. Throughout the delivery of my day-long leadership coaching program, there are many opportunities for managers to authentically coach with their peers. Inevitably, I can always recognize when a manager is trying to coach or close when I hear this feedback:

I had a hard time coming up with the question that would guide the person to where I want them to be. I tried asking the questions several different ways hoping they would get it, and I still didn't get the answer I wanted. I was getting impatient and frustrated from the conversation because all I want for them is to quickly get to the right answer that I already know!

Now, the coachee leaves this experience feeling unheard, undervalued, and they never want to be coached again!

When managers use leading questions, whether by intention or by habit, they simply try to hide their agenda in the questions they ask.

Consequently, this pushes the coachee to arrive at *the manager's* desired answer or solution, not their own. According to the manager, their direct report decided that the manager's ideas, activities, or approach are best. That, my friend, is closing, not coaching someone!

Then managers wonder why their direct reports don't want to be coached by them! This approach makes people feel judged and manipulated, further eroding the trust needed in every relationship for coaching to be effective.

TIP FROM THE COACH

You know you're coaching someone when the process is effortless, collaborative, enjoyable, often unpredictable, and exciting! You know you're closing someone when you feel frustrated, impatient, directive, and exhausted at the end of the conversation from exerting your energy, pushing the coachee in the direction you want them to go.

Instead of pushing your agenda and what you think the person should do, focus on creating new possibilities. You may be familiar with the expression, "No one likes to be sold but everyone loves to buy." A similar truth exists in coaching. "No one likes to be manipulated or told what to do, but everyone loves to arrive at a solution our outcome they proudly created on their own."

Interrogative Coaching—Leading the Witness

If they haven't come up with the ideas themselves or if you know the answer to the question you ask or ask a question to get the response you're looking for before hearing their opinion, it's *your* agenda! Here are nine questions that are prime examples of leading and loaded questions to avoid.

Leading and Closing Questions
- Don't you think it's a good idea to call the customer and give them a compelling reason as to why they should buy from you?
- Wouldn't it be a good idea if ... (you qualified your opportunities better the next time)?

- Did you try … (calling the customer yet)? These are the manager's ideas that stimulate a *yes* or *no* response and will feel like an interrogation rather than a collaboration. Instead, simply ask the open-ended, *how* and *what* questions. (For example: *What* did you try so far? *How* did you qualify? *What* did you say when you called up the customer?)
- Don't you think it's a good idea to follow the process you've been given?
- Why don't you include and leverage the account manager more often when it comes to working with and supporting this client? (Is this a fact, as in something they've told you, or is it your assumption dancing in this problem-focused question?)
- Is it that you haven't leveraged the resources and people involved in this deal, or do you really think it's procurement's fault why your deal won't close this quarter? (You've now created a question that clearly articulates your point of view, and the only two solutions you assume are best.)
- Would it help if I called up that account executive's manager to see what's going on?
- So, what do you want me to do to help you here? (Putting yourself in the situation to take on the problem and solve it yourself.)
- Looking at your numbers, it seems that you really need to improve the relationships you have with your customers, correct? (Sharing what you perceive to be true and then turning it into a closed-ended question, which, if the coachee didn't tell you firsthand, is an assumption.)

Closed-ended, judgmental questions feel like an interrogation or a competition, put the coachee on the defensive, shut down the conversation, and provide the manager with a *yes* or *no* response. Open-ended, objective questions create an environment of exploration, conversation, acceptance, exploration, and collaboration.

If you've regressed to this point in the conversation, you may as well just tell the direct report what you want them to do or give them the answer, instead of even bothering with asking these deadly, coach-killing questions.

COACHING CONUNDRUM

Manipulative, directive coaching, which is an oxymoron, is more damaging than no coaching at all.

SURRENDER CONTROL TO EMBRACE THE UNKNOWN

Managers avoid asking questions they may not know the answer to because they fear that, if the coachee doesn't have the answer, then they'll be exposed as a fraud! An imperfect coach! That's the ego getting in the way of being an authentic human and being comfortable with not knowing every answer. Besides, if you did know *everything*, then how do you enjoy the adventure and journey of lifelong learning?

If you're looking to create a new possibility, and you already know the answer to the question you're asking, *it's the wrong question*. The best questions are the ones you don't know the answers to. Those are the only ones that stimulate new thinking. After all, there are many ways to achieve a goal, train for a marathon, or travel to reach your desired destination.

Let's walk through the cycle of futility and see what happens when managers engage in this dastardly deed.

1. Looking for assistance around solving a problem, a direct report approaches the manager.

2. The manager assumes that they, as well as their direct report, understand the goal, objective, or challenge, believing it's one they've handled many times before.

3. Subsequently, the manager assumes the gap or root cause, stops assessing with questions, and provides an answer based on the manager's own experience, expectations, and desired outcome. The manager may also ask closed-ended or leading questions that guide the direct report to the manager's desired outcome or the solution. ("When I was in your role," "You should really …" "Don't you think it would be a good idea to …")

4. Because the core issue or root cause wasn't uncovered, managers now solve the wrong problem or treat only symptoms of the problem, resulting in repetitive, time-consuming conversations, impatience, failure, and frustration.

Figure 12.1 illustrates how this plays out in real time.

And so, this vicious and unproductive, damaging cycle continues. Then, managers wonder why they're frustrated, impatient, and spend most of their time dealing with recurring problems that have no business being there in the first place!

Conversely, if you ask the right open-ended questions and give your direct reports the space to problem solve or explore new ways of thinking, only then can you transform from a manager to a coach, and your salespeople can transform from salespeople to sales champions.

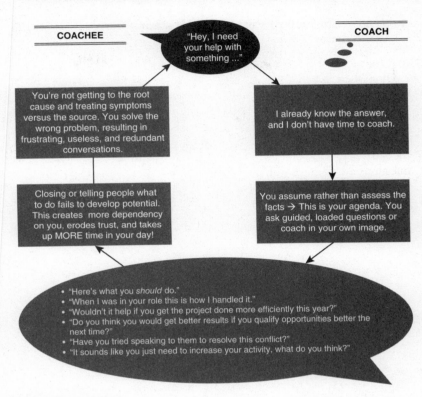

FIGURE 12.1 The Vicious Cycle of Closing Instead of Coaching.

TOXIC TACTIC #3: COACHING IN YOUR OWN IMAGE

Do you *should* on peers, customers, direct reports, family members, or yourself, instead of patiently respecting other people's ideas, abilities, talents, or opinions? If you err to the side of *should*-ing, then you're *coaching in your own image*. Consequently, you crush creativity, stifle personal growth, and obliterate innovation and new possibilities that could blossom from an authentic coaching conversation. Instead, you create mediocrity, and automatons rather than tapping into people's individuality and talents, even if your heart is in the right place. Here are a few common *shoulds*:

- When I was in your role, this is how I achieved my goals, so you *should* follow my strategy.
- "You *should* always present to your prospects this way …"

- You've been working here for how long? You *should* know this already!
- My other customers bought because of this feature, so you *should* too.
- I know what worked for me, so it *should* work for you.

Or, you *should* on yourself

- I *should* have known this would happen.
- I *should* have achieved my goals by now.
- I *should* be performing at a higher level.
- I've been a manager for five years. I *should* know how to coach my team!
- "I'm almost done with this damn book. I *should* be a coaching guru by now!"

When you *should* on yourself or others, it's one big invalidation where you're making everyone *wrong*! Realize a *should* is the excrement of your assumptive agenda. So, stop *shoulding*!

COACHING CONUNDRUM

Using manipulative, closing questions also translates into coaching in your own image because you're attempting to quickly get someone to where you think they *should* be, often based on where you've been or your experience and what has worked for you.

Coaching in your own image is just one big *should* we dump on others. What makes honoring each person's individuality so difficult is, if you don't know how to coach, you default to what you know, assuming what you do to attain success will work for others.

And if anyone continues to *should* on themselves, there's a strong chance they're suffering from a bad case of perfectionism. When the goal is to be flawless, we're certainly setting ourselves up for failure and disappointment!

We can choose *judgment* and make ourselves wrong or beat ourselves and others up by being a *should* master, or we can choose *acceptance* by honoring that who we are and where we are in our lives right now is exactly where we need to be on our path of personal evolution and self-discovery.

*Should*s capture the essence of what regret looks like and are a great example of what it sounds like if you're someone who lives in the past, or in the future, rather than living and being present in the moment. Our internal, self-talk sounds like, "If only I ... I *should* have (taken that other job, made that decision, found my soul mate, saved more money, bought that stock when it went public, approached my boss for a promotion, took better care of myself, etc.). Then my life would be so much better today!" This mindset keeps you stuck living in the regret of your past.

Rather than focusing on how you feel it *should* be or should have been, embrace how it is in the moment, because the moment is all we have. And in this moment, we always have the power to make the choices that create the life we want today.

TOXIC TACTIC #4: LIVING EVERYWHERE BUT NOW

With the insatiable drive to achieve aggressive results and the obsession over getting to what's next instead of being here in what's now, every company, every leader needs to start focusing on the biggest miss of all, the very thing that will determine your success or your failure. The present.

Managers are wired to be the chief problem solver, fix things, and consequently, approach practically every situation looking to offer a quick solution. They are conditioned to focus on their sales targets, look to fix what's wrong, and provide directive feedback.

Unfortunately, this very mindset comes at a great cost. If you are focused on the problem, the result, or what's next, then you are not focused on the *now*. And what is happening now? Your people, your process, your actions, your choices—your life.

Here's another personal story I share that illustrates this point and the importance of authentically living and being in the moment.

Not to be morbid, but death is a part of life. Unfortunately, I've been to my share of funerals. At some point during a funeral, friends and family members will often get up and stand in front of the congregation and talk about the person who passed. When this happens, every human being has two general reactions. First, especially if it's an elderly person who died, the reaction might be, "Wow, I didn't realize what an impact this person had made on so many people. I had no idea how much this person achieved in their life."

The second reaction is more commonplace. That is, you start thinking about your own life. You begin to reflect upon your mortality. When this happens, you experience a physical, as well as an emotional, even spiritual reaction or a feeling in the core of your soul. There's a tingling in your chest. You notice your breathing becoming slightly irregular. Your heart feels heavier than it normally does. At first, there are tears, then you begin to sob, a natural occurrence at a funeral. Initially, you may find your behavior surprising to yourself, even uncomfortable. But in the end, you realize you need to experience those feelings of sadness, grief, regret, and remorse, those human emotions everyone feels when honoring the loss of someone they love and care about. Then, as if it were scripted, you experience a sense of relief. You're acknowledging and reflecting upon something that's been growing inside you, taking up space. This internal conflict that many people struggle with—the eternal battle between honoring your core values, your priorities, and your life, with the unyielding obsession to win and achieve more in your career. Your competitive nature consumes you and engulfs your time, while simultaneously challenging your integrity, which is the very thing that makes you authentically complete, puts your life in balance, and tells you whether you're being true to yourself.

You reflect further and ask yourself, "Am I making the right choices? Am I making too many personal sacrifices to get ahead in my career or make more money? Have I given up too much of my life for what I perceive to be a means to an end? Am I doing what I want to be doing, what I'm passionate about? Am I relentlessly driven by the right reasons and the right goals and if so, at what cost? Am I truly happy?"

Immediately, you flash back through your life—where you were, where you are today, and where you may be going. For a moment, you are covered by a blanket of regret among a sky filled with your achievements— of things you did, wish you did, wish you did more of, and things you wish you didn't do. But then, you realize something. You realize that you can change things. That you are in control of your life. That the game is far from over. And so, you start thinking about what you need to change that would make your life more fulfilling, more worthwhile, more meaningful. You think, "Life is too short. I need to spend more time with my family and my friends. I need to spend more quality time with my kids. I need to take better care of myself, and the people in my life. I need to do more of the things that bring me joy, inspiration, and fulfillment. I've got to stop working so hard. Life is so fragile. There's no dress rehearsal. I need to make the most of it now. I need to put my priorities in perspective. I need to change where I'm spending most of my time and focus on my core values and what matters most. Life is way too precious, so fragile, and such a blessing."

For that defining and intimately honest moment during the funeral, your mind is quiet. The stars are aligned.

You have clarity.

Your priorities and values are top of mind.

You're clear about your values. You know what you need to do to start treating every moment like the gift that it is.

This emotionally triggered moment of self-reflection provided you with an invaluable perspective, as you place a higher value on where to invest your time, and your life. Everything makes sense. You're at peace. You feel fully present, connected to your values and priorities, and more engaged and present in the moment than you ever have been before.

Then, you leave the funeral, and your phone rings or you get the next text—and you're right back to living in the future, focused on what you need to do next: the next project, deadline, sale. The defining moment when you experienced that sense of clarity is gone, and you're consumed with everything else, except being present. Now, you're choosing to allow the daily pressures, tasks and responsibilities to pull you away from the moment and your peace of mind.

But don't lose hope. Ironically, it's a lifelong journey to be fully present and focus on what's now. It takes a conscious effort to be mindful of the goals, fears, pressures, or situations that pull us back into the past or propel us into the future and take us away from what's most important in the now.

To be clear, I'm not suggesting that achieving measurable, worthwhile goals is unimportant! However, we need to balance both, so be mindful of the *two conflicting truths that coexist simultaneously*.

Living in the present is challenging, especially when so much is being thrown at us. There are so many priorities competing for our limited time, dragging us in different directions.

Yet, instead of looking at life through the lens of a child, where everything is new and exciting, and every situation is a conduit to growth and learning, we become hardened by our experiences. We use our experiences to define us. We form our own truths that we fall in love with and forget we need to continually challenge them to see if they still serve us best. We take our past experiences and project them into the future, assuming our prior experiences are an indication of what will happen again.

What's missing? The present.

COACHING CONUNDRUM

Coaching is the art of creating new possibilities. You can't create new possibilities or actively listen if you're not present, and you're not present because you're attached to your future agenda goal and expectation or stuck in the past, assuming the same outcome. This creates destructive self-fulfilling prophecies and redundant, lackluster results. File under: big trouble.

To Be Present, Become Process Driven

If you want to see the impact that your result-driven mindset has on your communication and coaching, and what happens when you shift your thinking to become someone who is a process-driven thinker, look at these different sets of questions.

Result-Driven Questions

- What do you have confirmed that's going to close this month?
- You know we have to do more to sell into the company than just call on IT.
- How many outbound calls did you make to try to get into the C-suite?
- Are we going to get that project done on time and meet the deadline?
- How many calls are you making every day? How many meetings do you have scheduled?
- Is your pipeline and forecast accurate? How will you finish up the quarter?

Process-Driven Questions

- How have you handled that situation before?
- What are the steps you would take to resolve this? How would you do it?
- Walk me through the conversation you recently had with that person.
- What are the specific questions you ask to qualify every opportunity?
- What will the message sound like when you call the customer?

When you shift to process-driven questions, you ask better questions and the focus moves to the process—the how, the who, and the strategy, instead of results. You also remain focused on the present, not the past or future. Since the process lives in the present and the results live in the future, you also exist in the present—that is, in the moment—to the person who you're talking to. If you're not present,

- You're not listening or fully engaged.
- You erode trust.
- You miss coaching moments.

- You will assume versus assess the gaps.
- It will cost you more time, money, goal attainment, the present, living your values, honoring priorities, and the quality of your life.

Life happens today. Not being present means missing out on everything that matters most.

TIP FROM THE COACH

Coach the process (the *how*, *why*, and *who*), not the result.

Detaching from the outcome is difficult. When you attach your own agenda to a conversation, you:

- Limit the ability for a new or better possibility, solution, or outcome to surface.
- Create a filter in your listening, preventing others from contributing to you and to the conversation.
- Invalidate the other person by not respecting their point of view.
- Erode trust.

MINDFUL MOMENT

Note the distinction between a *doing* leader and a *being* leader. After all, beliefs precede experience. To detach from the outcome and create a better possibility, you need to *be* present. (You can't *do* present.) This is the inner game versus the outer, tactical game of leadership. Who you are versus what you do. Ultimately, how you think is what you do—and what you do is what you get!

THE PRACTICE OF NOW

Your daily pressures and responsibilities aren't going away. Your business objectives and aggressive sales targets are a reality. There will always be something in front of you that can pull you into the future, distract you from your present priorities, suck you back into your past, and take your eyes off what you value most.

Yes, we are all victims of our results-driven company culture. This environment forces you to drive for results, focus on and live in the future, and the sad part is, it's costing you your life.

However, now you have a choice. And I'm not suggesting that you can control outcomes, responsibilities you have in your position, or how things will turn out. I am saying that you always have choices around how you respond to each person, challenge, and situation.

TIP FROM THE COACH

Shut up, listen, and observe the miracles around you. That's often more valuable than anything you can ask or say.

I am fortunate that I was taught at an early age to live by a universal law that determines the quality of your life. That is, it's not the events in your life but how you choose to respond to them that defines who you are and creates the quality of your life.

What can you learn from this? Well, how effective are you at living in the present and being fully engaged in what is happening *now* while being mindful about what will happen *next*?

Here's something I do during the beginning of every delivery that drives the power of presence home: No matter where I am, if there are 50 or fewer people in the room, within the first hour of my delivery I'll know everyone's name without name cards—and that includes international names. When asked what my secret is, I simply say, "I'm being present. I pay attention. I'm focused only on you in that moment. I'm accepting you, not judging you."

Being present to recognize the daily miracles around us that make life worthwhile, whether at home or at work, is something we must be mindful of and focus on every day, and we will continually be tested throughout our lives to see if we got the lesson. I vote to get the lesson now, before it's too late.

Now, it's up to you. What choice are you going to make today?

MINDFUL MOMENT

Embrace dualities and surrender absolute thinking. Be mindful of the future, while engaged in the moment.

TOXIC TACTIC #5: COACHING MULTIPLE GAPS AT A TIME

Several years ago I was in Milan, Italy, delivering a coaching workshop for one of Google's management teams, and they had one of their biggest snowstorms in history. The four feet of snow didn't stop this team of managers from showing up for day two of our leadership coaching course. We were working through a peer-to-peer coaching real play. This is different from a *role play*, where one person puts themselves in the shoes of another person and acts the way they perceive that person would act. A *real play* is simply, well, real coaching—one peer goes to another peer for authentic, real-time coaching around an actual issue or goal.

While these managers were coaching each other, I stopped to listen in on one conversation between two managers. The coaching manager did a great job following the L.E.A.D.S. framework; however, it seemed that during their assess stage, the manager was under the impression she had to know *every* detail about the situation. While having this information is critical, the challenge came when the manager moved into the define stage.

By asking just one question, the manager was able to uncover the gap! And when I debriefed with her afterward, she said, "Keith, that one question revealed a coaching moment. But then, I wondered what else I could uncover by asking more questions.

"Well, the more questions I asked, the more gaps I uncovered. I was so caught up in the weeds, I didn't know which way to go!"

This manager successfully redlined until the point she overengineered her coaching. Sometimes, it just takes one question to expose the coaching moment or developmental opportunity.

COACH ONE GAP AT A TIME

I recently spoke with a manager who told me, "I had this incredibly long list of topics to discuss with one of my salespeople during our one-hour coaching session over the phone, but we only got through the first few."

As much as I wish this to be true, it will take more than one hour to solve world peace and hunger. This holds true for everything on your agenda, and your coachee's agenda, regardless of how much needs to get done or how many priorities you have. Get real. You're not solving and tackling every topic through to completion in one hour.

When it comes to a one-to-one scheduled coaching session, it's a best practice to see one or two topics through to completion, rather than starting ten conversations and getting closure on none. Agenda overload only succeeds at disrupting the focus of your team and creates confusion around what tasks and projects to prioritize.

FIGURE 12.2 Coach One Gap at a Time.

While in Cairo, Egypt, I had the memorable experience of touring the pyramids and the Great Sphinx on a camel. Did you know that to this day, they are still excavating and finding artifacts that are thousands of years old? Here's my point: If you keep using great coaching questions to continually dig deeper, and go beyond the first gap you uncovered, then you'll keep finding other coaching moments and gaps that will derail that coaching session (see Figure 12.2).

COACHING CONUNDRUM

Don't overengineer your coaching! If you keep digging, you'll keep finding more. Coach one gap at a time through to completion.

TOXIC TACTIC #6: DOUBLE-DIPPING ON QUESTIONS

Here's a quick lesson on etiquette: It's inappropriate and disgusting if you re-dip a chip after putting it in your mouth. (Unless you're by yourself or with someone who just doesn't care.) Bring this code of polite conduct and appropriate social behavior into the world of coaching and you'll find the same rule applies here as well. Ask one question at a time and do not ask the next one until the coachee answers the first one completely! Otherwise, what's the point of asking the question?

TIP FROM THE COACH

If you're intentionally and proactively listening, let each response become the springboard and inspiration for your next relevant question to guide the conversation forward.

To maximize the power of every question, no double-dipping! Besides, you don't want to be known as *that coach* whose social coaching graces are offensive and annoying.

In any conversation, ask one question at a time. When you *double-dip* and ask more than one question at once, several things will happen.

- People don't answer either question.
- They answer the easier question that they are more comfortable with.
- They provide an answer to a question you didn't ask.
- The answers they provide are diluted and there's a loss of focus in the conversation.

Consequently, the coaching goes sideways, along with a natural progression toward the conclusion of a coaching conversation. Rather than travel down one path, you and your coachee are now stuck at a crossroads, unsure which path to take. You'll always have the opportunity to ask that second question if needed.

So, if you find yourself vacillating between asking two questions, rather than ask them simultaneously, pick one. If you need to ask the other question, it will still be in your coaching playbook waiting for you. Respecting this coaching etiquette keeps you moving down the one-way path toward a breakthrough.

TOXIC TACTIC #7: COACHING IS FOR LOSERS

How did you set the expectations of coaching with your team before you read this book? Are you coaching only the underperformer or the problem child? Are you coaching only when you see a problem? Finally, are you coaching based on only results and activity?

In many cases the message the manager sends when coaching is, "Can all the underperformers please stand up! Here's your chance to redeem yourselves!" Ouch. This remedial notion of coaching doesn't create an atmosphere where everyone would want to be coached. It creates the very resistance you're looking to avoid. For example:

> **Manager**: I don't understand why the top performer doesn't want to be coached.
>
> **Coach**: Share with me a typical coaching experience …
>
> **Manager**: I typically coach when there's a problem.
>
> **Coach**: Tell me more …
>
> **Manager**: At some point when the problem escalates, that's when I jump in. So I spend most of my time coaching C performers, since they're the ones who need the most help.

If this was how the manager positioned coaching, imagine if you were a solid or top performer? You observe that your manager is coaching only the underperformer, so when he attempts to enroll you in coaching, resistance is imminent! The manager positioned coaching as a tactic, remedial approach or *punishment* meant only for poor performers! So, why would a top performer ever want to be put in that classification and embrace coaching?

Don't create a mentality that says, "I am coaching you because you're broken and need to be repaired."

To avoid this misconception, coaching must be positioned as an essential part of every person's career development. Therefore, everyone gets coached consistently and, when done well, everyone will find value and want to be coached. Note to self: Let people to know that coaching is for the elite. The champions. The rock stars. And more important, coaching is for the people who you care about most.

EVERYONE GETS COACHED

It's glaringly obvious to me when a team or company has negatively positioned coaching to the point that it's a dirty word in their organization. Once I hear a manager ask, "Do we have to call it coaching?" it's time for a coaching reset.

Well, you can call it eating or dancing or skiing, the fact is, it's coaching. You can either not coach, or you can reset the definition and expectations of coaching by having a reenrollment conversation. It can be as simple as a team or one-to-one meeting and enroll people on crafting a new definition of coaching that if everyone can honor, would make coaching a new and valuable experience for all.

TOXIC TACTIC #8: IN SEARCH OF THE PERFECT COACHING QUESTION

It was about five minutes into a coaching conversation between Tala and Michael. Tala was being extremely open and coachable as Michael followed the L.E.A.D.S. coaching framework we've been working on during our two days together.

Michael then asked Tala a fantastic coaching question. Tala answered but Michael just kept on going, asking question after question. After a few minutes, I stopped the conversation and asked him, "Can you rewind the conversation about three minutes? You asked a great question and Tala responded very clearly that you hit on something she needed to work on. Do you recall that?"

Michael clearly had no idea what I was referring to. When I asked him to go back and reference the question and the response he heard, he exclaimed, "Keith, I don't remember what I asked or what I heard because I was so focused on the next question I was going to ask!" Therein lies lessons in listening and coaching.

1. *There's no such thing as a _perfect_ coaching question*. If one question doesn't work, ask another!
2. If you're focusing on the next question to ask, you can no longer be proactively listening. And if you're not listening, then what's the question worth?
3. You will miss valuable coaching moments and derail the conversation based on where you assumed it needed to go.
4. You're making the coaching about you and how good you want to look as a coach, rather than humbling yourself and making it about the coachee.
5. The greatest coaching questions bloom from your heart not your head.

When you're hooked on the future outcome or on what you want to happen, and not in the present moment of insatiable curiosity and exploration where proactive, intentional listening occurs, the possibility of creating new possibilities is no longer possible.

> ## COACHING CONUNDRUM
>
> Searching for the perfect coaching question leads to failure. The perfect question is already within your heart and there's no restriction on the number of questions you can ask. So, get over your perfectionism and out of your head, or you can't coach like a guru.

TOXIC TACTIC #9: CARING TOO MUCH

Performance expectations in each person's role are one thing, and are for the most part non-negotiable. After all, according to the job description, the person was put into that position to be effective at their job function. However, it's each person's individual goals and motivations that we need to respect and coach to, not what we think their goals should be.

You can't care more about the other person's job than they do.

Otherwise, you're pushing your agenda and *can want more for the other person than they want for themselves* or what they're currently ready for. Even with your good intentions, you can push a solid producer out the door.

TOXIC TACTIC #10: IS EVERYONE TRULY COACHABLE?

At the end of day two of my program in Mexico, I asked each manager from PepsiCo to send me an update one week after delivering my sales and leadership coaching program, providing an update around how their enrollment on coaching went with their team.

Nine out of 10 managers reported great success. However, one manager emailed me and said, "Keith, you're not going to believe this, but no one on my team is coachable!"

It doesn't take a master coach to realize this issue isn't about this team but instead, is all about the manager! Clearly the accountability falls on the manager to find a more effective way to reenroll their team in a way that would create the alignment and buy-in needed for people to want to be coached.

To my point. There's only one thing that needs to be present for coaching to work: a *desire to change for the better*. That's it. If there's an inkling of this inside each person, then you can coach them and make a positive impact. And if you're wondering about that one manager I mentioned? Don't worry. He took accountability and successfully reenrolled his team.

TOXIC TACTIC #11: THE COACHEE ANSWERS THE QUESTION—NOT YOU!

I've witnessed managers ask a great question during a conversation, only to proceed with answering the very question they asked! Stop answering your own questions when coaching! If you do, you no longer need the coachee in that conversation!

Another common trap managers fall into has less to do with the question they ask, and more to do with the answer they receive from the coachee. I've heard managers ask some amazing coaching questions to which they did not get a response from the coachee. And subsequently, they move to the next question or answer the very question they asked! I believe this would fall more under the category of self-coaching. However, when I stop the coaching and ask the manager, "Wait, did the coachee actually answer the question you asked?" the answer is always, "No." If that's the case, the strategy is simple: Ask the question again.

Imagine a salesperson skipping over their discovery questions. Then, when they ask for the sale, they're shocked to discover several new objections they never heard, all because of the gaping hole in their discovery process.

TOXIC TACTIC #12: GETTING SUCKERED BY THESE TWO COMMON PHRASES

It seems that managers do have a weakness that comes in the form of two comments they frequently hear from their peers, customers, and direct reports.

1. **I don't know.**

What does "I don't know" even mean? It could mean:

- I really don't know.
- I know but I don't want to tell you.
- I know but I'm afraid to tell you.
- I know but I want you to tell me instead what to do.
- I know and want to validate it with you.
- I have an idea but I'm not 100 percent sure.

When faced with "I don't know," you have an opportunity to make the choice that a world-class leader would make:

1. Give the answer. Congratulations you took the bait.
2. Ask the question, "If you did know, what would it be." (Yes, it may sound like a ridiculous question, but it works. Just say it with a straight face and be prepared for an answer.
3. Use the 60-second coaching strategy, because everyone has an opinion (Chapter 4).

Options two and three create a coaching moment and an opportunity to develop the coachee's skills, self-awareness, and confidence. The second comment is:

2. I've tried everything.

When you hear this, what is your reaction? Do you gloss over it? Continue with your conversation or soapbox delivery of pontificating prowess? Do you think they *actually tried everything*? Did you assume that even if they did, it was done following best-in-class practices? Or do you think they've done things the way you would do them, which, of course, would make you sleep well at night?

Break this statement down to its stupidity. *Trying everything* is a mathematical impossibility. Especially when it comes to coaching and communication, I'm sorry to say that you have not, in fact, tried everything.

While this can shut down the exploration of new ideas, allow it to open the conversation to create a new coaching moment instead. You can respond with, "When you say you've *tried everything*, can you say more about what exactly you tried and how you did it?" "When you did (X), what exactly did you do? How?" "What did it sound like when you spoke with ..." These questions incorporate coaching best practices and the principles around coaching phraseology, assumptions, language, and one gap at a time.

TIP FROM THE COACH

"I don't know" and "I've tried everything" are diversionary tactics. Don't take the bait. Peel the coaching onion back further to get to the root cause. And that goes for you, too, coach. Telling your coach (me), "I did something like that," or "This won't work" is a load of crap. Don't *assume* something won't work until you try it, especially every coach track and coaching question in this book. Do it first, then email or reach out to me.

TOXIC TACTIC #13: THINKING YOU'RE SUPER COACH

This experience took place in Toronto, Canada, at the regional office of American Express, where the manager's ego inhibited his transparency with his team due to some perceived fear about being vulnerable and less than perfect.

Most often, there's an assumption being made about what it means to be a great leader. As such, there's a perceived level of weakness some managers feel they would display if they appear less than perfect or don't know something they feel managers should already know or be expected to know.

When I address this, quite often managers say, "Well, if I let my people know I'm just learning how to coach, I'm essentially admitting that I don't already know how to coach effectively, which is something I should know how to do, being a manager. I can't let my people know this. They already expect me to know how to manage. Sharing a message like this is a sign of weakness and a surefire path to discrediting me and my value as a manager."

Let's follow this line of thinking through to completion. You approach your team and position yourself as the master coach, even though you're at the apprentice stage. Your team now thinks you're Super Coach and expect that level of value from your coaching. Fast forward to the first coaching interaction you have.

When you don't deliver on this expectation, or if the first coaching conversation is not effective, what message did you send? If you're now the self-proclaimed master coach, you don't have any margin for error or room to course correct.

Subsequently, what experience and collateral damage have you now created? Your staff now feels that coaching doesn't work, or that you are a horrible coach! Do you think your people are now looking forward to their next interaction or coaching session with you?

Moreover, if a manager truly feels they know how to coach, and finds the coaching they deliver is ineffective or is met with resistance, I often see managers evaluate this experience not from the position of, "Hmm, maybe there's more to this coaching than I thought. Time to reevaluate my approach and skill set," but from the egomaniacal position of, "It's not me, *it's coaching*. Coaching doesn't work for me, my team, my company."

Coaching is then perceived as negative or ineffective, so the face of coaching is now tarnished. Effectually, the value of coaching is discredited because of faulty positioning and delivery; poorly set expectations; and subjective, inaccurate assumptions.

Get over yourself and get comfortable with saying and thinking, "I don't know" rather than "I do know." *I do know* fuels the assumptive, chief problem solver. *I don't know* stimulates curiosity and the thinking of a truly great coach. If you don't know, you then seek to understand. This creates trust, reciprocity, and better results.

TOXIC TACTIC #14: LOSING PATIENCE IN COACHING

If you reexamine any of the damaging behaviors or practices we've discussed, that's where you'll find the root cause of your impatience.

It is not up to your employees, regardless of age, to adapt to you and embrace your style of leadership, communication, or your behavior and thinking. It is the manager's job to adapt to their team and who they are, not just what they do.

One of the core pillars and principles of coaching is *respecting and coaching to each person's individuality*. If you're detached from your own agenda, and care enough to respect each person's individuality, strengths, thinking process, communication style, skills, goals, values, motivators, how they like to be managed, and their position in the company, you will naturally become more *patient*. It's a natural by-product of letting go.

However, if you're *coaching in your own image*, or feel what is often self-imposed pressure to get results fast, patience is lost, the *should*-ing begins, the directive manager emerges, and the erosion of trust follows in its wake.

A GPS FOR YOUR PATIENCE

Managers share dozens of reasons why they lose their patience. That's when I say this: "What if you never lose your patience again because you use a GPS for patience. Now you can always track it, find it, and get it back.

Take a reflective moment. Think about the last time you may have become a bit impatient. It shouldn't be too much of a stretch. Now, stop and ask yourself *why*?

Here are some typical reactions I hear from managers.
- I already know the answer.
- I don't have time.
- It takes too long to keep asking questions.
- They're not getting it.
- They're not getting it fast enough.
- They should already know this stuff.
- My leading, closed-ended questions keep the conversation moving to where they need to get.

Here's what managers don't share until I dig it out of them.

- If I ask a question I lose control.
- What if I don't have an answer?
- What if this drags on forever?
- What if we don't arrive at the right solution?
- What if they don't think this is valuable?
- Why go through the time-consuming process of coaching, when they should just listen to me because my strategy works?!

This is the very attitude that is the root cause of and breeds impatience!

MINDFUL MOMENT

Acceptance is the opposite of judgment. Judgment causes the demolition of patience. Therefore, acceptance is the gateway to eternal patience.

NEVER LOSE YOUR PATIENCE AGAIN

Your patience is in your thinking. Patience doesn't require an external shift but an internal shift.

During a coaching conversation, you're either 100 percent present and focused on the other person or you're not. You have already made a defining decision on the outcome of this conversation by going into it leading with one of two of the following beliefs.

1. *I already know.*
2. *I don't know.*

Let's ride these statements to their inevitable conclusions:

1. **I already know** ➔ I'm not curious because I already know the answers. ➔ I already know where they need to be, so I'm no longer listening. ➔ I'm living in the future; no, I can no longer be living in the present. ➔ I'll ask some questions but assume most of the facts. ➔ They're not getting it. ➔ I have other things to do. ➔ I'll stop asking questions and write out a prescription for my solution. ➔ Prescribe the same painfully monotonous answers. ➔ Trust is lost. ➔ Coaching is tarnished. ➔ The coach and coachee both leave frustrated over a useless conversation.

2. **I don't know** ➜ I'm curious to find out. ➜ Being curious causes me to be in the moment. ➜ If I'm in the moment I can be patient. ➜ If I'm patient I can intentionally listen. ➜ I'll ask relevant questions to ensure I gather all the facts rather than make assumptions. ➜ Trust and the value of coaching is strengthened. ➜ We co-create something greater together. ➜ The coach and coachee both leave empowered and inspired over a high-value conversation.

THE TAO OF PATIENCE

Here's the summarized formula for maintaining eternal Zen-like patience.

No assumptions/judgments/agenda + being present + being process driven + insatiable curiosity + proactive listening + intentional coaching questions = Developing the timeless patience of a masterful coach.

Patience is a gift you give to others—and without it, all your coaching efforts will be destroyed. Without patience you can't honor the core competencies of a coach, especially the ability to actively listen.

Impatience is due to the inability to be present. It signals a failure to detach from your own outcome and expectations and instead give your undivided attention to the coachee. Allow the flow of the moment to take its natural course without aggressive intervention or pushing for something to happen. Resistances causes erosion, and erosion destroys trust.

When you let go of your self-serving agenda, you'll notice that you'll naturally have more patience, enjoy the coaching process more, and create the results you ultimately want.

MINDFUL MOMENT

If you're present, you're patient. Patience only lives in the present. If you're anywhere else, you're pushing for something to happen, rather than letting something unfold naturally.

TOXIC TACTIC #15: DISHONORING THE ABCs OF LEADERSHIP

If you've read both of my coaching books along with my blogs, the concept of the ABCs of leadership is probably etched in your brain: Always be coaching. But don't lose sight of these additional cornerstones of leadership.

- **ABC:** Always be coaching.
- **ABPC:** Always be peer-coaching.
- **ABE:** Always be enrolling.

When these three core pillars stand together in a natural, complementary, and cohesive way, what happens next? The extraordinary. The implausible. The unprecedented. You might refer to them as miracles, especially if you've ever had a top performer that, at one point, you almost terminated before they became your golden child.

There's no doubt that avoiding these 15 toxic coaching practices will lead to greater personal and organizational success. Yet, while the excitement of coaching takes hold, the concern of balancing consistent coaching with every other responsibility follows in its wake. In the next chapter, you'll find six strategies that will make coaching as habitual as breathing.

13

Culture-Shift: Sustaining The Habit of Coaching

While waiting to board my flight to Singapore, I was excited to bump into a manager who I had coached a few years ago. I asked her how things had been progressing with her sales team and their performance.

She said, "Keith, things are finally getting better." Now, as a coach, naturally, I asked her, "Why? What's changed?"

And this manager's response, which is still rare to hear today was this: "Because *I'm* getting better."

This is the foundational thinking of great leadership. If you want your people to change; if you want them to have a positive attitude and be more accountable, coachable, transparent, loyal, collaborative, driven, open to feedback, fearless, caring, vulnerable, trusting, productive, inspired, focused, organized, supportive, respectful, and innovative—change starts with you. And that's good news because creating a team of champions and a culture of coaching is all in your power.

Are you modeling the behavior you want to see in others? Every morning, look yourself in the eye, and make a commitment. What's the one change or improvement you can make today that would positively impact and help others succeed, while building a personal brand and legacy you would be proud of?

If you want to make people more valuable, it starts with making yourself more valuable; that will always be your choice.

SIX STRATEGIES TO NOURISH THE COACHING HABIT AND PRESERVE YOUR COACHING CULTURE

At this point, you have everything you need to introduce the L.E.A.D.S. coaching framework and methodology; enroll your team in coaching (E.L.A.D.S.); schedule time with each person on your team for individual enrollment; conduct your first coaching and observation session; uncover how people like to be motivated, coached, and held accountable; think like a transformational leader; and make every conversation a coaching or enrollment conversation.

Congratulations! You have everything you need to build your own team of champions and become an exceptional leader and coach!

Here are a few additional ideas to ensure your coaching efforts produce a measurable return on investment. These simple, effective strategies will help sustain and embed your coaching culture and efforts, so you can spark the continued evolution of your company and your team for the long term.

Coaching must maintain its positioning as *the* ongoing priority. You'll need a sufficient structure in place to sustain the momentum you're beginning right now. Here are seven strategies you can implement immediately to drive adoption, sustain positive change, build companywide accountability, and avoid slipping back into unproductive habits and a fear-based, result-driven culture.

1. PEER-TO-PEER COACHING

When engaged in an authentic, peer-to-peer coaching session, managers are always surprised how the conversation changes for the better, as well as how they feel when someone is fully engaged and interested in what they have to say. They find themselves sharing more information than ever by having the space to work through an issue and then arrive at a new idea, solution, or an outcome they never thought possible.

That's why at the end of every program I deliver, I conclude the program by making the following statement:

> Look at the person to your left who is sitting next to you. Now, look at the person to your right. These are your peers. These are the people who, during our time together, shared the same challenges and goals that you did. The same people who also want to build a successful career and discover the best way to navigate within the organization and collaborate with other teams and

departments. The same people who often feel isolated and disconnected from the company. The same people who admitted they are leaving with practical, valuable ideas, strategies, and a healthier way of thinking, all because of their coaching experience. The same people who are 100 percent committed to becoming best-in-class coaches because they care enough to bring out the best in others and themselves. And the same people who felt validated, heard, and acknowledged throughout the course.

You are the glue and the foundation that will ultimately determine whether world-class coaching takes root, flourishes, and grows organically within your culture. If you really want to create a thriving culture, then this change starts with you, the leaders of the organization. And that will require each of you to make an unconditional commitment to consistently and effectively coach each other, your peers.

This is *your* coaching moment. Leaders conceptually understand that it's up to them to ensure the coaching is well received and sustained among their team and throughout the company. But they rarely stop and consider putting themselves in the shoes of the coachee, let alone be coached by their peers.

Every manager needs to create alignment and set expectations around coaching, then coach their team to greatness. The same is true for peer-to-peer coaching. Other than continuing education, training, videos, webinars, or online courses, coaching will continually build your coaching acumen, the most essential skill that will determine your success and impact as a leader. That's why the most powerful coaching resource you can leverage, regardless of your position, is right in front of you: your *peers*.

When being coached, you'll be exposed to a new and different perspective and approach you never considered. And it can be from someone who may not be as close to the issue as you are, who understands the subtleties, logistics, and inner workings of your organization, or someone from an entirely different department. In addition, you'll get the validation that you are, in many cases, already doing what's best.

Be the Accountability Partner: Be the Change

Without peer-to-peer coaching, companies incur a great cost. I know there are many managers who experience pushback from their direct reports around being coached as a result of ineffective enrollment or poor coaching.

As the leader, if you don't make an authentic, trusting connection with your peers, how can you expect your team to do the same? If you're struggling to trust your peers to coach you, imagine the reaction your direct reports may have when you attempt to coach them.

When managers develop a trusting relationship with their peers, it allows for authentic coaching to flourish. Then, others take notice, especially your direct reports. They think, "Wow! My boss is reaching out to another manager for help and for coaching? If they see value in coaching, maybe it's time for me to take advantage of more coaching."

Now your peers and direct reports start coaching and supporting each other. That also includes having your direct reports coach up to you! This can only occur within a coaching culture, where you're supportive of one another, reinforcing best practices and building a deeper level of trust throughout your organization.

TIP FROM THE COACH

Buddy up once every few months with a different peer coach to experience a different style of coaching, which leads to the creation of alternative possibilities.

2. CROSS-TEAM COACHING AND OBSERVATION

Aside from the observation managers must always be doing (Chapter 11), some managers have created an opportunity for their team to be coached and observed by another manager who can see things through a fresh, new set of lenses.

Here's where another manager can connect with someone on your team in a way that you may not have been able to. As you can imagine, for this to occur, it's critical to enroll and set clear expectations with the person who may be coached or observed by another manager, so they are clear about what the benefit would be for them.

3. MONTHLY COACHING MINDSHARE SESSIONS

To best sustain the changes that your management team, sales team, or any other department wants when it comes to creating a coaching culture, scheduling a monthly onsite or teleconference meeting is essential. The peer-to-peer team session is focused only on coaching results, wins, experiences, challenges, and opportunities for development. This keeps each person accountable around consistently coaching, while being exposed to different perspectives and best practices from their coworkers around how they can improve as a coach.

Not only will you be able to share experiences and reinforce core coaching competencies that everyone can learn from, but you will also have the opportunity during this time to receive additional coaching and support from your peers.

Once again, if this essential mindshare meeting isn't on everyone's calendar, it's a safe bet that it may never materialize.

4. GET YOUR OWN COACH

To reinforce best practices, develop your ideal and balanced life, honor your values and priorities, and maintain your championship status at work, every great coach and athlete hires a personal coach to continue their evolution and growth, while addressing problems, fears, or challenges they may not be comfortable working on with a peer. As Gandhi said, "Be the change you want to see in others."

Are you authentically modeling the behaviors you want to see in others? Even the best coaches need a coach who acts as an accountability partner, a safe sounding board, or someone to challenge them and call them out when they're wrong on their own Stories. Cons. Assumptions. Meaning. Mindset. (S.C.A.M.M.) (refer to Chapter 3 of *Coaching Salespeople into Sales Champions*), and keep them focused on the goals they want to achieve.

5. CREATE COACHING EVANGELISTS

I have a client in Greece who created a Coaching Culture Committee on his team. This consortium is a volunteer position, where each person (or one person) is responsible for maintaining and building upon your newly formed culture of coaching. This committee will ensure coaching is consistently happening throughout the team and with the people assigned to a specific team coach.

This person does not necessarily have to be your team leader, if you happen to have one. It can be someone else who has a passion for coaching and supporting others, while holding all coworkers accountable for receiving and delivering coaching, upholding the clearly defined company and team vision, supporting each other, and honoring the characteristics of an ideal employee and coach.

Here's a friendly reminder. Every time you introduce something new, people initially need to be enrolled, so intentions and benefits are clear to all.

6. LEVERAGE TECHNOLOGY OR BUILD RECIPROCATED ACCOUNTABILITY

Technology evolves too fast for me to comment. By the time you read this book, they'll probably be some new platform available to support your coaching efforts. There are many so-called coaching platforms out there that provide greater visibility and accountability around coaching. However, most are simply stripped down, basic customer relationship management tools (CRMs). Others are so cumbersome or redundant that you're probably better off using your current CRM to manage the coaching process.

Finally, if you do find an intuitive and easy platform to integrate into your company, most of the time there's no coaching content, tips, resources, or coach tracks to use when a coaching moment presents itself. I know this to be true, because I get at least one call a week from these types of companies, asking if it would be possible to license my content so they can embed it into their coaching platform.

While some of these platforms, if leveraged and rolled out correctly, will complement your coaching efforts, what other options do you have to manage the coaching process, track progress, and validate the value and results achieved through coaching?

If you review the Coaching Prep Form and Coaching Action Plan (Chapter 5), and combine it with a program like OneNote, that may very well be enough.

After all, if you're looking to hold people accountable, track progress, and measure results, you can simply go back in time, review all the coaching prep forms and action plans, and easily identify the personal growth and results the coachee has achieved through coaching.

However, if you're compelled to explore a coaching platform, just do your research to make sure any coaching platform you invest in complements your CRM. If it's too cumbersome and the value isn't clear to the coach and coachee, you'll need a lot of luck to reach full adoption, and you'll probably spend more time trying to convince people to use the tool than helping them maximize it as a useful resource.

Before signing up to use a coaching platform, start with the Coaching Action Plan and prep forms. After a few months, you may find that they are all you'll need.

PART I

YOUR JOURNEY BEGINS HERE

CHAPTER 14

The Final Transformation

We were wrapping up the second day of my leadership coaching program in Dublin, Ireland, for a team of Oracle leaders throughout the EMEA region. As we went around the room, listening to people share their *aha* moments, one manager said, "Keith, I totally believe in coaching and how important it is to develop this skill and mindset to effectively coach my people so they can develop their talents and gifts to achieve excellence. However, I'm struggling with trying to fit coaching around all of my other responsibilities."

Before I could respond, another manager jumped in and said, "Wait, you need to look at this in a different way. You can't ask yourself how you're going to fit coaching around all of your other responsibilities. You have to ask yourself how you're going to fit all of your other responsibilities around coaching."

That's the fundamental shift managers need to make in their thinking to truly make coaching your number-one priority. Don't ask yourself where you want to be or where you want your team to be tomorrow. Ask yourself, "Where do I want to be in a month from now? Three months from now? A year from now?"

You see, the choices you made in the past created your life and your career today. The exciting part is, the choices you make today, will create the life and career you want tomorrow.

MINDFUL MOMENT

With anything new, you're going to focus primarily on the mechanics and how you need to think. Initially, this requires conscious effort to use the coaching framework, ask the right questions, and develop the patience and mindset you need to become a transformational coach. So, be mindful that, in the beginning of the coaching journey, every manager, salesperson, or professional coach starts by coaching from their head, consciously thinking about what they need to do. As you evolve as a coach and make this part of who you are, the greatest coaches intuitively and naturally coach from their hearts, not their heads, which now makes this part of your anatomy who you are.

As we near the end of our journey together, ponder this. "Why do you want to be a manager?" It was one of the first questions I asked you when we began our voyage of transformation.

Now, ask yourself, "Who created the culture and environment that exists within your team?" Look in the mirror. You did. That's great news because it's all in your power!

Don't lose sight of the fact that it's not only your responsibility to create a coaching culture, it is entirely your choice to create the team of champions you want!

Now you can enjoy the journey throughout your career, since coaching people makes them exponentially more successful. When this happens, and you find your job deeply gratifying and, yes, actually enjoyable, you know you've crossed to the other side and are now coaching and communicating with intention, with heart, and with habit! You no longer have to think about coaching someone, because it's naturally who you are.

Many managers respond to this by saying, "Keith, you don't understand. I work for a global company. We are a results-driven, metrics-driven organization." So is virtually every company on the planet. Especially if you work for a large organization, trying to change a culture sometimes feels like trying to quickly turn a battleship, or manage a team of 50 salespeople! It can feel very overwhelming.

Can one leader change the world? It's the only way the world can change. Do you remember how to transform a culture? How do you coach and develop champions?

One person at a time. One conversation at a time.

COACHING CONUNDRUM

How long have you been a manager? Whether one month or 30 years, as with anything new, give yourself a break. Besides, there are many salespeople and leaders who, while they may be in their role for 20 years, don't necessarily have 20 years of experience and learning. Instead, it's quite common that they have one year of experience, just repeated over 20 years! Said a different way, if you've never learned how to coach effectively, then you've simply been repeating the same ineffective or mediocre habits and behaviors throughout your career! This is why salespeople and managers often ask me, "Keith, where were you 20 years ago when I could have really used you!" You're not changing 30 years of conditioning, or mastering coaching in a week. Give yourself at least two weeks to become a coaching ninja. Seriously, consider it will take at least a year to earn your coaching black belt.

If you've gotten this far, embraced what you've read, and are committed to changing your thinking and style of leadership, then I applaud you. You deserve the acknowledgment and recognition for being a committed, caring leader destined for greatness.

Honoring this philosophy organically creates the changes you want within your team, because regardless of your culture, your people interact with you every day.

That's why *you are the culture*. As I've said before, avalanches roll downhill. So does greatness. You create the culture you want on your team. This is all in *your* power to become the elite leader who will stand out, who will make an impact, who realizes that who you are is always more important than what you do, who has a team of loyal, talented, and committed people leading change, who always puts their people ahead of results, who quietly leads change from behind, who puts the spotlight on their people to highlight their achievements instead of letting your ego get in the way of doing so. If you honor these best practices and develop the habit of coaching, you will always be remembered as an extraordinary leader.

Personally, I'll forever remember the people who have made an indelible, defining impact in my life, one of them being the great Zig Ziglar. It was a privilege and an honor to spend a day with Zig Ziglar and his son, Tom, at their corporate office in Dallas, Texas. We did a series of interviews back in 2009, which you can still find on my blog.

Fast forward to November 28, 2012. I was exploring the streets of Denmark, Copenhagen. I just left Frederiks Kirke, popularly known as The Marble Church. It was a gray day, and night had begun to fall. A soft mist filled the air. As I continued my exploration through Denmark, I received a text from one of my sales directors. It read, "I know how much Zig Ziglar means to you. I have terrible news. He died today." Sadness immediately consumed me. The world suffered a great loss, and I lost a mentor, a role model, and a friend. Zig was, and will continue to be a beacon of inspiration and an example of how personal success comes from helping others succeed. As the tears began to roll down my face, I remembered what Zig had once told me. "Keith, the two most important days in your life are the day you were born and the day you find out why."

I'm grateful to have had those precious moments with Zig. His message goes beyond what it means to be a leader and sales champion but a champion of humanity.

I hope by now you've uncovered your *why*—your purpose as a leader and your reason for being on this path of self-discovery that will unleash your fullest potential so that you can become the leader I know you can be. Congratulations on your significant accomplishments to date, and for allowing this book to be your guiding light as you become a true coaching prodigy! To become a beacon of leadership in every area of your life, remember that no behavior is changing until you change your mindset.

The most successful leaders I know are effective, engaging communicators. That is the power they harness through coaching. Technical knowledge, while essential, is not what makes a great leader. It is merely one of many other characteristics leaders may possess. That's why great leaders lead from the center and surround themselves with people who are often more talented and knowledgeable.

MINDFUL MOMENT

You don't have to be great at coaching to start, but you have to start to be great at coaching.

Look where you started. Maybe you, like many managers, began on the beaten path of mediocrity, learning the wrong leadership lessons and letting others steer your ship of life toward an undesirable destination.

Look where you are now. Traveling down the path you've created, one that leads to your greatness, your goals, and your personal vision.

My only objective for this book is that it exceeds your expectations and overdelivers. I trust that my passion, intentions, unwavering commitment, and steadfast purpose are unquestionably clear.

Your genius is already within you. I hope this book sparked the fire to expose your brilliance.

16 FINAL GUIDANCE PRINCIPLES TO BECOME A COACHING PRODIGY

As you close this book (for now), remember these guiding principles that outstanding leaders and coaches embrace.

1. Be open to change. Change is scary, even for you. Stay strong to your purpose.
2. Be caring.
3. Come from a place of "I don't know," not, "I already know."
4. Be patient.
5. Be present.
6. Stay focused on your *why*.
7. Be the gift of coaching.
8. Talk and advise less.
9. Ask more and better questions so you assess instead of assuming facts.
10. Be selfless.
11. Be creative.
12. Be a proactive, intentional listener.
13. Be courageous, confident, and vulnerable.
14. Be detached from the outcome.
15. Be coachable by anyone.
16. Be human first.

Most important, be authentically human rather than trying to achieve a state of perfection. Resist your ego's desire to speculate on how you compare to others. You are the only comparable measurement of success. Otherwise you surrender your own personal power and put the control of your life in the hands of those to whom you compare yourself.

Never stop asking questions to challenge status quo. And most important, always follow your heart, because that's where you will discover your purpose, your gifts, your creativity, and your inspiration. Remember, life has no remote control. You **must** get up and change it yourself.

TIP FROM THE COACH

Motivation is the ignition that gets you started. Habit is the fuel that keeps you going. The behavior change that enables you to achieve leadership and coaching mastery is simply this:

Be insatiably caring and curious to lead with questions rather than answers.

After all, there are only three things we can control in our lives: our actions/communication, our reactions, and our thoughts/attitude. How ironic that we spend most of our time trying to control the things we can't, rather than master the things we can. By focusing on the three things your can control, only then can you truly master your life.

MINDFUL MOMENT

Show me a leader who embraces their humanity, their fear, and expresses their vulnerabilities, and I will show you an influential, inspiring leader who is invincible. Once you own and embrace what you perceive to be your weaknesses, fears, and vulnerabilities so they become your strength and heart of coaching excellence, what else can stop you?

From this point on, it's up to you. Keep striving for better questions; always challenge status quo; and never, ever let anyone rob you of your personal power. Don't give up on yourself; always honor who you are and your core values, in order to create the extraordinary you.

I mean this with the utmost sincerity. Thank you for allowing me to contribute to your success. If I did, then it made writing this book worthwhile.

Please stay in touch and feel free to reach out to me anytime at www .KeithRosen.com or our corporate site at www.Coachquest.com, my personal email, which is KeithR@KeithRosen.com. And feel free to connect with me on any social media. My website is also where you'll find a treasure of resources. I'd be honored to hear from you and would love to discuss coaching wins and even the challenges you may experience along the way. I'll always be in your corner to support you on your continued journey.

FROM THE SIDELINES

Three rabbits are sitting on a log. One decides to hop off. How many are left? Three. Because there's a difference between deciding and doing. It's easy to decide this book provides the path that is indisputably the only way to master sales leadership. However, motivation does not always result in transformation. It's time to take action.

Honor the coaching code; the L.E.A.D.S. and E.L.A.D.S. frameworks and the transformative questions. Soon enough, you'll find your coaching language and voice, voice and personal style that will help further develop your coaching habit.

Congratulate yourself. You've embraced the habit of coaching and made it part of who you are. Let your individuality and magnificence shine brightly. Stick to this new, daily cadence of coaching, this new way of leading others with intention, purpose, and passion to achieve things they never thought possible.

I leave you with this final thought: Be present to embrace the daily miracles around you and the ones you create; never compromise who you are and who you want to be; and always honor the language and the ABCs of leadership. Always be coaching! I look forward to staying in touch, and I wish you extreme success.

Seven Steps to Creating a Top Performing Coaching Culture

What follows is the leaders' outline to successfully roll out coaching to their team or their company. It also contains the essential conversations for introducing the different components of coaching to your team. You'll find this outline goes hand in hand with Chapter 7, as it contains all of the templates and coaching tracks you'll be using throughout this implementation.

While some managers may read through this and find this timeline to be aggressive, others would rather expedite the process. Much of this has to do with your current company culture, the relationship you already have with your team, how effective and consistent your coaching has been to date, and the size of your team.

1. **Week one: Send a coaching enrollment email.**

   I'd suggest sending a brief, preliminary email preparing for the meeting, establishing the topic, and outlining what's in it for them. See Chapter 7 for the template you can use.

2. **Week one: Schedule a team meeting for team enrollment in coaching.**

   Take a few minutes toward the end or beginning of a (positive) meeting and do a brief team enrollment. You can share your experience during my sales leadership coaching mastery course you participated in or what you've learned from this book. Use the team enrollment template in Chapter 7.

   Let everyone know they will be receiving a meeting invite to discuss this individually to set individual expectations and alignment around coaching and ensure it's a valuable experience for each person on your team. Some managers use a few slides in a brief presentation to highlight some of the main points around coaching, a brief description, and overview. (Warning! This is not mandatory and is just another suggestion. Don't get caught up on feeling you have to overengineer this by developing a PowerPoint presentation!)

3a. **Weeks one and two: Schedule individual meetings for enrollment in coaching.**

   Enroll in coaching (see templates in Chapter 7), set expectations, introduce the coaching prep form, Coaching Action Plan, discuss note taking, situational versus scheduled coaching, the structure of coaching sessions, being their accountability partner, setting expectations of the coach and coachee, when you coach (ABC), where you coach, confidentiality, communication platforms, (phone, face to face, email, text, etc.). You can also mention there will be a deeper discussion around observation.

3b. **Schedule the first coaching session.**

   Steps 3a and 3b happen during the same meeting. At the end of your one-on-one enrollment conversation, schedule your first one-on-one coaching session with each coachee. Make sure they complete the coaching prep form, the Coaching Action Plan, and have their goals and expectations set prior to your first coaching session, as that will initiate your first conversation.

   Remember, you're always better off adding coaching sessions than canceling them. If you cancel coaching, the caustic reaction from your coachee will be to think, "Coaching isn't important.

I'm not important." So, start with one or two sessions per month per person, depending upon the size of your team. As we discussed, the communication platform and number of *scheduled* monthly coaching sessions will vary depending upon the situation and each individual.

TIP FROM THE COACH

Develop your coaching cadence and schedule it into your calendar. When will you conduct scheduled coaching sessions? Midday, every day, assigned days, early mornings, after work hours, in person, on the phone? Block the time and make it non-negotiable or it won't happen. This is your number-one priority. If you don't have the appointment, you don't have the commitment.

4. **Week three: Enroll in a motivation exercise and schedule the debrief.**

These two distinct exercises can be combined into one, one-hour meeting with each coachee. Because this is something you want for them, and it's an empowering conversation, in the spirit of efficiency, you can *suggest* making this a topic of one of your coaching sessions to avoid scheduling a separate meeting, but you can't force it.

Refer to the enrollment templates and exercises in Chapter 7. At the end of the meeting, schedule a follow-up meeting to discuss what they've learned.

5. **Weeks three and four: Discuss the motivation exercise.**

As per step 4, schedule time to review the exercises, so you know exactly what their goals, passions, values, motivations, and priorities are. Use the questions in Chapter 8 to facilitate this debrief, whether it's during their next coaching session or a separate meeting.

6. **Week four: Enroll in observation.**

You can take the same approach in step 2. A brief team enrollment, then schedule a time to set up the rules of engagement during a scheduled coaching session or a separate meeting. Use the enrollment coaching track in Chapter 9, then schedule your first observation session.

7. **Execution—Sustainability—Transformation—Results**

Honor the language and habits of the world's most well-respected and influential coaches and leaders. ABC, ABPC, and ABE; that is, always be coaching, always be peer coaching, and always be enrolling!

Become the Model
— of Exemplary Sales —
Leadership

BRING THIS COACHING HABIT AND FRAMEWORK INTO YOUR COMPANY

Seventy-five countries, hundreds of companies, and three million business leaders and going. Since 1989, that's how many managers and salespeople we've had the privilege of working with, so they can transform from a directive, chief problem solver to an influential, respected leader and effective, inspiring coach.

What would be possible if you had everything in this book come alive and be a reflection of your organization? What if you, personally, could achieve all the benefits that hundreds of thousands of other managers and coaches have experienced? What if you can do this all by *coaching in ten minutes or less*?

Sure, you now have one, if not two (*Coaching Salespeople into Sales Champions*) of the most tactical, relevant, and widely used sales leadership coaching books to make you the sales leader you want to be. But you can't ask a book questions, and the book can't hold you accountable, even with your best intentions.

Even with good intentions, with all the pressure in our lives, it's easy to slip back into the directive, perceived, time-saving habits and let the coaching muscle atrophy. And trying to track the impact or consistency of coaching by making it part of your scorecard, key performance indicator, or what you're measured against based on activity isn't helping change behavior. Ultimately, this initiative will then mistakenly be branded as another short lived, flavor of the month.

We help managers and leaders develop a champion mindset and skill set so that coaching becomes a fulfilling and impactful part of their daily lives and every conversation. When coaching becomes a natural, healthy habit and part of your daily cadence, you can truly make the difference you want and create the legacy you're proud of.

Whether it's delivering one-to-one coaching, a half-day workshop, virtual or onsite coaching and training, or at your next retreat, send me a personal email at KeithR@KeithRosen.com or visit www.KeithRosen.com. I'd be happy to talk about how we can work together, including our other programs on time management, personal productivity, and, of course, how to develop your salespeople into top-performing consultative sales coaches so they now coach customers to succeed.

Finally, if you're a coaching evangelist and want to get a bunch of these books to share this gift with others, we can help with discounted pricing. We can also co-brand and customize this book specifically for you or your organization, and you may even qualify for a complimentary workshop with me. For bulk sales, email me at KeithR@KeithRosen.com. It would be my honor and privilege to contribute to your success.

Acknowledgments

To every person and the millions of managers and salespeople who I've had the privilege of meeting, coaching, and sharing my life's work with. To every caring, selfless leader who authentically wants the very best for his or her people. To every organization that truly puts its people over results. Thank you for disrupting the status quo and making the workplace a great place. I thank you for showing us that work can be a close, trusting community where people can thrive; contribute; grow; have fun; build timeless, lasting relationships; innovate; collaborate; do fulfilling and meaningful work; and make the impact people want in their home and in our world. Thank you for inviting me around the world to over 75 countries to collect the stories, global adventures, and experiences that were the impetus for this book.

Thank you to all of my clients and the great leaders I have had the privilege of working with, coaching, and learning from. Thank you for making my job the best, most fulfilling, enjoyable career in the world. You have given me my greatest gift: allowing me to be your coach and express my core value of making a positive impact that enhances the quality of your life. It's been an honor, a remarkable journey, and a joy to watch you grow and achieve what you never thought possible, especially when it comes to the type of teams you can develop. Please know you'll have me as your coach in your corner forever.

My hope is that this book will continue to support you on your journey to become a world-class, legendary leader and to serve others who are in pursuit of their dreams and goals.

Thank you to Wiley, my publisher. If patience, support, and collaboration were a picture, you'd see Wiley's logo, and then a picture of Shannon Vargo, Kelly Martin, Vicki Adang, and the rest of the committed team at Wiley. As an author, I feel like part of their family. You guys simply rock. Thank you for your endless patience and support to make this a glowing success.

About the Author

Keith Rosen, MCC, is the founder of Coachquest and CEO of Profit Builders, named one of the best sales training and coaching companies worldwide.

Since 1989, Keith has delivered his transformational programs to hundreds of thousands of salespeople and managers in practically every industry, on five continents, and in over 75 countries. He teaches caring, busy managers and salespeople how to coach masterfully in 15 minutes or less, and creates extraordinary results.

Inc. magazine and *Fast Company* named Keith one of the five most influential executive coaches. Keith has written several best sellers including *Own Your Day* and the globally acclaimed *Coaching Salespeople into Sales Champions*, winner of five international best book awards, which has reigned as the number-one best-selling sales leadership book on Amazon.

He's been featured in *Entrepreneur, Inc., Fortune, The New York Times*, and *The Wall Street Journal*. Keith was also featured on the award-winning television show *Mad Men*, and was one of the first coaches who earned the distinguished Master Certified Coach designation credentialed through the International Coach Federation.

As a leader in the coaching profession, Keith was inducted in the inaugural group of the Top Sales Hall of Fame. Keith was named The 2009 Sales Education Leader of the Year and is consistently honored as having one of the top 25 sales and leadership blogs. He was also named one of the 50 best salespeople of all time, along with Zig Ziglar, Steve Jobs, Dale Carnegie, and Jeff Bezos.

When Keith isn't coaching and creating, he invests his time in his family, friends, philanthropy, personal evolution, disrupting the status quo, and challenging the rules and conventional wisdom. His team still gets frustrated when he answers all the inbound calls, but why should they have all the fun?

Keith also values, adventuring, doing hot yoga, playing guitar, trying to sing, making an impact, biking, golfing, embracing every moment he has—and enjoying the ride. Finally, Keith believes that music, literature, and the arts can create world peace, and that coaching, like music, is truly a universal language and the greatest gift we can give one another.

INDEX

Page references followed by *fig* indicate an illustrated figure; followed by *t* indicate a table.